FEMALES AND AUTONOMY

A Life-Span Perspective

Edited by

Margot B. Nadien
Fordham University

Florence L. Denmark
Pace University

Allyn and Bacon
Boston • London • Toronto • Sydney • Tokyo • Singapore

Senior Editor: Carolyn Merrill
Series Editorial Assistant: Amy Goldmacher
Vice President, Director of Field Marketing: Joyce Nilsen
Composition and Prepress Buyer: Linda Cox
Manufacturing Buyer: Megan Cochran
Cover Administrator: Jenny Hart
Production Editor: Christopher H. Rawlings
Editorial-Production Service: Omegatype Typography, Inc.
Electronic Composition: Omegatype Typography, Inc.

Library of Congress Cataloging-in-Publication Data
Females and autonomy : a life-span perspective / edited by Margot B.
  Nadien and Florence L. Denmark.
      p.   cm.
   Includes bibliographical references and index.
   ISBN 0-205-19856-2
   1. Women—Psychology.   2. Autonomy (Psychology)   3. Developmental
psychology.   4. Life cycle, Human.   I. Nadien, Margot B.
II. Denmark, Florence.
HQ1206.F427   1999
155.3'33—dc21   98-12181
                                                        CIP

Printed in the United States of America

10 9 8 7 6 5 4 3 2 1   03 02 01 00 99 98

To all the significant people who inspired this work.

CONTENTS

PREFACE

The importance of love to an individual's psychological health and well-being has been widely recognized in various social science disciplines, including psychology and psychiatry, during much of the past century. It is only in recent decades, however, that research has pointed to another personality feature as being essential to a person's psychological health and well-being—namely, an individual's perception of possessing autonomy, a personality construct variously conceptualized in terms of a sense of independence, competence, personal control, and perceived self-efficacy.

Several excellent books have grown out of research on autonomy and related constructs. Many of these have focused on the effects of a sense of personal control, especially among the elderly or among the very young. However, this work is unique in that it studies some causes and effects of females having (or lacking) a perceived sense of autonomy at each of five major phases of development. It also devotes attention to cross-cultural differences all across the life span, and includes references to ethnic and gender differences. Because of this unparalleled combination of features, this volume can serve not only as a reference work for professionals, but also as a supplemental text in three types of graduate and undergraduate courses: developmental psychology, personality, and the psychology of women.

This book comprises eight chapters. Chapter one sets the stage by presenting differing concepts and theories about autonomy, noting the purpose and plan of the book, and providing an overview of each chapter's focus, as well as its authors. The second chapter explores cross-cultural perspectives, examining female autonomy in diverse societies at each major phase across the life span. The next five chapters examine autonomy among women during each of the five major phases of the life span: infancy and childhood, adolescence, early adulthood, the middle years of adulthood, and old age. The final chapter reflects on more general considerations raised throughout the book. It analyzes current issues bearing on gender and autonomy within women's studies and within developmental and life-span psychology, and it comments on adaptive and maladaptive strivings for autonomy by females at different junctures across the life span, including those of differing groups of women of color.

ACKNOWLEDGMENTS

We wish to express our appreciation to our editor at Allyn and Bacon, Carolyn Merrill, for her many constructive suggestions. Much gratitude is also owed to Khaya Novick Eisenberg, Nicola Holder, and Erica Heitner for their assistance in the preparation of this book.

We would like to thank all the people who wrote reviews of the manuscript: Claire Etaugh, Bradley University; Vera Dunwoody, Chaffey College; Yvonne V. Wells, Suffolk University; Carolyn I. Spies, Bloomfield College; M. Betsy Bergen, Kansas State University.

MBN
FLD

ABOUT THE CONTRIBUTORS

Editor: Margot B. Nadien

Dr. Margot Nadien is Associate Professor of Psychology at Fordham University in New York City, where she has also been the Director of the Gerontology Certificate Program. She has authored two texts on human development, many chapters and journal articles, and over 30 papers and workshops given at regional, national and international meetings and conventions.

Dr. Nadien was elected to *Phi Beta Kappa* (Hunter Chapter) and *Psi Chi*. She was a finalist for the Cattell Award given by the New York Academy of Sciences, and the winner of the 1995 Kurt Lewin Award as well as a 1996 service award given by the New York State Psychological Association. Margot Nadien is cited in *International Who's Who in Education, World's Who's Who in Women, Directory of Distinguished Americans, Who's Who of American Women,* and *Who's Who in the East.*

Margot Nadien is presently involved in 12 professional societies at international, national, regional, and state levels, including the *International Council of Psychologists,* serving on the Scientific Program Committee and as New York State area chairperson; the *American Psychological Association,* with membership and participation in panels in Divisions 1, 7, 9, and 20; the *Eastern Psychological Association,* the *New York State Psychological Association,* including the presidency of the Social-Psychology Division and subsequently the presidency of the Academic Division; and the *New York Academy of Sciences,* where she is the current vice-chair of the Advisory Committee of the Psychology Section. Also, she participates in several gerontological organizations, including the *Gerontological Society of America,* the *National Council on Aging,* and the *State Society on Aging.*

Editor: Florence L. Denmark

Dr. Florence Denmark is Robert Scott Pace Distinguished Professor and Chair of Psychology at Pace University, and Adjunct Professor, Graduate School, City University of New York. She has authored or edited 15 books, almost 100 articles and book chapters, and has given 50 scholarly presentations at universities in the United States, Europe, and Israel. One of her recent publications, *The Handbook of the Psychology of Women* (co-edited with

Michelle Paludi), was selected by the journal *Choice* in January, 1995, as an academic book of excellence.

Dr. Denmark has been honored on numerous occasions, is a member of *Phi Beta Kappa, Psi Chi, Alpha Theta,* and is cited in *World's Who's Who of Women in Education, Who's Who in the East, Who's Who of American Women,* and *American Men and Women in Science.* Innumerable awards include several from the American Psychological Association for distinguished contributions and outstanding achievement in psychology, and for service to women in psychology; from the *New York State Psychological Association,* including the Kurt Lewin Award, the Wilhelm Wundt Award, and awards for national and international achievement in psychology; from *Psi Chi,* the First National Distinguished Service Award; and various honors and awards for outstanding achievement and contributions from such groups as the *Organizations for Professional Women,* the *Association for Women in Science,* and the *Association for Women in Psychology,* among others.

Florence Denmark is a past president of the American Psychological Association (and also of its Divisions 1 and 35), and president-elect of Division 52. She has also been president of the *International Council of Psychologists;* of the *Eastern Psychological Association;* and of the *New York State Psychological Association* (as well as of its Academic and Social-Psychology Divisions). She has also been vice president of the *New York Academy of Sciences* (and chair of its Psychology Section), and vice president of the *International Organization for the Study of Group Tensions.* Florence Denmark is currently fellow of the *American Psychological Association* (and eight of its divisions) and of the *New York Academy of Sciences.*

Leonore Loeb Adler

Dr. Leonore Adler is Professor of Psychology and the Director of the Institute for Cross-Cultural and Cross-Ethnic Studies at Molloy College. She has edited eight books, published 48 chapters and journal articles, and has presented papers in many symposia held in the United States, Canada, Europe, and Asia. Dr. Adler has been a consulting reader for *Psychological Reports* and *Perceptual and Motor Skills,* and has contributed to the *International Journal of Group Tensions,* first as associate editor, then as managing editor and, currently, as a member of the editorial board. She has been a columnist for the Social Psychology Division of the *New York State Psychologist* and is presently a consulting editor for *World Psychology.*

Dr. Adler has been honored with the Molloy College President's Medal along with awards for leadership from the *Queens County Psychological Association,* from the *New York State Psychological Association,* the Wilhelm Wundt Award, the Kurt Lewin Award, and several distinguished service awards.

Dr. Adler is a fellow of the *American Psychological Association* (and also of Divisions 1 and 35), and has been Treasurer of Division 52. She works on the APA's Committee on International Relations in Psychology. She is also a fellow of the *New York Academy of Sciences,* where she serves as a member of the Advisory Committee of the Psychology Division. She is also a member of innumerable other organizations, including the *Eastern Psychological Association, New York State Psychological Association, International Association of Cross-Cultural Psychology, International Organization for the Study of Group Tensions, International Council of Psychologists, International Society for Comparative Psychology, World Federation of Mental Health Societies for Cross-Cultural Research,* and the *Association for Women in Science.*

Georgia Babladelis

Dr. Georgia Babladelis is Professor of Psychology at the California State University at Hayward. She has authored two books, 12 articles, and four reviews. She has published over 25 articles on computer use and software programs; and has given almost 20 presentations at scholarly societies in the United States, Canada, and Europe. After founding and becoming editor of the *Psychology of Women Quarterly* (1974–1980), Dr. Babladelis served as its consulting editor throughout the 1980s. She has also been a reviewer for the *Journal of Personality.*

Dr. Babladelis was elected fellow of the *American Psychological Association* and its Divisions 9 and 35. She has also been honored for her work as the first and founding editor of the research journal of APA's Division 35, and was included as one of the 100 Outstanding Women in Psychology for the APA centennial celebration in 1992 in Washington, D.C.

Dr. Babladelis has been a member of the AAAS and of the Western Regional Association of Women's Studies. She has served as the United States director of research on a UNESCO sponsored investigation of cross-cultural studies and sex-related attitudes, and has served on the advisory committee of the International Women's Studies Program at the University of Haifa, Israel.

S. Patricia Clark

Dr. Patricia Clark is both Associate Professor of Gerontology and the Director of the Institute of Gerontology at Molloy College. In addition to several published works, Dr. Clark has participated in over 30 workshops on health and education in the United States.

Dr. Clark is an active participant on the *Membership Committee of the Association of Gerontology in Higher Education.* She is also a member of the *Gerontology Society of America,* the *American Society on Aging,* the *New York State Society on Aging,* the *Nassau Coalition for Health Reform,* and the *Therapeutic Recreation Association* for Nassau County and also for Suffolk County in New York.

Virginia Smith Harvey

Dr. Virginia Harvey is Assistant Professor of Counseling and School Psychology in the Graduate College of Education at the University of Massachusetts at Boston, where she has taught both undergraduate and graduate courses since 1993. In addition to a work published by the *National Association of School Psychologists,* Dr. Harvey has published 13 chapters and articles and has given more than ten presentations at national and regional meetings.

Dr. Harvey was awarded by the *National Association of School Psychologists* a "Certificate of Appreciation and Recognition for Professional Activity Leadership and Dedication in Promoting Government and Professional Relationships." She was chosen by the *New Hampshire Association of School Psychologists* as a winner of the New Hampshire "School Psychologist of the Year" Award.

John D. Hogan

Dr. John Hogan is Professor of Psychology at St. John's University, where he has taught since 1965. The Associate Editor of *World Psychology* since 1995, Dr. Hogan has also been a consulting editor since 1984 for the *Journal of Genetic Psychology* as well as for *Genetic Psychology Monographs.*

Dr. Hogan is co-editor of two books and of a third currently in press, and has co-authored six book chapters, two monographs, and more than 20 articles. In addition to delivering papers at conferences in Canada and England, he has given presentations at innumerable meetings held all across the United States.

Dr. Hogan has received certificates for service to *Psi Chi* in 1987, 1991, 1993, 1994, and 1996. He was also elected to *Kappa Delta Pi,* the national honor society in education, and to the *Skull and Circle Honor Society* of St. John's University. Dr. Hogan is a long-time member of the *American Psychological Association* and is a fellow of its Divisions 1, 2, 7, 10, 20, 24, 26, and 46. Dr. Hogan is also a member of the *American Psychological Society,* the *Eastern Psychological Association,* the *Committee of Undergraduate Teachers of Psychology,* the *International Council of Psychologists, The Cheiron Society* (the International Society for the History of Behavioral and Social Sciences), and the *Society for the Psychological Study of Men and Masculinity.* Dr. Hogan has been especially active in the *New York State Psychological Association,* where he has served at different times as the president of the Academic Division and president of the Division of Adult Development and Aging.

Judith Kaufman

A state certified school psychologist in New York State, Dr. Judith Kaufman is Professor of School Psychology in the Psychology Department of Fairleigh Dickinson University at Teaneck, New Jersey. Dr. Kaufman has authored or co-authored 18 publications and has been a presenter or co-presenter of over 40 papers and workshops. She was a winner of the James McKeen Cattell Award given by the New York Academy of Sciences, and is listed in the *American Men and Women in Science, Who's Who of American Women,* and *National Register of Health.*

A member of the *American Psychological Association* (Divisions 2, 15, 16, and 27), Dr. Kaufman has served on several committees dealing with children, youth, and families. As a member of the *National Association of School Psychologists,* she has been its treasurer, its northeast regional director, and the founder and director of its Children's Fund. She is also active on various committees of the *National Association of Student Personnel Administrators,* the *Association of Independent Colleges and Universities of New Jersey,* the *New York State Psychological Association,* the *New York Association of School Psychologists,* and the Committee on Continuing Professional Development.

Barbara A. Mowder

A certified school psychologist, Dr. Barbara Mowder is Professor of Psychology and is both the Director of Graduate Psychology Programs and the Associate Director of the Psychology Department at Pace University in New York City. She has authored over 20 journal articles, a book, and six chapters, and has presented or co-presented over 60 papers.

Dr. Mowder is a fellow of the *American Psychological Association* (Division 15), and a member of Division 16. She is a member of the Academic Division of the *New York State Psychological Association.* She is currently president of the *New York Association of Early Childhood and Infant Psychologists.* Barbara Mowder belongs to the *New York Academy of Sciences,* where she is the current president of the Psychology Division's advisory committee; and she is a member of several school psychology associations, including international, national, and New York State associations of school psychology, and societies for research in child development and adolescence.

1

FEMALES AND AUTONOMY: SETTING THE STAGE

MARGOT B. NADIEN
Fordham University

FLORENCE L. DENMARK
Pace University

Females and Autonomy: A Life-Span Perspective examines the way females experience autonomy at successive stages of development across the life span. The focus is specifically on females, but some gender similarities and differences are also explored.

Within personality and developmental psychology, autonomy connotes effective personal control and self-direction. Such feelings grow out of a clear sense of self and identity and enough confidence in one's values and beliefs to allow for relative independence in one's decision making and actions (Erikson, 1950, 1968).

Following this overview is a separate chapter presenting cross-cultural perspectives on autonomy and gender during each of several broad segments of the life span. Thereafter, individual chapters consider autonomy and related issues during each of five major life-span phases—infancy and childhood, adolescence, early adulthood, middle adulthood, and old age. The book concludes with a final segment touching on general notions about autonomy and adjustment, and some factors which may influence them.

This overview will first examine early views about autonomy, including the clinical approaches of Freud, Murray, White, and Erikson, and then the social learning approaches of Rotter, Seligman, Bandura, and Rothbaum and his colleagues. Attention will then be directed to early perspectives on autonomy as they bear on differing phases across the life span.

Finally, we shall comment on the essential features of the subsequent chapters—the chapter on cross-cultural perspectives across the entire course of life, the five following chapters exploring female strivings for autonomy during each of the life-span phases, and the final chapter on current trends in studies of autonomy, gender, and development.

EARLY VIEWS ON AUTONOMY

Clinical Views

As concerns personality growth, notions about autonomy trace to Freud's view that, as a consequence of ego development during the anal stage, toddlers seek to take independent action so as to gratify their needs more quickly and completely than would occur if they had to rely on their caregivers for such gratification (Hall, 1954). Thereafter, Henry Murray advanced the idea of autonomy as a major need when he defined it in terms of the independence that comes from breaking free of restraint or control by others (Murray, 1938).

Expanding on this broad view of autonomy, Robert White, a student of Murray, related autonomy to a child's need for competence or efficacy in exploring and mastering the environment (Monte, 1991; White, 1959, 1975). Within this same time period, Erikson's elaboration on Freud's theory linked autonomy to a child's wish to exercise personal control over such daily events as walking, dressing, self-feeding, and toileting (Erikson, 1950, 1968).

Social Learning Views

Rotter's "Locus of Control" Construct

As a complement to the clinical views of Murray, White, and Erikson, social learning theorists forged a research-oriented perspective on autonomy. The first of these social learning positions to be introduced was Julian Rotter's (1954, 1966) view of "locus of control," a construct centering on two opposing perceptions of the source of control over situational outcomes. According to Rotter, an *internal locus of control* refers to people who have a generalized expectancy that they can exercise "personal control" over future happenings, whereas an *external locus of control* (i.e., "nonpersonal control") exists when there is a generalized perception of situational outcomes being determined either by chance or by powerful others (Rotter, 1954, 1966).

Seligman's Learned Helplessness

What happens when people feel bereft of control? Such circumstances are explored by Martin Seligman (1975). Focusing on events that are both uncontrollable and aversive, Seligman found empirical support for his idea that repeated failures to control painful events may instill a generalized expectancy of *learned helplessness*. Such feelings may breed depression and low self-regard (Abramson, Gerber, & Seligman, 1980; Abramson, Seligman, & Teasdale, 1978).

Bandura's Perceived Self-Efficacy and Outcome Expectancy

Notions of personal autonomy were further advanced when Albert Bandura (1977, 1982, 1986) distinguished between two features of personal control. One of these, *perceived self-efficacy,* deals with a person's perception of having (or lacking) the requisite skills to cope well with specific problem situations. The other feature, *outcome expectancy,* concerns expectations about the environment's responsiveness to one's personal actions. Bandura held that a nonresponsive environment may be so deleterious as to cause a generalized expectancy of failure, even in persons who normally have a perception of self-efficacy.

Rothbaum, Weisz, and Snyder's Primary versus Secondary Control

Yet another refinement of Rotter's construct was introduced by Rothbaum, Weisz, and Snyder (1982). They reconceptualized Rotter's "internal locus of control" as *primary control,* the belief that one can make outer events conform to one's own personal needs. They used *secondary control* to designate the form of personal control which occurs when a person accommodates to her or his environment.

These differing concepts of control are explored in much greater detail in the chapter on aging women by Nadien and Denmark. However, comments about these and other forms of autonomy are also discussed in other chapters. For example, Virginia Harvey speaks of authors who separate autonomy of thought and autonomy of action, and who distinguish between *instrumental autonomy,* the freedom to make choices and act without guidance from others, and *emotional autonomy,* the ability to act independently of the social approval or support of significant others.

Distinctive views of autonomy derive in part from differences in orientation among psychologists (i.e., whether they are psychoanalytic, cognitive–behavioral, phenomenological, or eclectic in approach). Yet, even within a given orientation, concepts about control vary according to the age and stage being considered. In other words, even though a sense of autonomy (and of identity) first takes root in infancy, the manifestations of control (or noncontrol) change at the differing phases of development across the life span (Wood, 1997).

Having said this, what, then, are the theoretical views about the bases for autonomy during major periods of development?

THEORETICAL POSITIONS

Henry Murray's Views

Reworking Freud's views on the residual effects of the birth trauma and of childhood fixations, Henry Murray linked desires for autonomy to complexes acquired during prenatal, oral, and anal stages. For example, strivings for autonomy were held to emerge shortly after birth among those infants whose prenatal experiences spawned a wish to avoid any reminder of the confinement and restrictiveness of the womb. Alternatively, infants who have had bitter or painful oral sensations may want to escape the dependency of the oral phase. Of course, drives for autonomy could also arise during the anal stage because of a wish to break free of parental control or to resist the strictures imposed by outside controlling figures (Murray, 1938).

Robert White's Views

White (1959, 1975) offered a slightly different perspective on the relationship between autonomy and development. He held that, aside from the innate mechanisms for meeting basic survival drives, infants are gripped by helpless feelings. These foster an attachment to the mother and a dependency on her. Yet, as infants become more capable of independence, and as parental figures lessen the extent and immediacy of their care, children's frustrated needs generate anxiety. This mobilizes the wish in growing children to manipulate and explore their world—and to become competent in doing so. For the greater the skill in coping with the world, the less the sense of helplessness and fear (White, 1975, p. 298).

Along with other developmentalists, White believed that independence and competence are stifled if dependency behaviors are over-learned during infancy or if, during childhood, assertiveness is punished and conformity rewarded (White, 1959).

Erik Erikson's Views

Erikson provided a third perspective on the origins of personal control in his life-span theory of development. He held that autonomy becomes central to growth in childhood, and continues to be important in adolescence, adulthood, and old age.

For Erikson, strivings for independence clearly emerge in the second year of life, at which time children seek to become masters of themselves and their environment. Yet, in striving for self-rule, children must also recognize and cope with parental authority. Parents, for their part, must avoid the over-protectiveness that fosters continued dependency, but, at the same time, must refrain from undue criticism of their children's lapses in control. Otherwise, feelings of self-doubt or shame may prompt one of two compensatory behaviors from their children. The first is the defiance and impulsiveness characteristic of anal-expulsive children who rebel against parental authority and injunctions that they show more personal control than they can or wish to show. Alternatively, when children accept parental authority but fear lapses in self-mastery, they may develop obsessive and compulsive trends (Erikson, 1968).

Strivings for autonomy often become linked with other personality traits and other features of growth. For example, Erikson believed that a *sense of autonomy* gained in early childhood establishes a sound foundation on which to build a healthy ego. A sense of autonomy fosters the beginnings of will power in toddlers. Once acquired, children's feelings of mastery over themselves and their world encourage the exercise of initiative during the preschool years, and feelings of competency during the elementary school years.

If they possess these sources of ego strength, adolescents are better able to cope with the "identity confusion" wrought not only by their pubertal change but also by the social pressures to renounce childhood interests and move toward adult roles. At the same time, if adolescents are to succeed in overcoming their identity confusion, they must elaborate the autonomy of childhood into an *autonomous identity*. This occurs when, independently of the family of origin, adolescents choose social and vocational roles that are meaningful to them, and evolve a personal ideology by which to guide themselves during times of conflict and change throughout the rest of their lives (Erikson, 1968).

By adulthood, an autonomous identity requires that continuing needs for personal control be reconciled with the ofttimes contrary desires for control sought by a partner and by offspring.

The links between autonomy and other features of personality vary during later stages. In the early and middle years of adult life, feelings of identity and self-worth rest, in part, on being able to exercise some personal control over one's activities and social relationships. But, in old age, the wish to retain some measure of personal control may run afoul of realistic declines in health and sensorimotor functioning (Erikson, 1986). In support of

Erikson's view, research indicates that even though cognitive capacities often remain intact, such changes as dimming eyesight, weakening strength, and diminished health may undermine the capacity of some elders to function independently (Nadien, 1995, 1996). When this is true, optimal adjustment may require a new view of control—one focusing on "autonomy in the choice one makes." Thus, most elderly persons exercise independent judgment when they recognize those activities over which they still have some personal control and when they acknowledge those activities that require help from other people or from such mechanical devices as wheelchairs, canes, and hearing aids (Erikson, Erikson, & Kivnick, 1986).

THE PURPOSE AND PLAN OF THIS WORK

The foregoing discussion of theoretical positions about autonomy across the life span suggests at least two things. First, owing to the biological and psychosocial changes that distinguish one phase from another, the bases for autonomy—and also the very meaning of autonomy—differ at each developmental phase or stage. Second, different phases of growth often bring shifts in the links between autonomy and other features of personality, such as the person's sense of identity and self, and also of self-worth and emotional connectedness with others.

Awareness of these possible developmental shifts prompted our resolve to undertake a life-span study of autonomy. We chose to have individual authors, according to their specific expertise, explore the theory and research associated with autonomy and related personality traits.

This book is marked by a number of distinct features. First, since developmental phases are not always discrete and instead flow one into the other, some behaviors and influences may be prominent at several phases of growth. For this reason, major themes of development are often addressed by more than one author. A second characteristic of the book is that each chapter focuses specifically on females. However, comparisons are also drawn between females and males when existing research permits such comparisons. Third, cross-cultural studies are the focus of the second chapter, and are also incorporated into several of the other chapters. So as to orient readers to the scope of this study of female autonomy across the life span, we shall give a brief survey of the chapters which follow—as well as their authors.

Cross-Cultural Perspective

Following this introductory chapter is one that provides a broad overview of the differing ways in which females strive to achieve autonomy in childhood, then in adulthood, and finally in old age. In examining female autonomy (or non-autonomy), however, special weight is given to the similarities and differences found among peoples living in diverse cultures and different locales around the world.

The chapter highlighting cross-cultural perspectives is co-authored by Leonore Loeb Adler, a cross-cultural psychologist and the Director of the Institute for Cross-Cultural and

Cross-Ethnic Studies at Molloy College in New York, and S. Patricia Clark, a Professor of Gerontology and also the Director of the Gerontology Institute at Molloy College.

In exploring autonomy and gender in diverse cultures, Adler and Clark present studies which suggest that, with increasing age, children who fail to achieve primary (direct) control over environmental events will settle for secondary control (accommodation to uncontrollable events). They also note how the rearing patterns in differing cultures help to determine whether children will exhibit overcontrolled or undercontrolled behavior.

With respect to early and middle adulthood, the authors speak of gender differences resulting partly from polygamous practices (i.e., polygynous versus polyandrous types of marriage) and partly from other gender-typed marital behaviors prevailing in a given society. Finally, the authors suggest that possibilities for female (as well as male) autonomy in old age may be linked to the extent of androgynous trends within a given culture—and, hence, to the roles which each culture assigns to its aging women.

In chapters three through seven is found an examination of female autonomy at each of the five succeeding developmental phases across the life span: infancy and childhood, adolescence, and the early, middle, and late phases of adulthood. Interwoven through all these chapters on childhood, adolescence, and adulthood are links (or distinctions) between two complementary trends: autonomy and affiliation.

Infancy and Childhood

The connection between *autonomy-related behaviors* (e.g., independence and achievement) and *affiliative behaviors* (e.g., lovingness, connectedness, and responsiveness to others) is first examined in the chapter on infancy and childhood by Barbara Mowder, Professor of Psychology at Pace University in New York City and a specialist in early childhood and parenting.

Mowder comments on the interdependence of autonomy and emotional bonding, noting that attachment, a precursor of affiliativeness, precedes signs of autonomous behavior. Children require emotionally secure relationships before they feel free to move away from their chief caregiver and explore unknown features of their environment. But once such exploration does take place, children acquire new skills that engender a sense of mastery. This, in turn, instills the self-confidence needed to form new relationships and thereby extend connections with others.

Mowder points to yet other links between autonomy and affiliativeness. Children who achieve *emotional* autonomy tend to have closer and more harmonious relationships with their parents. Such relationships help to forge a firm foundation on which to form positive relationships with teachers and peers.

The differing socialization of girls and boys affects their early development of autonomy and affiliativeness. For example, Mowder notes how the process of instilling autonomy starts in infancy for boys (but not for girls) because mothers lessen or cease cuddling their sons when they reach about 6 months of age, and encourage them to move away from them and function on their own. Girls, by contrast, tend to be cuddled throughout infancy and discouraged from wandering away from their caregivers or from showing other signs of independence. This may explain why, in our culture, females show a prolonged period of dependence, and a delay in their progress toward autonomy.

Adolescence

The chapter on adolescence is by Judith Kaufman, Professor of Psychology at Fairleigh Dickinson University in Teaneck, New Jersey, and a specialist in adolescent development.

After dealing with the physical, cognitive, and situational events that generate adolescent confusion, Kaufman notes that adolescent friendships and close family relationships help not only to promote intimacy and affectional ties, but also to facilitate the processes of separation, self-reflection, and self-definition, all of which are very important in establishing an autonomous identity.

Judith Kaufman provides an extended discussion of factors contributing either to continuity or to change in an adolescent's physical, cognitive, and psychosocial functioning, including gender differences as well as a range of other factors that may lead to dissimilar responses in adolescents, in other words, historical, racial, ethnic, and social–class influences.

The crucial issue of identity formation is also explored in terms of theory and research that bear on gender differences and on factors that may be conducive either to a negative adaptation (e.g., suicide, depression, eating disorders, and inappropriate sexual behaviors) or to a positive adaptation (e.g., acquisition of coping skills).

Early Adulthood

The issue of gender differences in autonomy and affiliation is brought into very sharp focus in the chapter on early adulthood by Virginia Harvey, Assistant Professor at the University of Massachusetts at Boston, and an expert on early adult development.

Harvey speaks of the need for young adults to find a balance between their sense of autonomy (self-definition along with independence in thought and action) and their feelings of affiliation (their involvement with and commitment to social others). This necessitates differing tasks for women and men. Indeed, by early adulthood, the effects of childhood and adolescent socialization engender in young women a sense of intimacy that is more developed than their sense of autonomy. By contrast, the childhood socialization of males fosters in young men a developed sense of autonomy, along with a need to further expand their capacity for affiliativeness.

In addition to presenting theories about young adult women (and men), Virginia Harvey examines research on female autonomy in diverse cultures with respect to abortion, birth control, and fertility treatment; young women's civic, economic, and political rights in comparison to those of men; the degree of continuing dependency versus individuation from parents; and questions of physical and psychological health, spousal relationships, and career activities.

The Middle Years

That many young women and men strive to enlarge their behavioral repertoire to include *non-gender-typed* traits is suggested by the chapters dealing with the middle years and old age.

The examination of traits and trends in the middle years is undertaken by Georgia Babladelis, Professor of Psychology at the California State University at Haywood, and a founder and first editor of *Psychology of Women Quarterly*. Babladelis points to research suggesting that an increase in *androgyny* (in desirable traits associated with the opposite sex) was achieved mainly by women showing an increase in gender-typed masculine traits (e.g., assertion, aggression, and achieving behaviors), but without sacrificing their nurturing tendencies. More generally, Babladelis points to middle-aged women's sense of autonomy being bolstered by the successful enactment of multiple roles.

Old Age

Exploring theory and research bearing on old age are Margot Nadien, Associate Professor of Psychology and the Director for five years of the Gerontology Certificate Program at Fordham University in New York City, and Florence Denmark, the Robert Scott Pace Distinguished Professor and Chair of the Psychology Department at Pace University in New York.

In probing the issue of continuity or change in the autonomy of women (and men) in old age, Nadien and Denmark explore two general trends. They note that in the case of healthy old-agers, the personality and adaptive patterns of middle age tend to continue in old age. This means that, aside from a greater incidence of depression and neuroticism in females, old-agers of both sexes exhibit the same moderately high degree of autonomy they had exhibited in their middle years when androgynous trends governed much of their behavior in terms of control-related behaviors (e.g., assertion, aggression, and effective coping behaviors). However, a second general trend is also found among some old-agers. This entails a decline in actual and perceived autonomy. Its source is not gender difference. Rather, it springs from the perception in both women and men of their personal control being eroded by declines in physical or cognitive functioning, and/or in the quality of their life situation, as occurs when the elderly are involuntarily institutionalized or robbed of prized activities and persons.

Further Reflections

Our final chapter is by John Hogan, a long-time member of the division of the Psychology of Women within the *American Psychological Association*. Professor of Psychology at St. John's University in New York City, John Hogan is a developmentalist, a specialist in the history of psychology in general and the history of developmental psychology in particular, and a strong supporter of the women's movement.

Drawing on a broad framework within which to discuss the book's chapters, Hogan analyzes questions of gender and autonomy in terms of existing trends, both within developmental psychology and women's studies. He considers adaptive and maladaptive strivings for autonomy across the life span and within the context of current developmental issues. Finally, he provides an overview of autonomy among differing groups of women of color, thus elaborating on a theme weaving through many of the book's main chapters.

To sum up, autonomy is crucial to an understanding of human development and adaptation. For most females, the sense of self and feelings of well-being and self-worth at each phase across the life span are intimately tied not only to a feeling of connectedness with valued others, but also to a perception of having some autonomy or personal control over one's acts and their environmental outcomes.

REFERENCES

Abramson, L. Y., Garber, J., & Seligman, M. E. P. (1980). Learned helplessness in humans: An attributional analysis. In J. Garber & M. E. P. Seligman (Eds.), *Human helplessness: Theory and applications* (pp. 3–34). New York: Academic Press.

Abramson, L. Y., Seligman, M. E. P., & Teasdale, J. D. (1978). Learned helplessness in humans: Critique and reformulation. *Journal of Abnormal Psychology, 87,* 49–74.

Bandura, A. (1977). Self-efficacy: Toward a unifying theory of behavioral change. *Psychological Review, 84,* 191–215.

Bandura, A. (1982). Self-efficacy in human agency. *American Psychologist, 37,* 122–147.

Bandura, A. (1986). *Social foundations of thought and action: A social-cognitive theory.* Englewood Cliffs, NJ: Prentice-Hall.

Erikson, E. (1950). *Childhood and society.* New York: Norton.

Erikson, E. (1968). *Identity: Youth and crisis.* New York: Norton.

Erikson, E., Erikson, J., & Kivnick, H. Q. (1986). *Vital involvement in old age.* New York: Norton.

Hall, C. S. (1954). *A primer of Freudian psychology.* New York: The World Publishing Company.

Monte, C. (1991). *Beneath the mask.* Fort Worth, TX: Holt, Rinehart and Winston.

Murray, H. A. (1938). *Explorations in personality* (chapter 2). New York: Oxford Press.

Nadien, M. B. (1995). Elder violence (maltreatment) in domestic settings: Some theory and research. In L. L. Adler & F. L. Denmark (Eds.), *Violence and the prevention of violence* (pp. 129–145). Westport, CT: Praeger.

Nadien, M. B. (1996). Aging women: Issues of mental health and maltreatment. In J. A. Sechzer, S. M. Pfafflin, F. L. Denmark, A. Griffin, & S. J. Blumenthal (Eds.), *Women and mental health* (Vol. 789, pp. 177–190). New York: Annals of the New York Academy of Sciences.

Rothbaum, F., Weisz, J., & Snyder, S. (1982). Changing the world and changing the self: A two-process model of perceived control. *Journal of Personality and Social Psychology, 42,* 5–37.

Rotter, J. B. (1954). *Social learning and clinical psychology.* Englewood Cliffs, NJ: Prentice-Hall.

Rotter, J. B. (1966). Generalized expectancies for internal versus external control of reinforcement. *Psychological Monographs, 8*(1) (Whole No. 1009).

Seligman, M. E. P. (1975). *Helplessness: On depression, development, and death.* San Francisco: W. H. Freeman.

White, R. W. (1959). Motivation reconsidered: The concept of competence. *Psychological Review, 66,* 297–333.

White, R. W. (1975). *Lives in progress: A study of the natural growth of personality* (3rd ed.). New York: Holt, Rinehart and Winston.

Wood, J. T. (1997). *Gendered lives: Communication, gender, and culture.* Belmont, CA: Wadsworth.

2

AUTONOMY IN A CROSS-CULTURAL PERSPECTIVE

LEONORE LOEB ADLER
Molloy College

S. PATRICIA CLARK
Molloy College

THE CONCEPT OF AUTONOMY

This chapter focuses on autonomy from a life-span point of view, reviewing the literature for accounts relating to autonomy in a variety of countries and cultures.

In the course of development across the life span, each phase brings along new situations and circumstances with regard to perceived and actual autonomy. In addition, a variety of considerations have to be taken into account because of the influence of different cultural backgrounds (see Adler, 1991, 1993). Therefore, each phase not only brings along changes in the individual's physiological conditions, but also leads to new adjustments and demands in the social environment. At every stage during the life span, new demands and challenges affect the person's autonomy and self-directedness.

It is tempting to suppose that all readers of this book cherish the thought of being autonomous and self-directed. It even seems that such a feeling might be a universal human trait. However, Schooler (1990) points out that, based on the evidence, this is far from the fact. Several scientists have shown that being an independent person in control of oneself is the desirable goal of only a small part of humankind around the world (Inkeles & Smith, 1974; Macfarlane, 1978, 1986; Redfield, 1956). The question occurs whether autonomy and self-directedness might be a North American phenomenon existing mainly in the United States and Canada. Schooler (1990) suggests that feelings of independence may not have the same effects in non-Western communities where autonomy and individualism are not as highly respected, such as among the Japanese, Javanese, or Iranians. However, very little cross-cultural research has discussed autonomy, and even less research has dealt with gender comparison, especially in the case of children. While at first glance the paucity of cross-cultural investigations seems appalling, an explanation may exist for the dearth of cross-cultural reports about autonomy, especially as it pertains to females and to gender differences. Interest in cross-cultural and gender studies has only recently increased. In addition, funds may not be available for research in developing countries.

A potentially promising revelation relative to this issue may be found in the work of a most authoritative anthropologist—Schlegel (1972), who wrote a book with an intriguing title: *Male Dominance and Female Autonomy.* Explaining her choice of the title, Schlegel comments that an alternate title, "Status of Women," would both neglect the functional disparities between the sex roles and describe female activities in comparison with male activities. Yet traditional women's activities center around the home; even in modernized countries the saying "a woman's place is in the home" still has meaning. It represents the traditional domestic component of a woman's lifestyle. Schlegel (1972) explains that she sees female autonomy not as equivalent to men. Instead it represents a woman's control over her thoughts and actions, and, in addition, her meaningful contributions to her family and the society "beyond breeding and feeding."

AUTONOMY AS IT RELATES TO CHILDHOOD

Primary Control versus Secondary Control

In his research in child development, Weisz (1990) initially set out to define the term *control* as causing an intended event. Weisz then elaborates on the meaning of this definition, pointing out that it contains two important dimensions: primary and secondary control.

Weisz explains primary control as follows: **primary control** represents an intended event. Causality by itself is not control. When the individual is the cause—either of intended or unintended events with desirable or undesirable outcomes—it usually signifies that the individual has internal or personal control (Weisz, 1990, p. 104). However, an intended event can occur whether or not an individual plays a causal role.

Secondary control occurs if the individual does not contribute the causal role, for then the situation is not under the individual's control. This is true even if the outcome is just what the individual had wanted.

Morris Rosenberg (1990) elaborates on Weisz' two-process model of control by explaining: "The first process, called *primary control,* involves the effort to act on the environment in order to produce desired outcomes. The second process, called *secondary control,* is an attempt to accommodate to objective conditions in order to effect a more satisfying fit with those conditions" (Rosenberg, p. 147).

A citation by Weisz and Stipek (1982) noted that when children had an opportunity to control some stimulation, they seemed to enjoy such an experience (Groos, 1901). Also in this vein was Piaget's (1963) observation that his own children in Switzerland tried to continue their control of the movements of objects in their cribs.

To test this concept of primary control, Weisz and associates conducted several studies. An interviewer asked schoolchildren, 6, 9, and 12 years old, to describe their experience with stressful situations and to report on their goals during these episodes (Brotman-Band & Weisz, 1988). The results of this investigation showed that only 3.5% of the children relinquished control. In other words, "giving up" was an infrequent response to a stressful situation. The authors also reported that one of their central findings turned out to be an overall age effect. They noticed that the ability to cope with secondary control increased with age. On the other hand, the reports with regard to primary control declined with age. Both of these effects were observed with the 6-year-olds as compared with both of the older age groups. However, the two older groups did not differ in their responses.

Overcontrolled versus Undercontrolled Behavior

Weisz (1990) also reports on two control-related styles: **overcontrolled** and **undercontrolled behavior.** He explains that these two styles are the most closely and immediately linked to clinical manifestations in children.

These behavioral styles could also be identified as children's behavior problems. The term *overcontrolled behavior* is applied to such conditions as fearfulness, sleep problems, headaches, social inhibition, sadness, and worry. On the other hand, *undercontrolled behavior* is identified in terms of the following behaviors: disobedience, fighting, swearing, impulsivity, and arguing. The former term suggests that stimulation and distress tend to be controlled excessively through internalization of parental prohibitions within the child. The latter term, in contrast, implies that stimulation and distress are not adequately controlled by the child.

While these two syndromes may be construed as behavioral styles, they appear in several studies investigating children's behavior problems using factor-analytic techniques (see Achenbach & Edelbrock, 1978). These two syndromes of overcontrolled and undercontrolled behavior seem to be widespread. Such behavior has been found not only in research conducted with people in the United States (Achenbach, 1978; Achenbach & Edelbrock, 1978), but also with the British (Collins, Maxwell, & Cameron, 1962), Sicilians (Peterson, 1965), Japanese (Hayashi, Toyanna, & Quay, 1976), and Greeks, Finns, and Iranians (Quay & Parskenopoulos, 1972).

Several studies investigated the prevalence of over- and undercontrolled behavior in the United States and Thailand. Both countries and cultures adhere to different socialization patterns and values. Weisz (1990) reports that:

> *Within this Buddhist tradition, and in Thai society generally, prohibitions against aggression, cruelty, and other forms of undercontrolled behavior are quite strong, relative to the traditions in the United States of America. Thai parents are intolerant of aggressive, abusive, disrespectful, or other uncontrolled behavior. (Weisz, p. 131). (See Gardiner & Suttipan, 1977.)*

Weisz also points out that in the culture of the United States other behaviors in children are tolerated; among these are independence, brashness, and rudeness. It therefore appears that the Thai culture is more attuned to overcontrolled behavior and less tolerant of undercontrolled behavior when compared to the culture of the United States. Perhaps this undercontrolled behavior contributes to the more autonomous behavior of people reared in the United States.

In her keynote address to a group in North Carolina, Kamii (1981) spoke of autonomy as the goal of education. She distinguished between *autonomy* (being governed by oneself) and *heteronomy* (being governed by somebody else).

In referring to the links made by Piaget between autonomy and morality in his book *The Moral Judgement of the Child* (1965/1932), Piaget conceived of autonomy as decision making in which relevant factors were considered whether or not they brought rewards or punishments.

AUTONOMY IN FAMILY AND WORK ROLES IN YOUNG AND MIDDLE ADULTHOOD

Marriage is one of the customs that is generally conceded to be practiced universally, although anthropologists do not agree with regard to the definition of marriage. Yet, Brown (1981) feels that the topic is so complex that until now cross-cultural investigations have been only fragmentary.

Among the cross-cultural research projects studying different aspects of marriage are the following investigations: Stephens (1963) offers a descriptive overview dealing with mate selection; Minturn, Grosse, and Haider (1969) investigate arranged marriages; and Ayres (1976) studies reproductive success by comparing monogamy with polygamy.

Another important study, done by Barry (1976), relates various aspects of marriage to childrearing practices. Barry based his findings on a sample of over 130 different societies. He notes that societies that have typically large sex differences in their childrearing practices, especially in the middle years of childhood, are also those societies that insist on the virginity of the bride at the time of the marriage. Barry (1976) also found that the custom of polygyny and the practice of offering a bride-price is related to the differential rearing of boys and girls. He suggests that such marriage customs prolonged the parents' control over their daughters. In addition, Barry feels that such demands for "stereotyped femininity" in childhood also reduce the opportunity for individual expression or rebellious attitudes (1976, p. 17); in other words, the possibilities of autonomous thoughts and behavior are stifled in the girls' childhood years.

The earliest cross-cultural study investigating premarital sex norms was research by Murdock (1964 and 1967), and was based on 180 societies, including the major cultural regions in the world. Murdock identified three distinct patterns in three kinds of society. In *restrictive societies,* premarital sex is not permitted and therefore is very rare. In *permissive societies,* sexual behavior by unmarried girls is more or less tolerated. There are also societies with an *intermediate attitude* between the two previously mentioned attitudes toward sexual expression. More recently, Goethals (1971) published a study which replicated Murdock's findings, although it used different measures for the independent and dependent variables (Broude, 1981). However, neither Murdock nor Goethals looked into the issue of the underlying autonomous control and self-directedness of the young women living in these three different social environments. Perhaps future research can further probe these three variations.

Types of Marriage

Some provocative and stimulating topics were opened by Loeb (1962) when he discussed *plural marriages*. There are several types of plural marriages. Each of them allows one spouse to have more than one marriage partner at the same time. In a *polygynous marriage* one husband has several wives; in a *polyandrous marriage* one wife has several husbands. There are also two types of polygynies: In a *sororal polygyny* the co-wives are sisters or are consanguinal (blood relatives), while in a *nonsororal polygyny* the co-wives are not related or only affinal kin (related by marriage).

Loeb (1962) suggests that polygyny is usually detrimental to women. In differentiating between limited and general polygyny, Loeb suggests that limited polygyny is more of a status marker for men (since the few polygynists represent high status) than for women (since enforced competition results in low status). However, sororal polygyny may enhance female autonomy as the women are supportive of one another. This contrasts sharply with the co-wives in a nonsororal polygyny who tend to be jealous of each other, particularly when competing for access to the center of power in the home, which is associated with the husband's authority.

Loeb hypothesizes that the polyandrous type of plural marriage is negatively associated with the status and dominance of the husband since the common wife could play one of the husbands (or brothers) against the others (also see Gielen, 1993, chap. 29).

Other Marital Customs

Some of the marriage customs are starting to change from a traditional form to a modern one. For example, in the People's Republic of China the Marriage Law was passed in 1980. This Marriage Law abolished the feudal marriage system which deprived women of the right to choose their spouses. This law has established a democratic marriage system, one that gives women free choice of partners, and mandates monogamy and equal rights for both sexes. It also protects the lawful interest of women and children, and outlaws bigamy, concubinage, child betrothal, interference in a widow's remarriage, and the extraction of money or gifts in connection with marriage (Yu & Carpenter, 1991).

Among the changes in Taiwan today are those that permit women to retain their family names after marriage. Women are also allowed to inherit property and to retain property and income in their own name. But in order for a woman to gain ownership of any property, a special contract must be drawn up. If this contract is not drawn up, all property acquired before and during the marriage will go to the husband (Yu & Carpenter, 1991). On the other hand, women are held responsible for their husband's debts (Diamond, 1973).

Female versus Male Rights and Roles

In societies where a wife felt that she had the right to use or dispose of her sexuality, she could be said to display a measure of personal autonomy. However, in a reversed situation, where the husband disposes of the wife's sexuality, the opposite would be the case. Wives have no control over their actions when the husband gives or lends his wife to another man for sexual purposes without her consent; her husband can force her to comply, or else she can be punished if she refuses (Schlegel, 1972).

In a similar way, regulations with regard to adultery might be weighted individually for the husband and the wife. One can probably expect that a double standard exists. For instance, it was suggested that in societies where the husband is dominant the attitudes toward him are more lenient. And vice versa, the wife might receive more lenient treatment in societies with other authority patterns (Schlegel, 1972).

Female versus Male Attitudes

A traditional men's attitude is reported from Mexico by Diaz-Guerrero and Rodriguez de Diaz (1993). They explain that, according to Mexican tradition, the undisputed authority of the male in the home and in all other functions in relation to the female may be explained by the fact that a man has testicles and a woman does not.

Incidents such as the following are very common among university students. If one of Mexico's relatively few career-driven women obtains high grades, one (or many) of the male students will suggest that he knows from reliable sources that this student has already missed several menstruations. United States citizens might leap to the conclusion that the young woman is pregnant; but in Mexico the implication is that "she is becoming a male" (p. 206).

Augmentation of such ideas and attitudes makes the home life for the lower-class Latin American woman quite difficult. Thus, Lefley (1991) notes that in some homes, men beat their wives as a prerogative of their *machismo,* which, they say, demonstrates their sexual love. There is no escape for the women but to suffer through these attacks. By doing so, these women can identify themselves with *la sufrida,* the woman who sacrifices herself for those she loves.

However, in a different vein, Lefley (1991) cites P. R. Sanday (1981) on the dual-sex political systems in Obamkpa, West Africa, where "each sex has its own autonomous sphere of authority and an area of shared responsibility" (Lefley, p. 116).

During recent decades many native Alaskan women have rejected their low status and their traditional roles. This is a major factor in the potential breakup of the native societies and the subsistence lifestyle. In coming decades Alaskan women are expected to be accorded greater equality, and hence, greater opportunities for autonomy (Fischer, 1991).

In general, women still follow the sex-stereotypical gender-specific roles in terms of being a homemaker, and a child- and family-care provider; only in the modern and industrialized countries do women take on salaried jobs outside the home.

In many parts of the world, the opportunity exists for women to accept employment outside their home and earn an independent income. Gardiner and Gardiner (1991) suggest that this new socioeconomic status may be a major contributing factor to the rapidly changing role of women, not only in Thailand, but in many parts of the world.

The working woman in India, as reported by Kumar (1991), seems to enjoy a more important status in her husband's family and takes pleasure in feelings of greater self-esteem. Because of this situation it turns out that in practice young, newly married wives are continuing their education. There exists currently a trend of a greater worth of a professionally trained working woman in the marriage market.

However, it is a different story for Tharu women, the tribal women of India (Singhal & Mrinal, 1991). Tharu women wield a considerable influence on their menfolk. They are industrious while the men are generally sluggish and unwilling. The Tharu women have greater responsibility in domestic life. Because of the dominance of Tharu women, chastity may not be a virtue and the Tharu men do not worry much on this account. Singhal and

Mrinal (1991) report that when Tharu women and men quarrel, the women always win. And when Tharu wives maltreat their husbands, the husbands may turn for help to their village chief. Yet here, too, the Tharu women have the final word. As is, the men are used to the behavior of their women and are generally yielding. It seems safe to say that the dominance of the Tharu women in their communities must have certainly bolstered their self-directedness, as well as their autonomy.

A current perspective is reported by Markoulis and Dikaiou (1993) about the social transition of Greek families moving to cities. They note that these families are nuclear. As a consequence, the daughter grows up with fewer adult female models with whom to identify. It thus seems that the woman in transition has to explore a new situation and lifestyle; but if she is goal-directed, she comes to grips with her heightened feelings of autonomy and her new status.

In the Greek urban family the father presents an ambiguous role model. He is still "father–provider." But he is not the only one who brings home a salary anymore; the mother, though she probably has a lower income, shares financial responsibility for the family. Despite this, the father probably does not help substantially with the household chores. While the mother most likely objects, she often has no choice but to perform her housework alone. In executing these chores, she might approach these duties with more efficiency.

There remain many areas where women follow traditional lifestyles. For example, the Yoruba wife in Nigeria is overtly submissive to her husband, though at the same time she is independent of him economically. Her housewifely behaviors include serving food to her husband on bended knee, yet she is free to secure a divorce (Okafor, 1991), and she is in control of her life and is free to be self-determined. In the case of a husband's death, the wife has the option to terminate the marriage or allow his marital rights to be passed on. When a man dies, his marital rights go to his younger brother, or to a son by another wife who can take care of the widow and her children (Okafor, 1991).

Until recently the situation was quite different in Portugal; de Mendonca Covas (1993) reports that "Once their spouse has died, men who have no one else to take care of them may give up on life. Yet, in traditional communities there were no remarriages after the death of a spouse—out of respect for the memory of the deceased. This philosophy is changing" (de Mendonca Covas, 1993, p. 297).

OLD AGE AND ISSUES OF AUTONOMY

Frequently the last phase of the life span has the aura of the "golden years." However, in recent decades this image often has been tarnished by reality. Bucher and D'Amorim (1993) report the results of the Educational Project for Senior Citizens (Projeto de Ensino para a Terceira Idade) conducted by the State University of Ceara in Brazil: "one of the greatest problems faced in conjugal relationships is due to the retirement of the husband, who begins to manage the household—the erstwhile prerogative of the wife" (p. 24). In response to the countless marital problems, the project enrolled the women in a course in preparation for retirement that included instruction in managing the power relationship and life or psychological space of the couple. This course restored the self-esteem of the wife, as well as her control and personal autonomy.

Merenda and Mattioni (1993) describe the situation for the elderly in Italy as follows: "Whereas in peasant culture the elderly had considerable status as the holders of wisdom and important practical knowledge, in modern industrial Italy the most that old people can hope for is a dignified autonomy" (p. 170). They continue, though, to explain that frequently this is a futile hope because, to a great extent, today's elderly receive pensions that have not kept up with the rate of inflation. This is why many are forced to live with children. One of the favorite pastimes of the elderly women is spending time with, and taking care of, their grandchildren, particularly in the case of working daughters and/or daughters-in-law.

Ragus and Pinzas (1993) also mention that elderly Chilean women are reliable in their nurturing role with children. In fact, judging by the many culturally different reports, it is quite apparent that just about everywhere elderly women can fall back on their nurturing skills, functioning as babysitters or taking care of grandchildren. The self-assurance that an elderly woman has, knowing that she is self-reliant if needed, certainly increases her feeling of self-esteem and self-directedness.

Half-way round the world, in Korea a somewhat similar situation exists. Tae Lyon Kim (1993) explains that "the philosophy of Confucius has traditionally been the primary influence on Korean behavior and customs. Under the teachings of Confucius, filial obligation has been regarded as the basic code of conduct and the most important moral principle" (p. 195). However, in modern times contemporary customs have shifted the power from the elderly to the nuclear family in general. Unable to keep up with the advancements of science and technology, the elderly have had to yield their position of experience and wisdom to the younger generation. Elderly men, especially, have lost their position as the center of power in the family. On the other hand, elderly women continue to exert their influence in the family, specifically in the realm of housekeeping, although to a lesser degree than was true during their earlier adult years. Many elderly women stay at home to take care of their grandchildren and help with the housework.

Korea also follows the trend of other countries with increasing standards of living and progressive developments in medicine, leading to a lower mortality rate and longer life expectancies. The result is a growing population of the elderly.

In most developed and advanced countries, life expectancy has increased steadily for the past decades. But today it is Japan that enjoys the world's longest average life expectancy of 74 years for men and 81 years for women. Sukemune, Shiraishi, Shirakawa, and Matsumi (1993) also point out that with longer life expectancy the younger Japanese wife may live with her mother-in-law until she herself is a grandmother.

Some interesting statistics are contributed for Israel by Safir and Izraeli (1991), who write about kibbutz life. Most of the kibbutzim were established by young people more than 50 years ago, and currently have a large elderly population. In addition, the life expectancy for women in the kibbutz is three years more than for their urban counterparts. And for the men in the kibbutz it is six years more. "While the economic structure of the kibbutz relieves its members of financial insecurity, social norms encourage the older members, both men and women, to continue working as long as they are able to" (p. 103). Elderly members, however, may move into less demanding jobs and reduce their working hours.

Safir and Izraeli also point out that the social status of the individual in the collective is greatly influenced by the person's contributions. Therefore, the kibbutz is faced with a dual problem. The first and the most obvious difficulty is the physical care of the aging members. The second problem is the task of finding meaningful social roles for the elderly so that they can function effectively in the kibbutz community. Certainly there seems to be an awareness of the importance of maintaining an active and positive self-image and sense of autonomy.

Conclusion

This chapter has focused on autonomy, in other words, on self-directedness, personal control, or self-efficacy from a developmental point of view as well as from a cross-cultural and cross-national perspective. Until now, very little cross-cultural research has been directed toward autonomy. Further research is needed in order to evaluate different approaches to autonomy under a variety of situations and conditions in varied environments.

Control is an important aspect of understanding autonomy in childhood. Control entails two important dimensions: primary and secondary control. Control-related styles include overcontrolled and undercontrolled behavior. Control styles in children have been studied cross-culturally in terms of their prevalence and also the attitudes toward these modes of behavior.

In young and middle adulthood, mate selection in different cultures is a central area of discussion pertaining to autonomy. Societies vary in terms of their acceptance of mate selection practices such as premarital sex, polygyny, and polyandry. Research on these topics, as well as on female and male roles and attitudes, provides insight into female and male autonomy cross-culturally in early and middle adulthood.

In old age, the self-concept and self-esteem of women may not reveal any deterioration—contrary to that of men after retirement—because elderly women continue to follow a maternal and nurturing role when they take care of grandchildren. In a cross-cultural perspective, elderly women follow the approved paths of sex-stereotypical and gender-specific roles. Yet their autonomy goes far beyond breeding and feeding, in Schlegel's (1972) words, as it includes the control over their thoughts and actions, as well as the many meaningful contributions they render to their families, their communities, and their societies.

Until recently, very little cross-cultural research has been directed toward autonomy. Further research is needed in order to evaluate different approaches to autonomy under a variety of situations and conditions in varied environments. While the cultural environment and its effect on autonomy is acknowledged, specific components of culture in relation to autonomy must be explored. For example, religious belief or the effects of religious practices play an important role in an individual's self-directedness and sense of personal control.

The following illustration describes such differences more succinctly. While discussing the topic of death and dying, a young Asian Indian woman who had been listening, responded spontaneously: "I do not know why there is such a fuss about death and dying; when you die you are reincarnated." This type of response reflects the tendency toward external attributions that is more typical of Eastern cultures. Thus, people's autonomous behavior will vary due to variations in religious upbringing as well as other differences in cultural backgrounds. It is necessary when pursuing cross-cultural research on autonomy to include the cultural dimensions that shape people's orientations, as well as channel and influence their behavior and lifestyles.

REFERENCES

Achenbach, T. M. (1978). The child behavior profile I: Boys aged 6–11. *Journal of Consulting and Clinical Psychology, 46,* 478–488.

Achenbach, T. M., & Edelbrock, C. S. (1978). The classification of child psychopathology: A review and analysis of empirical efforts. *Psychological Bulletin, 85,* 1275–1301.

Adler, L. L. (Ed.). (1991). *Women in cross-cultural perspective.* Westport, CT: Praeger.

Adler, L. L. (Ed.). (1993). *International handbook on gender roles.* Westport, CT: Greenwood Press.

Ayres, B. (1976). *Marriage systems as reproductive strategies: Cross-cultural evidence for sexual selection in man.* Paper presented at the meeting of the Society for Cross-Cultural Research, New York.

Barry, H., III. (1976). Cultural variations in sex differentiation during childhood. *Unpublished paper,* 17.

Brotman-Band, E., & Weisz, J. R. (1988). How to feel better when it feels bad: Children's perspectives on coping with everyday stress. *Developmental Psychology, 24,* 247–253.

Broude, G. J. (1981). The cultural management of sexuality. In R. H. Munroe, R. L. Munroe, & B. B. Whiting (Eds.), *Handbook of cross-cultural human development* (pp. 633–673). New York: Garland.

Brown, J. K. (1981). Cross-cultural perspectives on the female life cycle. In R. H. Munroe, R. L. Munroe, & B. B. Whiting (Eds.), *Handbook of cross-cultural human development* (pp. 581–733). New York: Garland.

Bucher, J. F., & D'Amorim, M. A. (1993). Brazil. In L. L. Adler (Ed.), *International handbook on gender roles* (pp. 15–27). Westport, CT: Greenwood Press.

Collins, L. F., Maxwell, A. E., & Cameron, A. (1962). A factor analysis of some child psychiatric data. *Journal of Mental Science, 108,* 274–285.

de Mendonca Covas, M. (1993). Portugal. In L. L. Adler (Ed.), *International handbook on gender roles* (pp. 281–300). Westport, CT: Greenwood Press.

Diamond, N. (1973). The status of women in Taiwan: One step forward, two steps back. In M. B. Young (Ed.), *Women in China.* Ann Arbor, MI: Center for Chinese Studies, University of Michigan.

Diaz-Guerrero, R., & Rodriguez de Diaz, M. L. (1993). Mexico. In L. L. Adler (Ed.), *International handbook on gender roles* (pp. 199–217). Westport, CT: Greenwood Press.

Dragonas, T. G. (1983). *The self-concept of preadolescents in the Hellenic context.* Unpublished doctoral dissertation. University of Aston, Birmingham, U.K.

Fischer, M. (1991). Women in the arctic (Alaska): A culture in transition. In L. L. Adler (Ed.), *Women in cross-cultural perspective* (pp. 20–25). Westport, CT: Praeger.

Gardiner, H. W., & Gardiner, O. S. (1991). Women in Thailand. In L. L. Adler (Ed.), *Women in cross-cultural perspective* (pp. 174–187). Westport, CT: Praeger.

Gardiner, H. W., & Suttipan, C. S. (1977). Parental tolerance of aggression: Perceptions of preadolescents in Thailand. *Psychologia, 20,* 28–32.

Gielen, U. P. (1993). Traditional Tibetan societies. In L. L. Adler (Ed.), *International handbook on gender roles* (pp. 413–437). Westport, CT: Greenwood Press.

Goethals, G. W. (1971). Factors affecting permissive and nonpermissive rules regarding premarital sex. In J. M. Henslin (Ed.), *Sociology of sex: A book of readings* (pp. 9–26). New York: Appleton, Century, Croft.

Groos, K. (1901). *The Play of Man.* New York: Appleton.

Hayashi, K., Toyama, B., & Quay, H. C. (1976). A cross-cultural study concerned with differential behavior classification: I, the behavior checklist. *Japanese Journal of Criminal Psychology, 2,* 21–28.

Inkeles, A., & Smith, D. H. (1974). *Becoming modern: Individual change in six developing countries.* Cambridge, MA: Harvard University Press.

Kamii, C. (1981, October). *Autonomy as the aim of education: Implications of Piaget's theory.* Keynote address at the Annual Conference of the North Carolina Association for the Education of Young Children, Winston-Salem, NC.

Kamii, C., & Joseph, L. L. (1989). *Young children continue to reinvent arithmetic—2nd grade: Implications of Piaget's theory.* New York: Teachers College, Columbia University.

Kim, T. L. (1993). Korea. In L. L. Adler (Ed.), *International handbook on gender roles* (pp. 187–198). Westport, CT: Greenwood Press.

Kumar, U. (1991). Life stages in the development of the Hindu woman in India. In L. L. Adler (Ed.),

Women in cross-cultural perspective (pp. 143–158). Westport, CT: Praeger.

Lefley, H. P. (1991). Foreword. In L. L. Adler (Ed.), *Women in cross-cultural perspective* (pp. xi–xvi). Westport, CT: Praeger.

Loeb, E. M. (1962). In feudal Africa. *International Journal of American Linguistics, 28*(3), pt. 2, 137.

Macfarlane, A. (1978). *The origins of English individualism: The family, property, and social transition.* Oxford, U.K.: Basil Blackwell.

Macfarlane, A. (1986). *Marriage and Love in England: Modes of Reproduction 1300–1840.* Oxford, U.K.: Basil Blackwell.

Markoulis, D.C., & Dikaiou, M. (1993). Greece. In L. L. Adler (Ed.), *International handbook on gender roles* (pp. 85–97). Westport, CT: Greenwood Press.

Merenda, R., & Mattioni, M. (1993). Italy. In L. L. Adler (Ed.), *International handbook on gender roles* (pp. 159–173). Westport, CT: Greenwood Press.

Minturn, L., Grosse, M., & Haider, S. (1969). Cultural patterning of sexual beliefs and behavior. *Ethnology, 8,* 301–318.

Moussourou, L. (1985). *Family and child in Athens.* Athens: Hestia.

Murdock, G. P. (1964). Cultural correlates of the regulations of premarital sex behavior. In R. A. Manners (Ed.), *Process and pattern in culture.* Chicago: Aldine.

Murdock, G. P. (1967). Ethnographic atlas. *Ethnology, 6,* 109–236.

Okafor, N. A. O. (1991). Some traditional aspects of Nigerian women. In L. L. Adler (Ed.), *Women in cross-cultural perspective* (pp. 134–141). Westport, CT: Praeger.

Peterson, D. R. (1965). Structural congruence and metric variability in a cross-cultural study of children's behavior problems. *Archivo di Psicologia, Neurologia, e Psichiatrica, 2,* 174–187.

Piaget, J. (1963). *The origins of intelligence in children.* New York: Norton.

Piaget, J. (1965/1932). *The moral judgement of the child.* New York: Free Press.

Quay, H. C., & Parskenopoulos, I. N. (1972). *Dimensions of problem behavior in elementary school children in Greece, Iran, and Finland.* Paper presented at the 20th International Congress of Psychology, Tokyo, Japan.

Raguz, M. M., & Pinzas, J. R. (1993). Peru. In L. L. Adler (Ed.), *International handbook on gender roles* (pp. 244–257). Westport, CT: Greenwood Press.

Redfield, R. (1956). *Peasant society and culture: An anthropological approach to civilization.* Chicago, IL: University of Chicago Press.

Rosenberg, M. (1990). Control of environment and control of self. In J. Rodin, L. Schooler, & K. W. Schaire (Eds.), *Self-directedness: Cause and effects throughout the life course* (pp. 147–154). Hillsdale, NJ: Lawrence Erlbaum Assoc.

Safir, M. P., & Izraeli, D. N. (1991). Growing up female: A life-span perspective on women in Israel. In L. L. Adler (Ed.), *Women in cross-cultural perspective* (pp. 90–105). Westport, CT: Praeger.

Sanday, P. R. (1981). *Female power and male dominance: On the origins of sexual inequality.* New York: Cambridge University Press.

Schlegel, A. (1972). *Male dominance and female autonomy.* New Haven, CT: Human Relations Area Files, Inc.

Schooler, C. (1990). Individualism and the historical and social-structural determinants of people's concerns over self-directedness and efficacy. In J. Rodin, C. Schooler, & K. W. Schaie (Eds.), *Self-directedness: cause and effects throughout the life course.* Hillsdale, NJ: Lawrence Erlbaum Assoc.

Singhal, U., & Mrinal, N. R. (1991). Tribal women of India: The Tharu women. In L. L. Adler (Ed.), *Women in cross-cultural perspective* (pp. 159–173). Westport, CT: Praeger.

Stephens, W. (1963). *The family in cross-cultural perspective.* New York: Holt, Rinehart & Winston.

Sukemune, S., Shiraishi, T., Shirakawa, Y., & Matsumi, J. T. (1993). Japan. In L. L. Adler (Ed.), *International handbook on gender roles* (pp. 174–186). Westport, CT: Greenwood Press.

Weisz, J. R. (1990). Development of control-related beliefs, goals and styles in childhood and adolescence: A clinical perspective. In J. Rodin, C. Schooler, & K. W. Schaie (Eds.), *Self-directedness: Cause and effects throughout the life course* (pp. 103–145). Hillsdale, NJ: Lawrence Erlbaum Assoc.

Weisz, J. R., & Stipek, D. J. (1982). Competence, contingency, and the development of perceived control. *Human Development, 25,* 250–281.

Yu, L. C., & Carpenter, L. (1991). Women in China. In L. L. Adler (Ed.), *Women in cross-cultural perspective* (pp. 189–203). Westport, CT: Praeger.

3

AUTONOMY DURING INFANCY AND CHILDHOOD

BARBARA A. MOWDER
Pace University

Autonomy is an interesting construct, but one which lacks consensus. Conventional views of autonomy often focus on an individual's acceptance of responsibility for personal decision making and behavior; but researchers vary as to the characteristics they select to define or describe autonomy. Among these are behavioral self-regulation, capacity for managing new situations, competence, individuality, internally mediated compliance, personal authority, self-assurance and assertion, self-regulation and control, and sense of agency. As can be inferred from theory and research noted in the first chapter by Nadien and Denmark, theoreticians also vary in their use of and meanings ascribed to autonomy. In general, however, autonomy is perceived as behavior which indicates some level of individual personal control.

AUTONOMY AND THE SELF

Historically, the idea of autonomy emanates from psychological theories focused on the self developed in Western culture. There is some question, however, about whether these theoretical views of autonomy accurately reflect the life experience of all individuals, particularly those of females.

For example, Lykes (1985) finds that views of the self as autonomous and separate ignore individuals' sociohistorical contexts (see Gergen, 1973; Sampson, 1978) as well as the social contexts which shape our psychological knowledge (Buss, 1975). Indeed, extensive evidence suggests that the experiences of females (e.g., Broverman, Broverman, Clarkson, Rosenkrantz, & Vogel, 1970), persons of color (e.g., White, 1984; Willie, 1979), and people from a lower socioeconomic status (e.g., Mishler, Amarasingham, Hauser, Liem,

Osherson, & Waxler, 1981) "are not faithfully represented by self-theories that emphasize autonomy and individualism" (Lykes, 1985, p. 357).

Lykes (1985) investigated alternative ideas about the self with regard to individualism, collectivity, and social individuality. Her notion of the self contrasts with both the position of autonomous individuals interacting with other autonomous persons and the view of the self as represented by the social whole (negating an appreciation of the individual). Lykes relies heavily on recent developments in psychological theory and gender research to argue for a self-in-relation position so as to give an accurate description of women's lives and experiences. She maintains that this is an important alternative to the prevailing view of the self assumed in notions of autonomous individualism as well as collectivist bases for ideas about the self.

Key elements for evaluating female perspectives come from research by Gilligan (1982), Chodorow (1978), Miller (1984), and others. For example, Gilligan (1982) debated Kohlberg's (1969) reliance on the constructs of autonomy and separation in defining and valuing moral development. For Kohlberg, the highest levels of moral reasoning depend upon abstract moral principles, consistent with a Western perspective of a moral hierarchy. Gilligan (1982), however, felt that women experienced a distinctly different sense of self, one which expressed itself in a separate form or basis for moral decision making. Because females' sense of self is housed within relationships, moral issues are also evaluated within that context. That is, relationships imply interactions, interdependence, and strong attachments, and it is through relationships that females come to know themselves and others. From this point of view, morality or responsibility depends on caring for others (Lykes, 1985).

Lyons (1983) examined gender differences in approaches to solving moral problems; she hypothesized that individuals would use one of two modes to describe the self-in-relation. From one perspective, the individual perceives relationships as essential, with the making, sustaining, and assisting in relationships as important, key features. From the other perspective, the self is described as being separate in terms of relationships with others. Even though both sexes use relational characteristics in describing themselves, females favor the orientation of making and maintaining relationships while men emphasize the self as separate from others.

Miller (1976, 1984) presents another alternative to the prevailing view of the self as an autonomous individual. Miller maintains that, in contrast to boys, girls rely, build on, and utilize their early attachment and affiliation experiences. Ultimately, females experience affiliation and relationships as strengths and enhancements in their lives. Interconnections and interdependence are part of their lives and form an essential part of their self-evaluation. Moreover, the individual decision making and autonomous behaviors of females grow out of and occur within a context of relationships. Miller finds that reliance on relationships, however, in no way detracts from females' sense of self.

Thus, the contemporary perspective is that the importance with which females hold relationships and define themselves does not detract from their autonomy or sense of individual personal control. On the contrary, the self-in-relation notion is supported by a substantial literature that documents the value of affiliation, connectedness, and relationships for women. Further, it assists us in understanding autonomy in females and how autonomy may develop differently for girls in contrast to boys.

Autonomy involves not only gender issues. There are also developmental implications in that children and adults are at quite different levels of physical, cognitive, and social-emotional growth. For instance, autonomous behaviors in a two-year-old may entail deciding what person to play with or how far to move away physically from the parents or guardians. Whereas autonomy for adults may center on issues such as making decisions about vocational choices or personal relationships. Thus, autonomy does not encompass the same factors over the developmental life span.

The demonstration of autonomy is bound to vary between the two genders and to display itself in behaviors which change somewhat over the course of life. Moreover, gender differences, related behaviors, and developmental changes are part of a broader picture. Autonomy is a social construct bound by social conceptions and conventions, and occurring within a historical context. For example, what may have been thought of as self-regulated behavior for a female at the turn of the century is surely different from that which is currently connected with autonomous female behavior. Therefore, autonomy is gender specific and developmental, and needs to be evaluated within its sociocultural and historical framework.

With these issues in mind, this chapter addresses the issue of autonomy as the construct relates to the developing female child from infancy through adolescence. Throughout this chapter the sociocultural and historical issues related to autonomy are interwoven and are integral to any discussion. This chapter, therefore, is organized so that there is a brief discussion of child development issues along with growth and development from infancy through early adolescence. Autonomy in girls is discussed in terms of the acquisition, possession, and manifestation of autonomy and the relationship of autonomy to parent-child interactions and child temperament. Finally, the need for further research in this area is discussed.

DEVELOPMENTAL ISSUES AS THEY RELATE TO AUTONOMY

Between birth and early adolescence, there is tremendous child growth and development. Infants are usually born with the full complement of sensory apparatus; but across childhood, the skills and abilities associated with taking in and using communications and information from the environment become more developed, integrated, and complex. *Development* refers to the pattern of change which begins with conception and continues throughout life. Development influences and is, in return, influenced by autonomy. Every aspect of child development, from physical and sensory development to cognitive and social-emotional development, is part of the growth landscape and merits at least a brief discussion with regard to the development of autonomy in young girls.

Gaining a sense of autonomy depends on the acquisition not only of sensory skills such as hearing and seeing, but also of the communication skills of attending to relevant stimuli, responding, and taking turns. But development is not limited to communication. At an early point, infants develop physically and learn to establish some degree of control over their bodies. Social skills, such as developing smiles in response to social interactions, develop as do cognitive skills. In the course of such development, children are integrating their skills and abilities, learning, and performing within their environment.

Developmentalists posit a number of questions regarding growth and development. Probably the most debated issue is that of nature versus nurture, the relative contribution of one's physical, biological constitution as opposed to the effect of environmental circumstances. Those who take a biological genetic position tend to perceive development as being determined from the outset by physiological predispositions. However, those who adopt the nurture position view development as being quite malleable and subject to variation due to familial and/or other sociocultural and environmental circumstances. This issue raises the following question with regard to autonomy. Is autonomous behavior the product of biological and physical changes in a child or is it subject to environmental and cultural manipulation and, therefore, the product of relationships, including family dynamics, and the social milieu?

Another issue is whether development represents changes which accrue quantitatively over time or whether it reflects characteristics that are qualitatively different from one time to another. The question is whether development constitutes a sum total of changes or whether the changes themselves represent something greater than the sum of its parts. Piaget (1929, 1951) exemplifies a theorist who takes the position that developmental changes are qualitatively different over time and represent more than a collection of learnings. Skinner (1972, 1976), on the other hand, believes that behavior is indeed a collection of learnings. He thinks, for example, that learning for the infant or toddler is no different than learning for the adult—the only difference is in the amount of cumulative learning that has occurred over time. The issue regarding autonomy is whether there is a development over time of accumulated behaviors that come to represent autonomy, or whether autonomy represents a qualitatively different aspect of behavior.

Another issue is whether children are active or passive in the developmental process. In other words, do children influence their development through their own actions or are they simply passive in terms of the activities and interactions occurring around them? Piaget asserts that individuals must be active in their development, whereas Watson (1930) argues that children are absolutely passive—events around them shape their world, their behavior, and their future. If one takes the passive point-of-view, the child simply comes to display autonomous behavior because of the events occurring around them which shape their behavior according to external expectations. If, however, one holds to the child as active in her or his developmental sequence, then the child's behavior is a factor which strongly influences the development of autonomy.

Past experiences and their effect on development constitutes yet another issue with which developmentalists grapple. For example, if infants have experienced a background of neglect, how might that affect their later behavior? Theorists like Freud might maintain that early deprivation and other experiences affect all subsequent aspects of child, adolescent, and adult development. On the other hand, such learning theorists as Skinner and Bandura assume the opposite position. They think that significant changes in behavior may occur based on different circumstances which occur over time. For example, the effects of early deprivation or neglect do not necessarily mean that the child will experience atypical social-emotional development. Applying this issue to autonomy, the question is whether the child's early experiences preclude, for example, the development of autonomous behavior, or whether the child's early experiences are, for the most part, irrelevant with regard to the development and display of autonomy and personal control.

Developmentalists also want to identify the end-goal of development. For learning theorists, there is no one specific expectation as the end-goal for development. Each person's development is to some extent different. For cognitive developmentalists such as Piaget, however, there is a very specific goal—attaining formal operational thinking. Similarly, for Freud and other psychodynamic theorists, development inevitably moves toward a specific goal; for Freud that goal is the stage of adult genital development. Regarding autonomy, the question is whether there is a final or achieved behavior which is indicative of an autonomous individual or whether there are a variety of behaviors which may come to represent autonomy with different individuals evidencing autonomy in somewhat different ways.

Finally, there is the issue of the stability of traits over time. In other words, once children have achieved a certain developmental milestone, does it become a part of their developmental repertoire? Or, on the other hand, are all behaviors to some extent modifiable? From a Piagetian point of view, for instance, once a child has achieved conservation (i.e., the understanding of equivalence), the child will not lose that skill. From a learning perspective, however, behaviors are substantially modifiable. No particular behavior is exempt from refinement and change. Applying this issue to autonomy, the question is whether autonomy is a trait, skill, or ability that, once developed, becomes part of the developing child, or whether autonomy is somewhat modifiable and is subject to environmental circumstances.

Thus, developmentalists grapple with many issues, most of which apply not only to autonomy but to many psychological phenomena which occur across the life span. Since our discussion focuses on autonomy as a developmental construct in infants, toddlers, preschoolers, and children, a brief review of some features of development from infancy through early adolescence follows.

NEWBORN AND INFANT DEVELOPMENT: DIFFERENT PERSPECTIVES

Infants start out with few of the resources needed for personal autonomy. For example, infants initially have little physical control over their bodies. As they develop muscle coordination, gross motor skills (large muscle activities) and fine motor skills (small muscle activities), their growth is rapid and the reflexes which predominate after birth give way to more sophisticated physical control over their bodies.

Language development is also a striking developmental feature that reflects some control over autonomy. Many psychologists think that communicative efforts begin at birth with the newborn's first cry. Others take the position that language starts when children make a distinct, deliberate communication effort, regardless of whether that effort is verbally based or not. In other words, smiles and other forms of communication represent integral aspects of language development. Regardless of its beginnings, children have acquired a significant vocabulary and an equally impressive set of receptive and expressive language skills by early adolescence.

Social–Emotional Development and Autonomy

Social–emotional development is an important area of child growth. For infants, attachment to parents is critical and forms the basis for much of the child's well-being and the model for the infant's later attachments and emotional relationships.

Well-being and attachment, in turn, have a bearing on the later development of autonomy. There is extensive research on attachment, much of it conducted by Mary Ainsworth (1973, 1982) and her associates (e.g., Main & Cassidy). Attachment as a construct was originally developed by John Bowlby (1969, 1973, 1980) and his thinking on this topic forms much of our understanding of attachment behaviors. For the infant, *attachment* is an invisible tie or bond of affection which develops between the child and the parent. As the child cries out, smiles, or establishes eye contact, the parent typically responds to the child's bids for attention. The attachment process has survival value; for if the infant's needs are not met, the developing young child, who lacks so many skills needed for survival, would surely die. By 18 months of age, the attachment relationship can be reliably measured. The results of a positive attachment outcome, secure attachment, are associated with children's abilities to initiate social contacts, engage in social play, and perform well in preschool.

Attachment is a precursor to autonomy. Attachment provides children with a secure base from which to explore their environment. The exploration, in turn, leads to greater examination of relationships, events, objects, and people. From the secure exploration, children tend to develop a sense of their own efficacy, of their abilities to move into unfamiliar areas with a sense of competence and impending success.

There are additional theories and related research regarding children's social and emotional development. The most relevant of the additional theories is that of Erik Erikson (1950), discussed in another section.

ACQUISITION OF AUTONOMY: DIFFERENT THEORETICAL PERSPECTIVES

Much of the research does not make comparisons between girls and boys, but instead deals with children in general. Thus, the acquisition of autonomy, irrespective of gender, suggests that at one point young children do not have autonomy, but at another point in time they do (see Allen, Hauser, Bell, & O'Connor, 1994). Depending on the theoretical framework selected, autonomy may be a characteristic which emerges gradually over time and therefore is considered a continuous developmental variable. In other words, behaviors accrue which build toward an overall demonstration of autonomous behavior. This position accommodates well to anticipated differences in demonstrated autonomous behaviors from childhood to adult development.

Taking a different perspective, however, one might assert that autonomy is a discontinuous variable in that there are not gradations or an overall shifting display of autonomy. Rather, one could argue that autonomy is a behavior which represents a complexity largely absent one day, but displayed and incorporated into the individual's cognitive and behavioral repertoire on the next. While this may be overstating the case, this perspective maintains that autonomy is a qualitative construct that has its own set of characteristics and is not just a combination of previously learned behaviors.

On the one hand, the notion of slowly developing skills that come to represent autonomous behavior represents a behavioral or social learning point of view. On the other hand, the presence of a qualitatively new behavior, autonomy, is characteristic of a more cognitively-oriented perspective. From each theoretical position, the same set of autonomous behaviors may be discussed (e.g., the young child's independent movement away from the parent or guardian), but the reasoning about how the behaviors come to be demonstrated starts from different premises and, therefore, each position explains the phenomenon differently. From the social learning perspective, the child attends to and retains the positively rewarded behavior of models, and then reproduces and displays that observed behavior. The imitated behavior will differ somewhat with child development because children differentially attend, retain, and reproduce observed behavior. Behavior is demonstrated that is appropriate to their developmental level, but that behavior changes according to differential observations and imitations of autonomous displays of behavior. For example, a 10-year-old child may readily approach a clown as she or he has seen another child do. A 3-year-old may readily move toward the same clown but stop before moving too far from its parent. And, for the cognitive developmental position, children develop schemas that represent their construction of their experiences. Their perceptions and related behaviors change as they assimilate new information or as the need for accommodation leads to changing schemata.

From a developmental standpoint, there are four prevailing positions—those of behavioral or social learning, cognitive developmental views, psychodynamic theory, and ethological theory. These four positions assist in the discussion of autonomy as a developmental issue.

Behavior and Social Learning Theory

As currently used, the behavioral position is well represented by social learning theory, especially in terms of Bandura's (1986) view of perceived control or self-efficacy. Bandura notes that self-efficacy is neither a fixed act, nor simply an issue of knowing what to do and when to do it. Instead, he finds that:

> *Efficacy involves a generative capability in which cognitive, social, and behavioral subskills must be organized into integrated courses of action to serve innumerable purposes. Success is often attained only after generating and testing alternative forms of behavior and strategies, which requires perseverant effort. Self-doubters are quick to abort this generative process if their initial efforts prove deficient (p. 391).*

Bandura is quick to point out that self-efficacy is not demonstrated by isolated, specific acts. Rather, self-efficacy is associated with more general, generative capacities. His theory is not specifically developmentally sensitive; however, his idea that subskills build integrated courses of action that serve a number of purposes provides room for different displays of autonomy developmentally. Even though Bandura uses a behavioral framework to describe human learning, it is clear from his description of self-efficacy that he incorporates a cognitive perspective. That is, behavior is closely related to an individual's cognitions and individual perceptions.

Piaget's Developmental Theory

Piaget is representative of a cognitively-oriented perspective. This point of view lends itself to the idea that a child develops a schema or schemas related to autonomous behavior. The young infant and toddler engage in behaviors that become routinized, forming a level of predictability from which the young child engages in more diverse behavior. Eventually, children come to develop cognitions and behaviors consistent with what one would describe as autonomous behavior. Once achieved, autonomy is built into a child's cognitive frame of reference and serves as a vehicle for further demonstrations of autonomous behavior. This view of autonomy as a discontinuous construct is nevertheless developmentally responsive. Once autonomy as a cognitive concept is achieved, the behaviors associated with it are assimilated into that schema. As the individual develops, the schemata related to autonomy accommodate more diverse, sophisticated views. For instance, the schemata accommodate changing perceptions of autonomy which, in turn, are related to the characteristics of the growing individual.

Psychodynamic Theory

From a psychodynamic perspective, the young child goes through a series of psychosexual stages. Freud is the primary representative of this theoretical perspective, but for the purpose of discussing autonomy, the views of Erikson, a neo-Freudian, are more useful. Indeed, Erikson is the only theorist who specifically uses the term *autonomy* developmentally and directly addresses the issue of autonomous behavior. For Erikson, autonomy is the primary crisis for young children in the second stage of development, when they are approximately 2–3 years of age. Autonomy represents the positive outcome of this second psychosocial crisis; the negative outcome is shame and doubt. The young child achieves the positive outcome of autonomy when parental responses encourage independence. Parental responses that are approving of independence or self-reliance give shape and meaning to the toddler's behavior and assist in the young child's sense of autonomy. Responses that continually offer the toddler a message of incompetence, on the other hand, lead to an outcome of doubt and shame.

The Ethological Position

In addition to the three prevailing developmental views on autonomy, an additional theoretical perspective that furthers our understanding of autonomy derives from ethological theory as expressed by John Bowlby (1969) and further advanced by Mary Ainsworth (1973). Bowlby's theory of attachment maintains that infants become attached to their parents or primary caregivers for survival reasons. That is, young infants need monitoring and protection in order to grow, develop, and survive. Therefore, young children display behaviors that adults, in turn, respond to. Ultimately, the attachment behavioral system leads children to internal working models of themselves, their caregivers, and their relationship. It is within their internal working models that children come to perceive themselves as safe and competent to successfully explore their surroundings. In so doing, they develop autonomy. The sense of autonomy, however, depends on a secure infant attachment to the mother. An insecure attachment leads to different behavioral manifestations, behaviors indicative of avoidance, resistance, or even disorganization.

From these four theoretical perspectives, it is clear that babies initially do not display what we would call autonomous behaviors, in other words, behaviors that demonstrate children's possession of some level of independence and control over their actions. Indeed, infants and their parents or caregivers are especially remarkable in their power asymmetry.

Parents or caregivers, in general, control the environment that the infants are brought into. Infants depend on their parents or caregivers not only for their well-being, but, indeed, for their very survival. From all four theoretical positions, however, typical young children around the age of 2 or 3 come to demonstrate what is called autonomy. Such behavior is characterized by independent movement away from caregivers and emerges when caregivers encourage and present such behavior in a positive framework.

In contrast to the paucity of research on gender differences in infancy with respect to autonomous behaviors or strivings, considerable empirical work has examined the effect that parents may have on the autonomy of girls as opposed to boys.

PARENTAL INFLUENCES ON AUTONOMY IN CHILDREN

Autonomy for the young child is also associated with responses to maturity demands. Baumrind (1968, 1971, 1973) finds maturity demands consistent with a degree of demanding and firm parenting practices. She refers to such practices as authoritative parenting. Baumrind (1971) defines maturity demands operationally as those parental expectations that by the ages of 2 and one-half, children are putting their toys away and that by the age of 3 they are assisting with household tasks.

Kuczynski and Kochanska (1995) hypothesized that children's personal and social competence develops from parental pressures for competent behavior. The parental demands arise out of harmonious reciprocal parent–child interactions. They conceptualized the parental portion of the parent-child in terms of:

> demands for competent action *as pressures for children to display behavior which benefits the self or others intellectually or instrumentally. These demands consisted of (a) prosocial action (e.g., chores and helping behaviors) and (b) cognitive and play demands. A second group of categories,* demands for appropriate behavior, *described controls that did not involve a tangible instrumental or intellectual action but were concerned with regulating behavior in accordance with standards of personal and social appropriateness. These demands included (a) social regulation and (b) appropriate use of objects. The third group,* caretaking demands, *concerned children's physical well-being and consisted of the categories (a) physical care and (b) monitoring. (p. 617)*

Kuczynski and Kochanska focus on distinguishing between commands requiring children to perform behaviors as opposed to injunctions requiring children to stop or prevent behaviors. Importantly, they found that the age of the child was an important influence on maternal behaviors. Like Gralinski and Kopp (1993), Kuczynski and Kochanska (1995) found that mothers' expectations changed with age during the period of toddler development. With the waning of pressures relating to physical care and protecting objects in the environment was an increase in the mothers' pressuring of their children "for both conventionally appropriate behavior and for socially responsible actions such as doing chores and providing help to others" (p. 625).

The parental behaviors associated with children's competent actions include demands having to do with the performance of behavior rather than the inhibition of behavior (Kuczynski & Kochanska, 1995). This presents children not only with specific behaviors to demonstrate, but also taps their motivational propensities. That is, children produce behaviors that parents specify and as a consequence are praised for their performance. The praise increases the demonstration of the requested behaviors and also the children's responsiveness to their parents. Early self-regulation and the pressures for competent behavior typically occur within a responsive social context. Kuczynski and Kochanska (1995) present findings that suggest parental behaviors which place "an emphasis on inhibitory functions and regulatory contents which predicts behavior problems rather than increased competence" (p. 626). Positive parental behavior in the sense of specifying behavior and rewarding the demonstration of that behavior begets competent, motivated, socially adept responses, whereas negative parental behavior, in terms of consistent negative feedback to children's behavioral productions, produces problematic child behavior.

Infants and toddlers continuously adjust to their parents' expectations. Some of the changes in behavior may reflect growth in children's capacities and attainments in conjunction with changes in parent's socialization goals (Kuczynski & Kochanska, 1995) and parenting perceptions (Mowder, Harvey, Moy, & Pedro, 1995). Gralinski and Kopp (1993), for example, found that parents' initial emphasis on safety shifts to a stress on self-care and on rules regarding chores and family and other social interactions for children between the ages of 13 and 48 months.

Studies of mother–infant interactions indicate that many mothers show different responses to their infants as a function of their gender. For example, girls receive more vocal and visual attention from the mother starting at the outset of their lives and continuing throughout their childhood (Goldberg & Lewis, 1969). By contrast, as Lewis (1972) observed, infant sons enjoy much more physical contact with their mother than do daughters, although this pattern persists only for the first half year of life. After 6 months, the amounts of tactile contact start to decrease for infant sons, but to increase for infant daughters.

With regard to fostering autonomy, parents tend to treat boys and girls differently. Independence training begins early for young boys, but not for girls. As young as 6 months of age, parents tend to discourage clinging behaviors in their boys and encourage independence. However, at 6 months, parents are still holding their daughters closely. By 1 year of age, boys are being encouraged to leave their mothers' side while girls tend to be warned about not going too far. In sum, boys are permitted to explore their surroundings while girls are discouraged from such displays of independence.

As to the possible motives for this gendered differential treatment of infants, Lewis (1972), along with Aberle and Naegele (1952), speculates that perhaps boys are touched more often in the first 6 months of life because, during this time period, they are more irritable than girls and are awake for longer time periods. However, as to the decreasing amounts of tactile stimulation of sons after they reach 6 months of age, one proposed explanation is that mothers withdraw from their sons so as to encourage their independence and motivate their exploration and mastery of their environment (Aberle & Naegele, 1952; Lewis, 1972). Certainly, by 13 months, boys start to differ from girls not only by venturing farther away from the mother, but also by remaining away for longer time periods (Lewis, 1972).

The expectation of dependent behavior in girls seems to increase with children's age. Kagan and Moss (1962), for example, found that prior to age 8, girls are not necessarily more dependent than boys. By late childhood and adolescence, however, such differences tend to be more stable. Lott (1978) offers some observations related to the finding of girls' increasing passivity.

Lott (1978) observed 4-year-old children during free play and found that girls' behaviors were more adult-oriented; girls tended to talk with, smile at, and follow the adults. She characterized one of the major differences between the girls and boys as the degree of the girls' adult-centeredness. The reliance on and susceptibility to adult influence has the potential of moving girls toward adult expectations for appropriate sex-role behavior. If adults, for example, indicate the appropriateness of girls' dependency, girls who are attentive to adults' expectations will tend to display that behavior.

Chodorow (1978) points out the importance of the family, especially the mother, in communicating to girls their gender role. This socialization process insures that girls grow up with appropriate characteristics so they will want to become mothers. Constantinople (1979) points out that parents and families are but some of the many social influences which enforce sex role behavior. And Weitzman (1979) confirms this point and notes the tremendous influence of books in conveying to children what boys and girls do and what is expected of them.

Indeed, Connor, Serbin, and Ender (1978) found that girls in grades 4, 6, and 8 increasingly judge passive behavior in positive terms while boys indicate a devaluation of this behavior. And, consistent with this finding, Maccoby and Jacklin (1974) found that girls, more than boys, comply with parental and teacher directives.

Parents with non-traditional gender-role beliefs, however, are more likely to grant early independence to their daughter than those who hold more traditional opinions (Barnett, 1981). Thus, girls receive messages regarding appropriate sex role behavior dependent on their own set of socializing agents.

Even before the age of 2, children internalize a variety of experiences from their many day-to-day interactions with their parents and others (Emde, 1994).

Much of the early development of the self is due to the knowledge children gain from the many procedural and affective routines they experience with their caregivers. Children's experiences range from actions associated with rules, standards, and empathy, to responses to parental prohibitions.

Shared cultural meanings, as well as children's unique experiences and perceptions, affect their development (Emde, 1994). Cultures add common features to an individual's experiences, yet each individual retains a uniqueness special to her or his own specific set of experiences. Emde (1994) further finds that "most of our developmental experience is nonconscious" (p. 731). This complicates the picture of children's displays of autonomy. The knowledge gained through development, or the behaviors displayed developmentally, may have to do with routines the child experiences, routines which are automatic and not necessarily accessible to consciousness.

As children move toward early adolescence, their autonomous behavior changes shape and form. For example, young pregnant adolescents, who were classified as autonomous, presented their early relationships in objective, lively, and poignant ways (Ward & Carlson, 1995). These adolescents were likely to have infants who were classified as secure at a later point in time. These young mothers were able to form adaptive attachments with their infants, even in light of difficult family and environmental circumstances.

MANIFESTATIONS OF AUTONOMY IN OLDER GIRLS AND BOYS

As children approach early adolescence, there is a shifting of the parent–child relationship. The shift is from a unilateral to a mutual authority (Youniss & Smollar, 1985). The shifts in authority, however, are not uniform across all domains. The primary shifts occur over issues regarding young people's personal jurisdiction; with increasing age, both the children and their parents view autonomy over personal issues and multifaceted issues as appropriate (Smetana & Asquith, 1994). In their research, Smetana and Asquith (1994) found that parental authority over multifaceted, conventional, and friendship concerns declined as these children grew older. They found that the sphere of autonomy for these young people is multidimensional and many aspects of control over their decision making, including such issues as their bodies, physical appearance, and choice of friends, are subject to parent–child negotiation. Thus, they assert that autonomy is a developmental issue for young people, with greater autonomy achieved with increased age.

The achievement of autonomy is not without conflict, however. Smetana (1988) states that parent–child differences in authority are a primary source of difficulty during late childhood, and that the disagreement occurs over young people's rights to personal jurisdiction over various aspects of decision making.

Allen et al. (1994) examined the mutually negotiated process of young people's autonomy in the context of a secure base of parent–child relationships. Their study considered ways in which autonomy and parent–child relationships interacted and predicted later ego development and self-esteem. They defined autonomy and relatedness as follows:

Autonomy and relatedness were defined and examined with respect to a paradigmatic challenge for families with adolescents: negotiating a difference of opinions. In this context, autonomy-exhibiting behaviors were defined as differentiating a person from others, reflecting independence of thought and self-determination in social interaction. Relatedness-exhibiting behaviors were defined as reflecting interest, involvement, and validation of another person's thoughts and feelings. (p. 181)

Their findings are consistent with predictions made from an attachment theory perspective. In optimal interactions between the parent and the child, the parent facilitates the growing child's autonomy from the secure base of a positive parent–child relationship. Therefore, by the time they reach the ages of 14 and 16, children exhibit behavior indicative of independence of thought and self-determination.

A further manifestation of autonomy is the development of identity exploration and formation. Grotevant and Cooper (1985), for instance, view late childhood as a period of gradual negotiation between parents and their children regarding the issue of authority and autonomy. They recognize the importance of both individuality and connectedness within families for the well-being of all members of the family. They use a model in which separateness and self-assertion in family interactions are key features for the growth of young people. The connectedness that growing children sense within the family provides a mutuality in terms of support, respect for the development of their own beliefs, and self-assertion. Their research embraces the view that identity formation is consistent with the development of a sense of self as different and distinctive from others. They hypothesize that family relationships afford young people the confidence and skills required to develop their sense of self and explore outside of the family. Their findings support the utility of examining individuality and connectedness within the family as predictors of individual developing competence.

Emotional autonomy also has received attention in the developmental literature. Lamborn and Steinberg (1993), for instance, describe emotional autonomy as a process that young people go through in which they relinquish their dependency on as well as their conceptions of their parents. Emotional autonomy is an adaptive process, begun in late childhood, in which young people shift from a reliance on their parents to their own internal resources (Steinberg & Silverberg, 1986). There is controversy, however, on the adaptiveness of emotional autonomy if it represents emotional detachment from parents, whom children need for support as they grow toward adulthood.

Fuhrman and Holmbeck (1995) argue that because young people develop within individual, family, and cultural contexts, the adaptiveness of emotional autonomy is best evaluated within these contexts. Consistent with this point of view, Sessa and Steinberg (1991) argue that emotional autonomy can be adaptive in cases where some emotional distance from the parents facilitates development. This occurs when young people live in environments that are either less supportive or more maladaptive. Indeed, Hetherington and Anderson (1988) and Sessa and Steinberg (1991) report that emotional autonomy may afford young people a degree of separation necessary during the course of marital separations and single parenting.

Fuhrman and Holmbeck (1995) anticipate that, with regard to ethnicity and socioeconomic status (SES), emotional autonomy would be less adaptive culturally in situations which stress interpersonal connection as opposed to those cultures which emphasize interpersonal separation. They find that much of the recent thinking about African American culture focuses on kinship (e.g., Boyd-Franklin, 1989; Hines & Boyd-Franklin, 1982; Ogbu, 1985). For African Americans, networks have served an important coping mechanism function.

Contrary to the findings of Lamborn and Steinberg (1993), who found that emotional autonomy has positive outcomes in supportive family relationships, Fuhrman and Holmbeck (1995) obtained findings suggesting the opposite contention. They assert that emotional autonomy is associated with negative adjustment in supportive family environments and with positive adjustment in less supportive families. They suggest that all of the family variables they studied, especially maternal warmth and intensity of child–parent conflict, influence the adaptiveness of emotional autonomy. In other words, to the extent that the child–parent relationship is positive, low emotional autonomy is associated with positive adjustment; when the child–parent relationship is negative, higher emotional autonomy is the positive adjustment outcome. Thus, the fit between young people's emotional autonomy and the nature of their relationship with their parents is the key variable in determining the adjustment aspects of these young people's emotional autonomy.

The Fuhrman and Holmbeck (1995) research also considered gender issues related to emotional autonomy. They found no differences between growing girls and boys with regard to their emotional autonomy and adjustment level. Further, family structure was also not a factor in considering emotional autonomy and adjustment.

Ryan and Lynch (1989) also examined the concept of emotional autonomy. They state that "autonomy, both etymologically and in current usage, refers to self-governance and self-regulation" (p. 340). They examined the construct of emotional autonomy, particularly regarding the distinction between detachment and independence. Ryan and Lynch debated whether emotional autonomy is similar to the concepts of autonomy and independence or whether this construct represents emotional detachment consistent with the adolescent's view of the parents as rejecting and unsupportive. They maintain that individuation by the time of adolescence is enhanced by attachment and not by detachment during childhood. And, further, they found that closeness with parents is positively related to measures of autonomy. Indeed, their research reveals that those who report more security in their attachment to parents also report more emotional security with their friends. And, those who are more emotionally detached from their parents may develop a more negative view of self. Thus, it is attachment as an emotional bond which optimizes individuation and enhances relationships with others.

AUTONOMY AND PARENTAL RELATIONSHIPS WITH OLDER CHILDREN

Older children's self reports of autonomy and their relatedness to their parents are associated with a number of positive outcomes. For example, those who report secure attachments to their parents also sense more emotional security with their friends (Ryan & Lynch, 1989). Further, support for autonomy is linked to more intrinsic motivation, more creativity, more cognitive flexibility, better conceptual learning, and higher self-esteem, among other things (Deci & Ryan, 1987). Smetana (1995) also studied parent–child relationships and the development of the growing child's autonomy by examining diverse parenting styles, including the following:

> authoritative *parents, who are both responsive and demanding,* authoritarian *parents, who are demanding but not responsive,* permissive *parents, who are responsive but not demanding… (p. 299)*

Her subjects were sixth, eighth, and tenth grade students and their parents; she found that parents' judgments of their parental authority differed according to their parenting style.

Permissive parents developed broader boundaries for older children's personal jurisdiction than did other parents. They also viewed rules regarding childrens' personal issues as less obligatory than did other parents. Authoritative parents considered moral rules as more obligatory than conventional ones; authoritarian parents felt that both moral and conventional issues were under the control of parents and that children were obliged to follow them. Smetana's (1995) research is consistent with the view that Steinberg and Silverberg's (1986) measure of autonomy development is a reflection of the degree of a growing child's detachment from their parents. She finds that her results "suggest the utility of reconceptualizing Baumrind's dimensions of parental demandingness and responsiveness in terms of the different domains in which parental expectations are enforced and autonomy demands are granted" (p. 314).

Kurdek, Fine, and Sinclair (1995) also examined the issue of family dynamics and autonomy granting behavior. They considered the number of times a child has experienced a change in family structure, termed a parenting transition, and the relationship of multiple parenting transitions and family characteristics (i.e., parental supervision, acceptance, parental autonomy granting behaviors, and conflict in the family) to adjustment to the school context (i.e., grades, achievement levels, and disruptive behaviors). They defined autonomy granting in terms of the extent to which parents are perceived as allowing their children (mean age of subjects = 11.86 years) to make their own decisions and encouraging them to be self-sufficient. The multiple parenting transition group considered their families as lower in acceptance, autonomy granting, and supervision compared to those subjects in the zero parenting transition group. Her research reveals that moderate levels of parental supervision may offer an appropriate degree of structure related to children's sense of responsibility for their own performance.

While not directly examining the issue of autonomy, Lamborn, Mounts, Steinberg, and Dornbusch (1991) explored the issue of competence and adjustment of children from four types of families (authoritative, authoritarian, indulgent, and neglectful). Those growing children who perceived their parents as authoritative received the highest scores on measures of psychosocial competence and the lowest scores on measures of psychological and behavioral dysfunction. Those from authoritarian homes scored reasonably well on conformity and obedience measures, were likely to do well in school, and were less likely to engage in deviant activities compared with their peers. However, these students were less self-confident and self-reliant in terms of their own social and academic skills. Those from indulgent homes presented a complex picture; they tended to be psychologically adjusted, oriented toward their peers, and engaged in activities valued by peers.

Kochanska (1990) examined maternal beliefs regarding rearing philosophy (i.e., authoritative-authoritarian dimension) and affective attitudes toward their children (i.e., positive-negative dimension) as long-term predictors of mother-child interactions. She studied two groups of mothers, "normal" and "depressed," and the original groups were assessed when their children were between 16 and 44 months of age. The two groups were assessed a second time when the children were 5 years old. Mothers who embraced an authoritative parenting style were associated with an avoidance of prohibitive interventions with their children. The authoritative parenting style was also associated with maternal autonomy granted to the child. In terms of predicting maternal parenting behavior, the parenting philosophy was a more important predictor of behavior for the normal group and the affective attitude was more predictive for the depressed mother group.

Since authoritative parenting is so highly linked to children's psychosocial competence and general well-being, Steinberg, Elmen, and Mounts (1989) decided to further examine this parenting pattern. More specifically, they considered school success in relation to the authoritarian parenting component characteristics of: warmth or acceptance; psychological autonomy or democracy; and behavioral control. Their results indicate that not only does the authoritative parenting style facilitate academic success, but each of the three components examined makes an independent contribution to student achievement. Importantly,

> the positive impact of authoritative parenting on achievement is mediated at least in part through the effects of authoritativeness on the development of a healthy sense of autonomy and, more specifically, a healthy psychological orientation toward work. Adolescents who describe their parents as treating them warmly, democratically, and firmly are more likely than their peers to develop positive attitudes toward, and beliefs about, their achievement, and as a consequence, they are more likely to do better in school. (p. 1,424)

AUTONOMY AND CHILD TEMPERAMENT

Children's temperamental processes are certainly involved in their growth and development and potentially influence the development and demonstration of autonomy. Rothbart, Ahadi, and Hershey (1994) maintain that temperament may affect how individuals perceive their environments and that different individuals learn different things even when presented with identical situations. With regard to children, they note that temperamental characteristics can influence children's approach and withdrawal tendencies and set the upper and lower limits for children's excitement levels. These temperament traits can affect help-seeking and other behaviors.

Caspi and Silva (1995) employed a longitudinal research design to examine personality traits from age 3 to age 18. They found evidence that childhood behavioral styles as assessed in their study may be heritable individual differences; genetic factors may contribute to the continuity of behavioral response styles across development. While not specifically related to autonomy, their research provides data pointing to genetic or biological factors that may be related to the demonstration of a variety of personality traits. In terms of the continuity of personality characteristics, they point to three forms of person-environment interaction which may be important to explore further:

> Evocative personal-environment interactions occur when an individual's behavioral style evokes distinctive responses from others. Reactive person-environment interactions occur when different individuals exposed to the same environment experience, interpret, and react to it differently. Proactive person-environment interactions occur when individuals select or create environments of their own. (p. 496)

These may be important avenues to explore further in the examination of the development of autonomy.

IMPLICATIONS FOR RESEARCH

There certainly needs to be more research on gender differences and similarities in children's autonomous and non-autonomous behavior. There are these, as well as many other research issues in the study of autonomy and gender. Emde (1994), for example, finds that the measures of competence are highly dependent on the child's context and age. He refers to Flavell (1992), in particular, who noted this problem in his review of recent cognitive developmental research. The issue of measuring competence is compounded especially when one considers the expression of competent behaviors in light of stressful, ambiguous, or culturally diverse situations.

Classification of variables is also an issue. Emde (1994) states that "it is not so much the differences among classes that is important to understand but rather the interplay among classified features of the personal as well as the background context of method that leads to classification in the first place" (p. 731). The example he uses is that of Kohlberg's moral dilemma technique. When one applies a different classification system, such as that of Carol Gilligan (1982), the picture of moral development changes appreciably.

Much of the research on autonomy relies heavily on self-report assessment; this approach has been useful but is subject to inherent biases. Allen et al. (1994) state that it is important to use diverse measures in considering the issue of autonomy. In particular, they point out the need to directly observe behaviors that are considered autonomous in nature.

Definitions are also an important issue. Allen et al. (1994) define autonomy-exhibiting behaviors as "differentiating a person from others, reflecting independence of thought and self-determination in social interaction" (p. 181). But researchers tend to characterize autonomy in strikingly diverse ways, thus contributing to differences in interpreting and comparing data.

Fuhrman and Holmbeck (1995) speak to the need for more complex models of relationships to assist in the study of issues such as emotional autonomy. They speculate on the usefulness of longitudinal data that would allow a consideration of the links between family environment, dysfunctional parenting, emotional autonomy, and alterations in adjustment. They also note the need to test for moderator effects in data sets. Always prevalent, according to their research, is the need to question whether findings are valid across different individual, family, and cultural contexts.

Kurdek et al. (1995) also suggest that, because research consistently reveals that older children's compliance to adult directives inhibits the development of children's sense of personal control, future research should consider whether highly supervised, structured family climates which produce high achievement levels are balanced by poorer socioemotional adjustment. They also regard exploring student characteristics, including control beliefs relative to academic performance and success, as worth exploring. These factors may mediate the influences among school performance, family dynamics, and peer influences.

Finally, Lamborn et al. (1991) used self-report measures of parenting practices and found a number of advantages regarding these measures. More specifically, these measures allow researchers to use large and heterogeneous samples in their research. They also note that their use of self-report data did not seem to result in unusual biases in the findings. However, others have debated the use of self reports particularly because of the inherent bias which may occur when individuals describe themselves in a socially desirable manner.

Conclusion

Autonomy is a multifaceted concept that has developmental characteristics. When applied to young girls, autonomy needs to be considered within the context of girls' experiential fabric. More specifically, most current research and writing reveals that girls grow up within a social culture of relationships and caring; their experience of autonomy and personal control therefore occurs within a relationship framework. Furthermore, the research on autonomy demonstrates that autonomous behaviors begin at about the age of two and one half as parents expect competence in terms of girls picking up their own toys and other playthings. Parents differ relative to their parenting style, yet most parents foster a sense of autonomy as children become 2 to 3 years of age.

The expectation of personal decision making assists girls in developing more complex, socially competent behaviors. Each of the developmental theoretical positions, including those of social learning theory, cognitive development, psychoanalysis, and attachment theory, contributes to an understanding of the developmental aspects of autonomy in girls. Social learning theory reveals that when girls view others performing socially competent behaviors, they imitate those behaviors which are rewarded, and avoid performing those which are not. From a cognitive developmental perspective, girls selectively perceive and integrate gender specific appropriate behaviors. These behaviors occur within their social milieu and are appropriate within their community or cultural group. From a psychodynamic perspective, autonomy is a positive trait significantly influenced by parental responses to the toddlers' attempts at exploration. When encouraged and rewarded, the youngster develops a sense of autonomy; but, when discouraged in her attempts at autonomy, the young girl feels doubt or shame. Moreover, from an attachment point of view, the girl who has achieved a secure attachment with her parents is in an excellent position to explore her surroundings and, in addition, to develop a sense of personal competence.

While each of the major developmental positions assist in the understanding of female development and the display of autonomous behaviors, there is much more research that would assist educators, psychologists, and mental health professionals in their application of an understanding of autonomous behavior. First, it would be useful to understand what professionals as well as parents perceive as autonomous or personally competent behavior. If autonomy has positive components consistent with females' own specific experiential base, then the issue becomes one of how to assist females in perceiving, understanding, incorporating, and displaying autonomy. Clearly, there are parent education as well as general education and psychological implications of such findings. If, on the other hand, there are aspects of autonomy which are relatively inconsistent with females' experience and value orientation (e.g., behaviors inconsistent with caring and relationships), then those components warrant further discussion among parents, educators, psychologists, as well as other interested parties.

While there are numerous aspects of autonomy that we understand, autonomy is a concept worthy of further exploration and research. Definitional issues abound and theoretical orientations, rather than being presented as disparate points of view, are quite amenable to an integrative approach. Such a theoretical integration would assist parents, professional practitioners, researchers, and other interested parties in their pursuit of psychological characteristics which assist young girls in optimizing their psychological and educational growth and development.

REFERENCES

Aberle, D. F., & Naegele, K. D. (1952). Middle-class father's occupational role and attitudes towards children. *American Journal of Orthopsychiatry, 22,* 366–378.

Achenbach, T. M. & Edelbrock, C. S. (1981). Behavioral problems and competencies reported by parent of normal and disturbed children aged four through sixteen. *Monographs of the Society for Research in Child Development, 46,* (1), Serial No. 188.

Ainsworth, M. D. S. (1973). The development of infant-mother attachment. In B. M. Caldwell & H. N. Ricciuti (Eds.), *Review of child development research* (Vol. 3). Chicago: University of Chicago Press.

Ainsworth, M. D. S. (1982). Attachment: Retrospect and prospect. In C. D. Parke & J. Stevenson-Hinde (Eds.), *The place of attachment in human behavior* (pp. 3–30). New York: Basic Books.

Allen, J. P., Hauser, S. T., Bell, K. L., & O'Conner, T. G. (1994). Longitudinal assessment of autonomy and relatedness in adolescent-family interactions as predictors of adolescent ego development and self–esteem. *Child Development, 65,* 179–194.

Bandura, A. (1986). *Social foundations of thought and action: A social cognitive theory.* Englewood Cliffs, NJ: Prentice-Hall.

Barnett, R. C. (1981). Parental sex-role attitudes and child-rearing values. *Sex Roles, 7,* 837–846.

Baumrind, D. (1968). Authoritarian vs. authoritative parental control. *Adolescence, 3,* 255–272.

Baumrind, D. (1971). Current patterns of parental authority. *Developmental Psychology Monograph 4*(1), Pt. 2.

Baumrind, D. (1973). The Development of instrumental competence through socialization. In A. D. Pick (Ed.), *Minnesota symposium on motivation* (Vol. 7), (pp. 3–46). Minneapolis: University of Minnesota Press.

Baumrind, D. (1989). Rearing competent children. In W. Damon (Ed.), *Child development today and tomorrow* (pp. 349–378). San Francisco: Jossey-Bass.

Baumrind, D., & Black, A. E. (1967). Socialization practices associated with dimensions of competence in preschool boys and girls. *Child Development, 38,* 291–327.

Bowlby, J. (1969). *Attachment and loss: Vol 1. Attachment.* New York: Basic Books.

Bowlby, J. (1973). *Attachment and loss: Vol 2. Separation: Anxiety and anger.* New York: Basic Books.

Bowlby, J. (1980). *Attachment and loss: Vol 3. Loss, sadness and depression.* New York: Basic Books.

Boyd-Franklin, N. (1989). Black families in therapy: A multisystems approach. New York: Guilford.

Broverman, I. K., Broverman, D., Clarkson, F. E., Rosenkrantz, P. S., & Vogel, S. R. (1970). Sex roles stereotypes and clinical judgments of mental health. *Journal of Consulting and Clinical Psychology, 34*(1), 1–7.

Buss, A. R. (1975). The emerging field of the sociology of psychological knowledge. *American Psychologist, 30*(10), 988–1002.

Caspi, A., & Silva, P. A. (1995). Temperamental qualities at age three predict personality traits in young adulthood: Longitudinal evidence from a birth cohort. *Child Development, 66,* 486–498.

Chodorow, N. (1978). The reproduction of mothering: Psycholanalysis and the sociology of gender. Berkeley, CA: University California Press.

Conner, J. M., Serving, L. A., & Ender, R. A. (1978). Responses of boys and girls to aggressive, assertive, and passive behaviors of male and female characters. *Journal of Genetic Psychology, 133,* 59–69.

Constantinople, A. (1979). Sex-role acquisition: In search of the elephant. *Sex Roles, 5,* 121–133.

Cortez, V. L., & Bugental, D. B. (1995). Priming of perceived control in young children as a buffer against fear-inducing events. *Child Development, 66,* 687–696.

Crowell, J. A., & Feldman, S. S. (1988). Mothers' internal models of relationships and children's behavioral and developmental status: A study of mother-child interaction. *Child Development, 59,* 1273–1285.

Deci, E. L., & Ryan, R. M. (1987). The support of autonomy and the control of behavior. *Journal of Personality and Social Psychology, 53,* 1024–1037.

Emde, R. N. (1994). Individuality, context, and the search for meaning. *Child Development, 65,* 719–737.

Erikson, E. (1950). *Childhood and society.* New York: Norton.

Flavell, J. H. (1992). Cognitive development: Past, present, and future. *Developmental Psychology, 28,* 998–1005.

Fuhrman, T., & Holmbeck, G. N. (1995). A contextual-moderator analysis of emotional autonomy and adjustment in adolescence. *Child Development, 66,* 793–811.

Gergen, K. (1973). Social psychology as history. *Journal of Personality and Social Psychology, 26,* 309–320.

Gilligan, C. (1982). In a different voice: Psychological theory and women's development. Cambridge, MA: Harvard University Press.

Goldberg, S., & Lewis, M. (1969). Play behavior in the year old infant: Early sex differences. *Child Development, 40,* 21–31.

Gralinski, J. H., & Kopp, C. B. (1993). Everyday rules for behavior: Mother's requests to young children. *Developmental Psychology, 29,* 573–584.

Grotevant, H. D., & Cooper, C. R. (1985). Patterns of interaction in family relationships and the development of identity exploration in adolescence. *Child Development, 56,* 415–428.

Harnish, J. D., Dodge, K. A., & Valenti, E. (1995). Mother-child interaction quality as a partial mediator of the roles of maternal depressive symptomatology and socioeconomic status in the development of child behavior problems. *Child Development, 66,* 739–753.

Hetherington, E. M., & Anderson, E. R. (1988). The effects of divorce and remarriage on early adolescents and their families. In M. D. Levine & E. R. McAnarney (Eds.), *Early adolescent transitions* (pp. 449–467). Lexington, MA: Lexington Books.

Hines, P. M., & Boyd-Franklin, N. (1982). Black families. In M. McGoldrick, J. K. Pierce, and J. Guirdano (Eds.), *Ethnicity and family therapy* (pp. 84–107). New York: Guilford.

Jacklin, C. N., & Maccoby, E. E. (1978). Social Behavior at thirty-three months in same-sex and mixed sex-dyads. *Child Development, 49,* 557–569.

Kagan, J., & Moss, H. (1962). *Birth to maturity.* New York: Wiley.

Kochanska, G. (1990). Maternal beliefs as long-term predictors of mother-child interactions. *Child Development, 61,* 1934–1943.

Kochanska, G. (1993). Toward a synthesis of parental socialization and child temperament in early development of conscience. *Child Development, 64,* 325–347.

Kochanska, G. (1995). Children's temperament, mother's discipline, and security of attachment: Multiple pathways to emerging internalization. *Child Development, 66,* 597–615.

Kochanska, G., Kuczynski, L., & Radke-Yarrow, M. (1989). Correspondence between mothers' self-reported and observed child-rearing practices. *Child Development, 60,* 56–63.

Kohlberg, L. (1969). *Stages in the development of moral thought and action.* New York: Holt.

Kopp, C. B. (1982). Antecedents of self-regulation: A developmental perspective. *Developmental Psychology, 18,* 199–214.

Kuczynski, L., & Kochanska, G. (1995). Function and content of maternal demands: Developmental significance of early demands for competent action. *Child Development, 66,* 616–628.

Kuczynski, L., Zahn-Waxler, C., & Radke-Yarrow, M. (1987). Development and content of imitation in the second and third year of life: A socialization perspective. *Developmental Psychology, 23,* 276–282.

Kurdek, L. A., & Fine, M. A. (1994). Family acceptance and family control as predictors of adjustment in young adolescents: Linear, curvilinear, or interactive effects? *Child Development 65,* 1, 137–1146.

Kurdek, L. A., Fine, M. A., & Sinclair, R. J. (1995). School adjustment in sixth graders: Parenting transitions, family climate, and peer norm effects. *Child Development, 66,* 430–445.

Lamborn, S. D., Mounts, N. S., Steinberg, L., & Dornbusch, S. M. (1991). Patterns of competence and adjustment among adolescents from authoritative, authoritarian, indulgent, and neglectful families. *Child Development, 62,* 1049–1065.

Lamborn, S. D., & Steinberg, L. (1993). Emotional autonomy redux: Revisiting Ryan and Lynch. *Child Development, 64,* 483–499.

Lay, K. L., Waters, E., & Park, K. A. (1989). Maternal responsiveness and child compliance: The role of mood as a mediator. *Child Development, 60,* 1405–1411.

Lewis, M. (1972). Parents and children: Sex-role development. *School Review, 80,* 229–240.

Lott, B. (1978). Behavioral concordance with sex role ideology related to play areas, creativity, and parental stereotyping of children. *Journal of Personality and Social Psychology, 36,* 1087–1100.

Lykes, M. B. (1985). Gender and individualistic vs. collectivist bases for notions about the self. *Journal of Personality, 53,* 356–383.

Lyons, N. P. (1983). Two perspectives: On self, relationships, and morality. *Harvard Educational Review, 53*(2), 125–145.

Maccoby, E. E. (1984). Socialization and developmental change. *Child Development, 55,* 317–328.

Maccoby, E. E., & Jacklin, C. N. (1974). *The psychology of sex differences.* Stanford, CA: Stanford University Press.

Maccoby, E. E., & Martin, J. A. (1983). Socialization in the context of the family: Parent-child interaction. In E. M. Hetherington (Ed.), *Handbook of child psychology: Vol. 4. Socialization, personality, and social development* (pp. 1–101). New York: Wiley.

Mead, G. H. (1962). *Mind, self, and society* (Vol. 1). (C. W. Morris, Ed.). Chicago: IL: University of Chicago Press.

Mellor, S. (1989). Gender differences in identity formation as a function of self-other relationships. *Journal of Youth and Adolescence, 18,* 361–375.

Miller, J. B. (1976). *Toward a new psychology of women.* Boston, MA: Beacon Press.

Miller, J. B. (1984). *The development of women's sense of self* (Work in Progress Papers, No. 84–101). Wellesley, MA: Wellesley College, The Stone Center.

Minton, C., Kagan, J., & LeVine, J. A. (1971). Maternal control and obedience in the two-year-old. *Child Development, 42,* 1873–1894.

Mishler, E. G., Amarasingham, L. R., Hauser, S. T., Liem, R. Osherson, S. D., & Waxler, N. E. (1981). *Social contexts of health, illness, and patient care.* Cambridge, England: Cambridge University Press.

Mowder, B. A., Harvey, V. S., Moy, L., & Pedro, M. (1995). Parent role in characteristics: Parent views and their implications for school psychologists. *Psychology in the Schools, 32,* 27–37.

Ogbu, J. U. (1985). A cultural ecology of competence among inner-city blacks. In M. B. Spencer, G. K. Brookins, & W. R. Allen (Eds.), *Beginnings: The social and affective development of black children* (pp. 45–66). Hillsdale, NJ: Erlbaum.

Parpal, M., & Maccoby, E. E. (1985). Maternal responsiveness and subsequent child compliance. *Child Development, 56,* 1326–1334.

Pettit, G. S., & Bates, J. E. (1989). Family interaction patterns and children's behavior problems from infancy to four years. *Developmental Psychology, 25,* 413–420.

Piaget, J. (1929). *The child's conception of the world.* New York: Harcourt & Brace.

Piaget, J. (1951). *Play, dreams and imitation in childhood.* New York: Norton.

Power, T. G., & Manier, S. H. (1992). Childrearing and internalization: A developmental perspective. In J. Janssens & J. Gerris (Eds.), *Childrearing and the child's prosocial and moral development* (pp. 101–124). Lisse, the Netherlands: Swets & Zeitlinger.

Rheingold, H. L., Cook, K. V., & Kolowitz (1987). Commands activate the behavior and pleasure of 2-year-old children. *Developmental Psychology, 23,* 146–151.

Rothbart, M. K., Ahadi, S. A., & Hershey, K. L. (1994). Temperament and social behavior in childhood. *Merrill–Palmer Quarterly, 40*(1), 21–39.

Rotter, J. B. (1954). *Social learning and clinical psychology.* Englewood Cliffs, NJ: Prentice-Hall.

Ryan, R. M., & Lynch, J. H. (1989). Emotional autonomy versus detachment: Revisiting the vicissitudes of adolescence and young adulthood. *Child Development, 60,* 340–346.

Sampson, E. E. (1978). Scientific paradigms and social values: Wanted—a scientific revolution. *Journal of Personality and Social Psychology, 36*(11), 1332–1343.

Sessa, F. M. & Steinberg, L. (1991). Family structure and the development of autonomy during adolescence. *Journal of Early Adolescence, 11,* 38–55.

Skinner, B. F. (1972). *Cumulative record: a section of papers* (3rd ed.). New York: Appleton-Century-Crofts.

Skinner, B. F. (1976). *About behaviorism.* New York: Vintage Books.

Smetana, J. G. (1988). Adolescents' and parents' conceptions of parental authority. *Child Development, 59,* 321–335.

Smetana, J. G. (1995). Parenting styles and conceptions of parental authority during adolescence. *Child Development, 66,* 299–316.

Smetana, J. G., & Asquith, P. (1994). Adolescents' and parents' conceptions of parental authority and personal autonomy. *Child Development, 65,* 1147–1162.

Stayton, D., Hogan, R., & Ainsworth, M. D. S. (1971). Infant obedience and maternal behavior: The origins of socialization reconsidered. *Child Development, 42,* 1057–1069.

Steinberg, L., Elmen, J. D., and Mounts, N. S. (1989). Authoritative parenting, psychosocial maturity, and academic success among adolescents. *Child Development, 60,* 1424–1436.

Steinberg, L., Lamborn, S. D., Darling, N., Mounts, N. S., & Dornbusch, S. M. (1994). Over-time changes in adjustment and competence among adolescents from authoritative, authoritarian, indulgent, and neglectful families. *Child Development, 65,* 754–770.

Steinberg, L., & Silverberg, S. B. (1986). The vicissitudes of autonomy in early adolescence. *Child Development, 57*(4), 841–851.

Tizard, B., Hughes, M., Pinkerton, G., & Carmichael, H. (1982). Adults' cognitive demands at home and at nursery school. *Journal of Child Psychology and Psychiatry, 23,* 105–116.

Ward, M. J., & Carlson, E. A. (1995). Associations among adult attachment representations, maternal sensitivity, and infant-mother attachment in a sample of adolescent mothers. *Child Development, 66,* 69–79.

Watson, J. B. (1930). *Behaviorism.* Chicago: University of Chicago Press.

Weitzman, L. (1979). *Sex role socialization.* Palo Alto, CA: Mayfield.

White, J. L. (1984). *The psychology of blacks: An Afro-American perspective.* Englewood Cliffs, NJ: Prentice Hall.

Willie, C. V. (1979). *Caste and class controversy.* Bayside, NY: General Hall.

Youniss, J. & Smollar, J. (1985). *Adolescents' relations with mothers, fathers, and friends.* Chicago: University of Chicago Press.

4

ADOLESCENT FEMALES' PERCEPTION OF AUTONOMY AND CONTROL

JUDITH KAUFMAN
Fairleigh Dickinson University

A woman, if she has the misfortune of knowing anything,
should conceal it as well as she can.
—JANE AUSTEN

Be all you can be.
—NIKE COMMERCIAL (1994)

AUTONOMY AND THE TRANSITION TO ADOLESCENCE

Any transition is a turning point which requires the development of new patterns of behavior or the restructuring of existing ones in order to meet changing perceptions, demands, and expectations associated with that transition (Schlossberg, Waters, & Goldman, 1995). Responsibilities, goals, identity, self-concept, and interpersonal relationships undergo significant modification during life-span transitions (Masten, 1991). The transition into adolescence, beginning at about age 11 or 12, is most significant, particularly for the female.

Adolescence is a normative, psychosocial transition precipitated by the onset of puberty, a chronologically regulated event. Society reacts to the event, thus facilitating or inhibiting psychological development. Although adolescence is typically regarded as a transitional *phase,* it is also a critical developmental *stage.* It involves the transition from childhood dependence to an independent and self-sustaining adulthood. This requires a clear-cut perception of having *autonomy* or personal control over events and one's behavior, along with a sense of *affiliativeness* or attachment to significant others.

Developmental challenges involve the application of physical, cognitive, and social skills learned in childhood, as well as those which evolve in adolescence to changing roles and expectations. The furtherance of autonomy is inherent in the transition, together with the integration of identity and self-concept.

Adolescence involves the process of exiting from childhood and creating a "new beginning." Pre-adolescent girls, according to Pipher (1994) are secure, confident, and capable. Then, "something dramatic happens to girls in early adolescence" (p. 19). Studies demonstrate that IQ scores drop, mathematics and science scores decrease dramatically, and resiliency and optimism diminish. Young adolescents report great unhappiness with their bodies and with themselves in general (Pipher, 1994). Therefore, the challenges of adolescent development include the incorporation of a new body image, the successful move toward greater independence, responding to changes in role and status, expansion of social networks, integrating identity, and enhancing self-concept. Thus, psychological development becomes a dynamic and interactive process between the self and the environment.

It is paradoxical that the illusion of control or "sense of omnipotence" (Elkind, 1967) manifests itself during the stage of life when dramatic changes take place in all domains of functioning, together with increased pressure for problem solving and personal decision making. Increased self-expectations focus on independence in thought and action and the ability to make meaningful choices. Learning to set realistic goals, consider alternatives, and make personally meaningful choices are essential skills necessary for adolescent development and the perception of personal control (Worrell & Danner, 1989).

Issues of choice versus control predominate during adolescence and often create tension. While the teenager has opportunities for choice, she may not perceive herself to have the control which may be essential for her psychologically. Thus, she may create situations and engage in behaviors which give her the illusion of control, but these actions are not necessarily the most productive or healthy responses.

A sweeping canvas has been painted of the adolescent years, emphasizing commonality in texture, theme, and variation. However, the adolescent emerges as a unique individual because of the interaction of developmental facts with the social, cultural, and historical context in which that development occurs. The essence of successful adolescent development and of the foundation for healthy and productive adulthood has three components: identity formation and the integration of "self" (Erikson, 1968a, 1968b); development of the skills of personal decision making that promote self-directed behavior; and the perception of personal control and autonomy.

This chapter will focus on the unique changes that occur in adolescence which challenge and strengthen perceptions of autonomy and personal control. A theoretical foundation is presented to provide a context for understanding the impact of the various changes. Factors that contribute to functional and dysfunctional adaptation and that contribute to autonomy, integrated identity, and self-concept are highlighted with specific application to uniquely adolescent issues. The development of autonomy will be examined by exploring internal factors, such as puberty, temperament, abilities, and values, as they interact with outer conditions, including those that arise out of the adolescent's significant social interactions with family and friends.

CONTEXT AND THE CONTINUITY OF CHANGE

The adolescent period has been characterized as one of multiple changes and transitions which affect all domains of behavior and functioning. Is adolescence inevitable and universal, or merely a cultural creation of the 20th century Western world (Mead, 1950)? Worrell and Danner (1989) suggest that adolescence is marked both by enduring features and changes occurring during adolescence, which are continuous threads through generations and throughout the world. What is expected or projected onto the adolescent period, particularly for the female, may be dependent on the social, cultural, and historical context in which these changes take place. Therefore, the processes may be comparable, but outcomes may vary considerably, given the time, place, and cultural context.

In order to understand the physical and psychological changes that take place and how these changes are perceived and integrated by the female as she struggles with issues of identity, autonomy, and personal control, this chapter incorporates interview material gathered from 250 adolescent females in order to highlight the issues in the adolescents' own words. Questions derived from Coleman's (1980) interview format were used as a basis for the hour-long interviews conducted by advanced undergraduate and graduate students as part of a course requirement in adolescent psychology (Kaufman, 1993, 1994).

PHYSICAL DEVELOPMENT AS AN IMPETUS FOR CHANGE

Physical changes, unique to adolescence, provide the impetus to move into puberty. These changes are visibly apparent and call attention to the developing young woman. She becomes attuned to changes in her body, both physically and symbolically. Awareness of the loss of childhood, together with gaining the capacity to bear children, enters her conscious awareness. What appears to be a rapid change in appearance and sexual capacity renders many young women with feelings of being out of control, poignantly sensing the loss of the familiar self.

Puberty is the beginning point for real physical and psychological differences between sexes (Group for the Advancement of Psychiatry, GAP, 1968). In the case of girls, puberty is not a single event and menarche is not its only signal. Rather, puberty specifically refers to the period of rapid physical change involving endocrine and somatic development that results in reproductive maturation. For girls, this process begins somewhere between the ages of 10 and 11 and takes an average of 4 to 5 years to complete (Tanner, 1962).

When the somatic changes are visible, it becomes the public signal for the onset of puberty. In terms of psychosocial consequences, pubertal change may be a direct effect on behavior or may be mediated through social or contextual factors (Peterson, 1988).

The male has a penis from birth and a clearly defined masculine make-up. But for the girl, menstruation may serve as an organizing force for mental and emotional functioning and also as the basis for acceptance or rejection of her femininity (GAP, 1968). Menarche and breast development are new to the female and, therefore, can precipitate a stronger identification with mother as a woman. This identification may then generalize to all females.

Menstruation causes the expansion of the ego-ideal to include reproductive function-ing. Symbolically, this may foster a change from being nurtured to providing nurture irre-spective of cultural context. This young woman is expected to learn how to work and how to love, activities essential to functioning as an adult.

Secondary sex characteristics are equally important and provide the basis for body image, self-image and feelings of attractiveness. The body for adolescent girls is seen as a reflection of the totality of self and becomes the focal point of many issues and concerns (Rosenbaum, 1993). Thus, how the body is perceived by others becomes critically impor-tant. For example, if the body is devalued and denigrated by others, it may become a source of shame and conflict.

Some of the struggles with personal control are enacted through reactions to physical change and body image, particularly once the changes become integrated with self-image. For this reason, pubertal timing becomes an important issue for the adolescent female. In this connection, whether physical development and the onset of puberty is early, late, or on time relative to one's peers becomes critical to the adolescent's self-concept, sense of belonging, and feelings of autonomy.

Three views of pubertal timing and its relationship to psychosocial aspects of function-ing have been generated:

1. All change is stressful. All girls regardless of pubertal timing will experience some dis-tress, particularly at the time of most rapid change.
2. Events that are considered to be occurring out of synchrony, either earlier or later than expected, become stressful.
3. Early maturing girls may be particularly vulnerable to adjustment difficulties, possibly because of a mismatch between societal expectations of their behavior and their level of cognitive and emotional maturity (Eichorn, 1973; Peterson & Stunkard, 1989).

The importance of pubertal timing differs for boys and girls. In the case of boys, advanced or early pubertal change enhances body image and status; but, in the case of girls, it brings decreased feelings of attractiveness (Crockett, Losoff, & Peterson, 1984). Delayed development has a negative impact on males in terms of acceptance by peers. This is suggested in the finding that late developing males are over-represented in the delinquent population. In contrast, girls who mature later demonstrate difficulty in separation, achieve-ment of autonomy, and integration of sexual self-concept (Dorn, Crockett, & Peterson, 1988).

Pubertal development is a universal feature, and the response and reaction to its changes, both personally and interpersonally, can change and modify a person's self-concept and perceptions of personal control.

The following stories about the onset of menstruation reveal a great deal. They reflect moods and attitudes, sexuality, independence, and perceptions of autonomy and personal control. They give insight into relationships with peers and parents.

Linda, 16, began menstruating at age 11. Reflecting upon that event, she says:

I didn't want anybody to know. I felt like it was embarrassing, horrible, disgusting. I especially didn't want my brothers and my father to know. And I got my period very early so I don't think other kids knew. It took me two years to mention it to my best friend. Telling secrets, we both confessed that we'd gotten our periods. I didn't want to mention it to anybody. I felt other people would be embarrassed by it if they knew I had my period…I definitely remember feeling differently, like my mom…Discovering I had my period was "Oh, I know what this is and an abrupt transition to feeling total self-revulsion and feeling out of control of my own body."

Yvonne, 15, states:

I think the first time I got my period I was 12. I was very excited about it, because I really wanted to get it and feel grown up. I remember running downstairs and telling my stepmother that I had my period and she said, "No, you didn't." She didn't even trust me about what was happening with my body!

Denise, 16, says:

I was embarrassed about having my period. I was 10 and the first girl I knew to get it. I mean, it was a terrible burden and took away my freedom. Things like carrying sanitary napkins and getting a pass to go to the bathroom and what you had to take with you. It was just terrible. I wouldn't admit I had my period because it was a stigma.

And Rachel, 15, says:

I felt proud, humiliated, scared, embarrassed, disgusting. I knew I was becoming a woman, but it really felt uncontrollable, my body bleeding like that. I never knew when I might have an accident and really feel mortified. I cried for four days. The first time I got my period was the worst, because I knew it had started and then I would have it for a long, long time.

The onset of puberty, particularly menstruation and breast development, has long been held as the hallmark of female development and the impetus for autonomy and personal control. Yet, in reviewing the personal reflections of these young women, it is apparent that these changes are welcomed and integrated in different ways, depending upon age, family environment, and psychological adjustment.

CHANGES IN OTHER DOMAINS

The adolescent years are characterized by multiple changes in domains other than physical ones. For the female, areas that particularly contribute to perceptions of personal control and evolving autonomy and competence include changes in cognitive development and changes in interpersonal relationships with family and friends.

Cognitive Changes

Piaget (1965) viewed early adolescence as the time when formal operational thinking begins to evolve. As the brain changes in its capabilities, the adolescent begins to formulate ideas and theories related to concrete phenomena. The ability to see logical relationships among diverse elements and the ability to reason abstractly begins to evolve and become solidified. Although cognitive and information-processing theorists have questioned Piaget's paradigm, it is clear that adolescent thinking is different from child thinking and includes abstractions and internal representations. Thought processes become relative rather than absolute and are characterized by multidimensional processing of information (Newton, 1995). Triggered by cognitive development, a higher level of self-awareness develops, often beginning with a reluctance to share oneself, in contrast to the general openness of childhood. This awareness involves concern about appearance, awkward growth, pubertal development, and the ability to look at oneself from another's perspective, often referred to as "playing to an imaginary audience" (Elkind, 1967).

Taking on another person's perspective and the gradual moving away from egocentric thinking are hallmarks of the transition from adolescent to young adult development. Whereas changes in most other domains are not dependent upon intellectual ability, the transition to higher-order thinking appears to be dependent on cognitive ability. There are individuals who never achieve formal operational thinking, nor move away from egocentric thought (Piaget, 1965).

Reflections of how some females view their thinking emerge from a series of interviews (Kaufman, 1993, 1994). Lyssa, 16, says:

> *Now I can see two sides of an argument; it was always my parents' side or my teacher's side or my friends' side. Now I can take a little bit of each. My thinking has changed. I thought I was Queen of the World. I knew more than anyone. Before I was an adolescent, I thought everything was perfect. Now I know that alot of things don't work out the way you want them to. I realize that I can't control the world…not even myself.*

Comments Susan, 13:

> *My thinking is really changing. I think about everything now. Now I think about my grades and know if I don't do my work, my grades will go down. Before I didn't care what happened with my school work. Now I know that I can control what happens by doing my work and asking questions. I ask other people if I don't understand something, rather than forget about it and not do it.*

LeShawn, 17, explains:

> *I think with more depth now, more realistically. Normally, I would think about what the crowd, my friends would do, now I have to think about what is good for me and my future. I am more in control of myself.*

These reflections indicate that changes in cognitive capacity affect perceptions of personal control. Gaining a broader perspective and greater insight enhances feelings of control for some, while being aware of too many issues and nuances, simultaneously, may be overwhelming for others.

Interpersonal Relationships—Family and Friends

In order to develop a sense of autonomy and self-control, relatedness and interpersonal relationships are critical for the female adolescent (Gilligan, 1982; Brown & Gilligan, 1992). With the onset of adolescence, the role in the family structure alters and perceptions about being a daughter change as friendships begin to take on new and broader meaning.

The Role of the Family

Family relationships are thought to be laden with conflict for the teenager. Contemporary theory, however, supports the positive contribution of family life to healthy adolescent development. Recent studies demonstrate that adolescents do not necessarily rebel against their parents (Youniss & Smoller, 1985; Offer, Ostrov, & Howard, 1981). Parental approval is often sought long after emancipation has begun. Even when adolescents shift their focus to friends, they retain a cooperative relationship with family.

Both parents and adolescents participate in the transformation of roles, thus making it possible for participation in the family to continue. Negotiations and changes in power relationships and roles are evolved through a continuous series of minor, although significant, confrontations. Serious problems, crises, and disorganization within the family structure are not necessarily typical (Csikszentmihali & Larson, 1984; Hill, 1987). Conflicts *do* take place, but they are not of the magnitude and intensity often reported in the theoretical literature. Conflicts are not, typically, about issues of major consequence, but about family chores, curfews, eating practices, dating, and personal appearance (Montemayor & Van Kormer, 1985; Santrock, 1990). Research suggests that there is a temporary increase in family conflict during early adolescence, particularly around issues of autonomy (Meece & Eccles, 1993). These conflicts, of mild to moderate intensity and with some degree of frequency, may give parents the impression of ongoing major crisis and indeed a period of disruption and "storm and stress." As the young woman renegotiates her role and exerts personal control, parents may experience a loss of control as authority figures.

Mothers and daughters engage in interactions that differ from those of fathers and daughters (Youniss & Smoller, 1985). Conversations with fathers are less frequent and tend to be limited to seeking or discussing practical information or objective social issues. They are lacking in intimacy, understanding, and acceptance.

The mother/daughter relationship is more complex and is invested with authority, equality, intimacy, and conflict. Mothers are viewed as flexible, approachable authority figures. Daughters perceive their mothers as needing their help as well as perceiving them as helpers. Daughters talk to mothers about personal as well as impersonal issues and, in some cases, the mothers reciprocate (Youniss & Smoller, 1985). However, there may also be heightened conflict between mothers and daughters, particularly if the daughters are early maturers and/or the mothers are uncertain, unhappy, or unfulfilled in their own gender role and personal self-concept.

The Role of Friends

The family provides a foundation for later relationships and is essential for healthy growth and development. However, self-understanding and self-reflection require reference points beyond the individual and her family. Adolescent friendships are critical and serve to facilitate separation, contribute to self-reflection, and self-definition (Gilligan, 1982). Close friendships in adolescence serve many functions, such as companionship, stimulation, social comparison, and intimacy or affection (Parker & Gotman, 1989).

The peer group often becomes a reflection of the social and cultural values that are compatible with the adolescent, and reflect "normative" expectations. Lack of a supportive friendship network can lead to feelings of isolation, self-doubt, depression, and perceptions of loss of control. Peer cliques and groups serve an important function by providing a means of social comparison as well as a source of information outside the family. Fitting in with desired groups or being rejected are acutely felt experiences, and for some result in feelings of serious depression (Garrod, Smulyan, Powers, & Kilkenny, 1995).

In reviewing interview material, peer pressure is not particularly emphasized, except for those who do not have a well-established social network. However, in terms of standards of dress and behavior, consider the following common statements from adolescents:

Unless you dress like everyone else, you are considered a neb.

You have to dress cool and act and behave accordingly, otherwise you are seen as weird.

Fitting in with my friends is important. Sometimes I don't feel like I belong and that makes me crazy.

The best thing about going to school is being with my friends and feeling like I am part of a group, where I matter.

Interaction of Parent and Peer Relationships

Parents and peer group both play an important part in the development of autonomy and control. Parke (1988) emphasizes the connectedness between the quality of family relationships and the quality of close peer relationships. Well-negotiated family relationships provide the groundwork for positive and supportive friendships and ultimately lasting intimate involvement (Gold, 1980). When conflict arises in the consideration of substantive issues between the peer group's opinion and parental opinion, young women with higher self-concepts will seek and follow parental advice (Robinson, Ruch-Ross, Watkins-Ferrel, & Lightfoot, 1993). For example, consider these statements:

"My parents really care about ME."

"They have more experience than my friends do."

"My mom will be my mom for the rest of her life."

While the need to belong is critical for role testing and independence, or what Blos (1962) calls "uniformism," perhaps the changes in the relationship to parents and to peers do not radically alter (Offer, Ostrov, & Howard, 1981; Youness & Smoller, 1985), but are renegotiated to meet the challenges and modified needs of the adolescent. When the relationships remain fixed, rigid, and inflexible, radical and extreme measures are taken and extreme behaviors evidenced in order to force the renegotiation.

Meece and Eccles (1993) maintain that optimal development takes place when there is a good stage/environment fit between the needs of the developing individual and the opportunities offered by the environment. The environment needs to allow for opportunities of self-determination and autonomy, not on an all-or-none basis, but with a gradual increase in opportunity as the young woman increases in competence. These opportunities need to be provided at home, at school, in the community, and in the wider social network. The need for more developmentally responsive environments is essential so that the girl can effectively move into young womanhood, preserving a sense of personal control.

HISTORICAL, RACIAL, ETHNIC, AND CLASS FACTORS

Considering universal developmental issues in a cultural, historical, and social context is fundamental to our understanding of development. Changes that the adolescent female undergoes may have no meaning or perhaps different meanings given her personal reference group, the neighborhood she lives in, and the geographic region or the historical time frame she comes from.

Adelson (1964) writes that the adolescent serves as a projective figure in the American mind. We attribute more idealism and feeling to the adolescent than she is capable of, and we are invariably disappointed. Adelson, in 1975, likened the pursuit of adolescent idealism to the search for the Loch Ness monster: a search that may tell us more about what we want to believe about adolescents than what they are really like.

The adolescent becomes as much a product of the media, the environment, countertransferential issues, hopes, dreams, and unrealized fantasies as she is of her character, personal, and developmental issues.

Adolescents of 50 years ago were not necessarily part of a visible subculture and the term *teenager* was just coming into popular usage. When the young woman came home from school she was probably greeted by her mother, and then set about to complete her daily chores. Most likely she was reminded about the value of appearance, behavior, and hard work. The family unit was a clearly defined structure, where the family always came first and the young woman was a valued member of that structure. Values were clearly communicated with many opportunities to observe and model parental behavior.

Contrast those assumptions with the young woman who returns from school today with a group of her friends, arriving home to an empty house. Her mother is employed outside the home, taking advantage of the expanded opportunities for women of today. Every high-tech gadget is present and MTV prevails. Values, character, and attitudes are manipulated daily through the media, and if there are any chores to complete and homework to be done, a monetary incentive is usually attached. While there may be good intentions, there is lax communication between parent and child, and the young woman rarely has the opportunity to observe her parents solving problems. Role models often emerge through media stereotypes reflecting limited ethics and, therefore, no clear sets of rules or values are communicated. The adolescent is thrust into a complex world with a limited amount of information, practice, and skill in making realistic decisions (Galotti, 1989).

Although the contrasting portraits may be exaggerated, there is validity in the characterization. Technology, media, economic demands, changing lifestyles, and sexual freedom have all served to foster change in the values and expectations of today's youth. Therefore, it is essential to consider the context and the times in understanding issues of personal control.

The protection and enhancement of self are two fundamental individual motivations. Different contexts have different effects on individuals who may otherwise be the same (Rosenberg, 1975). "Contextual dissonance tends to have a deleterious effect on the individual's self-concept if that [given] trait or status is devalued in the broader society or in the immediate group" (p. 112). The reference group becomes essential for comparison and contrast. Self-esteem is very much affected by identity, context, and dissonance or consonance of the individual with her environment.

Exposure to a diversity of contexts may have positive consequences on self-concept, yet most adolescents tend to cluster together with individuals of similar characteristics (Blos, 1968). There is evidence, for example, that African Americans who attend historically black institutions may have fewer racial issues to deal with on a daily basis and thus experience a higher sense of self-esteem. By contrast, African Americans on predominantly white campuses report feeling isolated and alienated, and are plagued with feelings of marginality (Helms, 1990). Similar observations have been made about women attending women's colleges, as compared with heterogeneous institutions (Wasserstein, 1993).

Race, ethnicity, and social class are factors which impact on personal characteristics. During the adolescent years, they take on even more significant meaning as the young woman struggles to "fit in" (Helms, 1990). There is a paucity of research which systematically studies the impact of such variables on adolescent development and personal control (Hamburg & Takanishi, 1989). Nevertheless, some theoretical assumptions and the highlights of the more recent studies are summarized below.

Individuals form part of their identity through social interaction. Different sociocultural influences become important at different developmental points and it is particularly true that, for the adolescent, the peer group is a primary factor in socialization. Racial identity can be considered to be formulated in much the same way as personal identity, where initially family and other authority figures become the primary source of identity formation. For the adolescent, the peer group becomes the reference point (Helms, 1990). The difference between racial and personal identity is that typically, in racial identity formation, it becomes a group's characteristics that are applied to the individual by society as differentiated from the individual's unique skills and abilities. Therefore, in part, racial identity is formulated based upon the family's values and the environmental reaction to racial characteristics.

It is particularly important, when working with minority adolescents, to consider the acquisition of ethnic group patterns and a sense of belonging to that ethnic group. Ethnic identity may vary, and be more salient in certain situations and less in others (Canino & Spurlock, 1994). Prejudice and discrimination can directly affect self-concept and self-esteem.

Acculturation can be a significant stressor, especially when the young woman is rooted neither in her mother culture nor in the new culture. This can become a significant problem when the adolescent is struggling to assimilate and acculturate, while parents are firmly rooted in their native culture. In a Puerto Rican family a core value is *respecto* to the parents and cultural values; yet, in the American family, assertiveness and independence are valued (Canino & Spurlock, 1994). How does the young woman reconcile these differences and remain attached to her family, and yet belong to her peer group? Who does she have to offend in order to feel in control?

If an individual grows up in a multi-racial environment where differences are celebrated, the individual can establish a pluralistic and positive racial identity; but when an individual grows up in an environment which denigrates the racial group, the individual may find racial identity difficult to establish in a positive way. Limited exposure to positive role models may often lead to the selection of inappropriate media personalities to identify with. If an individual receives conflicting messages about race, conflicting feelings about race may predominate.

How adolescents view themselves with regard to race can impact directly on academic functioning. Impaired ethnic identity can disrupt intellectual performance and academic functioning, and thereby lead to interpersonal and disciplinary problems. The student's level of ethnic identity development is believed to influence a personal sense of reality and emotional well-being, which in turn affects the response to the environment (Gay, 1985).

Allen (1992) also supports the importance of the role of ethnic group in the developmental process. In writing about Native American women, Allen indicates that Native American culture is gynocratic and not patriarchal. Tribal gynocratic systems accept a wide range of behaviors and personalities. The social order is based on social responsibility and not privilege. It is possible for the young woman, therefore, to grow up in a culture where nurturing can be valued in males, and self-determination in females. Native American women are deeply engaged in the struggle to redefine themselves and must reconcile traditional tribal definitions of women with non-Native industrial and post-industrial definitions.

In contrast to Gay's (1985) findings and Allen's (1992) discussion, Gibbs (1985) examined the psychological adjustment of urban African American females and concluded that ethnic or racial membership has less influence on adolescent self-concept than does socioeconomic status. Jessor (1993) suggests that most studies of adolescence have focused on middle-class youth without accounting for the psychological impact of poverty.

While accepting that culture and ethnicity are important variables, Chen and Yang (1986) suggest that the challenges of adolescence for Chinese Americans are similar to all adolescents. They therefore conclude that, from their research, ethnic group membership is not as salient a factor as age group membership.

It becomes apparent that there is limited and conflicting data demonstrating how race, ethnicity, and economic status impact on an adolescent's perceptions of personal control, and minimal research to support the assumptions that do exist. As our environment becomes more and more pluralistic, it becomes important to conduct well-controlled studies so that our assumptions do not breed continued stereotyping and unsubstantiated generalizations.

AUTONOMY AND DEVELOPMENTAL TASKS, STAGES, AND CONTEXT

Coleman's (1980) "focal point theory" suggests that there are different tasks to be mastered at the different stages of adolescence. Integrating changes in physical development and a new body image is the initial task of adolescence, followed by the expansion and mastery of interpersonal relationships, and concluding with negotiating relationships with one's parents, reflecting a future orientation and developing an attitude of independence.

New challenges arise and different issues come into focus at the different phases, and therefore the young woman needs to deal, one at a time, with each set of challenges and its consequent stressors. However, for those who have more than one major issue to resolve simultaneously, serious psychological concerns may emerge. For example, if a young woman is a late developer, she must balance the stressors of physical development at the same time that she attempts to develop meaningful interpersonal relationships. Most of her peers have already begun to integrate their changed physical and sexual selves, while she remains challenged by both sets of issues. A young woman who experiences the loss of her mother in her early teens may be forced to consider issues of independence, responsibility, and her future while still integrating the impact of physical changes.

Most researchers support the stage or critical task theory of adolescence, although they may give the specific challenges different labels (Lewis, 1987, Adatto, 1991, Hauser, Powers, Noam, Jacobson, Weiss, & Follansbee, 1984; Wagner & Compas, 1990). Adolescent development is characterized by both continuity and change, and is embedded in a socio-cultural context that shapes our views of the changes taking place. The interaction of age, stage, developmental tasks, context, and the universal changes that take place are all significant factors in the evolution of personal control and autonomy.

THEORETICAL APPROACHES

It is a fallacy to think that the development of autonomy, identity, and personal control is a uniform process. Although the major task of adolescence is the development of an integrated identity or self (Erikson, 1968a, 1968b), identity is made up of many fragments and pieces, some of which may be highly developed, while others are less so. This uneven development is particularly seen in female adolescents, and is embedded in and influenced by contemporary culture and expectations.

The Concept of Self and Identity

The self, and ultimately identity, is defined in many different ways. William James (cited in Adelson, 1964) made a distinction between the "Me" and the "I." "Me" is the self as known, and comprises the material self, the social self, and the spiritual or psychological self. By contrast, "I" is the self as knower, the ego personality which defines the meaningful aspects of "me" and organizes and interprets those aspects.

Anthropologist Margaret Mead (1950) saw the self as a concept reflecting symbolic interaction. According to Mead, self-reflection is a social construction, reflecting on the self through others' perspectives. Carl Rogers (cited in Adelson, 1964) talked of the real self versus the ideal self, where a self-image disparity can occur when there is a difference between the individual's assessment of self and the ideal self. Robert Selman (1980) identified three levels of the developmental progression in understanding the self. In early childhood, no distinction is made between internal and external life and understanding is based on physical terms. In later childhood, differences are recognized between internal and external states. Children begin to describe their true self in terms of internal, subjective states. In adolescence, the full level of self-awareness evolves, where the self as knower emerges. The young woman develops the ability to integrate the various disparate components of "me" into an internally consistent self-concept.

In Harter's (1986) theoretical model of self as knower, in early adolescence self-understanding is based upon social personality characteristics, while in late adolescence the focus shifts to a personal belief system and philosophy.

In order to understand the evolution of self, autonomy, and the perception of personal control, two contrasting theoretical approaches are discussed and integrated: the psychosocial/psychodynamic view characterized by the work of Blos (1962), Erikson (1968a), and Marcia (1980), and the cognitive/behavioral, social learning approaches of Seligman (1991), Gilligan (1982), and Rotter (1966). Clearly, no one theory by itself gives a complete view of the developing adolescent in a social context. However, the theories selected provide a foundation for the understanding of the development of autonomy and personal control.

Psychodynamic and Psychosocial Approaches

Erik Erikson's work (1968a, 1968b) and its extension by Marcia (1976, 1980) is thought to be fundamental to understanding the development of identity—in other words, a clear and consistent sense of self (Sul,1994), which in turn is essential to a sense of personal control.

The journey toward identity formation—an identity autonomous of the family of origin—becomes most salient during adolescence, according to Erikson (1968a). The psychosocial crisis is precipitated by the seemingly dramatic changes in the internal and external environments. The "crisis" of adolescence is self-discovery, and the resulting end product is identity formation or identity confusion. Making choices for identity consolidation involves renouncing a host of possible selves. A young woman living in a restricted and limited environment may be caught in a myriad of cultural and/or gender stereotypes. Therefore, she may have insufficient information and experience to make choices and may incorporate the identity she has been exposed to in her limited milieu.

There are several pitfalls in identity development. *Identity foreclosure* refers to the selection of an identity too quickly—settling on a path pushed by others, rather than choosing a path for oneself. Premature identity resolution is the result and the young woman limits her opportunities for role experimentation or choosing alternative directions.

Identity confusion or *diffusion* comes about by not making any choice. The young woman may drift without making a commitment to values or people. Role experimentation is limited because extended commitments are not made.

According to Erikson (1968a, 1968b), individuals experiencing role confusion tend to be self-centered and emotionally immature and to lack stable, committed friendships. Erikson believes the journey toward identity formation must include a psychosocial moratorium, which is defined as an extended time period to experiment with roles without excessive pressures to fulfill obligations. Erikson's model does not fully take into account the context of contemporary society and the realistic demands placed upon young women. A psycho-social moratorium may be relevant for a few, but may not be a realistic expectation for the majority of young women today who live in a highly complex and demanding environment (Gilligan, 1982; Brown & Gilligan, 1992).

The adolescent's journey toward identity solidification results in a clear sense of self. These adolescents feel confident about their values and their ability to live independent, autonomous lives and to develop intimate relationships with others.

Marcia's (1982) research evolved from Erikson's theory of identity formation. He clar-ified, defined, and operationalized identity status so that it could be measured and evalu-ated. Each level of status development is defined in terms of the presence or absence of a sense of commitment. Marcia's research rests on the assumption that a person achieves an integrated identity status by resolving the psychological crisis of adolescence.

The journey toward an autonomous identity is marked by anxiety, moments of feeling lost and out of control, and the hope of making meaningful choices. Crisis, in this context, refers to whether the individual has struggled over making personal decisions that are self-chosen and not externally imposed. Marcia's identity statuses include (1982):

- *identity diffusion* when the individual makes no commitments, appears to be drifting through life, and reports no sense of need to search for answers to questions about existence.
- *identity foreclosure* when the young woman has accepted values espoused by others, particularly parents, and accepted values without any struggle over personal choice.
- *identity moratorium* involving searching for persuasive answers to questions about per-sonal and communal existence. Such an individual is in a struggle over issues of com-mitment and existential meaning.
- *identity achievement* when the individual evolves a clear sense of self and feels confi-dent about her values. She is able to develop intimate relationships with others while living an independent and autonomous life.

Although Marcia specifies four identity statuses which form a developmental sequence, the only necessary requirement is that the moratorium be experienced before identity achievement. Identity diffusion, foreclosure, and moratorium are normal phases of adolescence and become problematic only when they extend into adulthood. Some people never develop through all four steps. A person may be in one status in one area of life, and in another in some other aspect. For example, a person may have an established identity concerning personal values and relationships, but may still be searching for the right college major. Thus, identity status is not a unified concept (Marcia, 1982).

In his research, Marcia found that neither IQ nor self-esteem relate to identity status. However, it must be noted that Marcia's primary research, having been comprised of all male, all white college students, could hardly be described as a representative sample.

Adams and Jones (1983) did study females in middle adolescence using Marcia's assessment instrument to determine the relationship between identity status and the adoles-cents' perceptions of the way they were parented. Identity achievement and moratorium women reported that their parents encouraged independence and exerted less control. Those reflecting a diffuse status reported that their parents used inconsistent child-rearing practices, exerting control but encouraging independence. The foreclosed status girls indicated that their parents exerted control as well as discouraged independence. Parenting practices, it would appear, influence the type of resolution adolescents give to the crisis and commitment of identity formation.

Phinney (1989) studied the extent to which reflections about ethnicity influence identity formation and concluded that both Hispanic and Native American families place a high value on the acceptance of traditional roles and values. Adams and Jones (1983) found that minority culture parents consistently enforce cultural values and roles. Therefore, in ethnocentric families, foreclosed identity is often seen as the ideal outcome of responsible parenting. Other identity statuses are seen as aberrant and a violation of cultural expectations. It is important to remember that identity formation takes place in a complex social context.

Gender Differences in Identity Formation

Traditionally in Western culture, women were expected to assume the roles of wife, mother, nurturer, and caretaker. As women become an essential part of the workforce, obtain higher-level degrees, and postpone marriage and parenting, expectations and opportunities are slowly changing. Gilligan (1982) argues that the developmental course for males and females differs as to the order of establishing identity achievement and personal commitment. Males are first to establish independence and personal achievement, whereas females must first establish emotional bonds of interpersonal attachment.

Gilligan feels that both Erikson and Marcia acknowledge only male patterns of identity formation and that their theoretical formulations are biased against women. Waterman (1985) contends that males and females are more similar than different in the way they make decisions. However, there have been research studies which support Gilligan's theory regarding female identity formation.

Orlofsky (1978) demonstrated that females interpret success differently than do males. Women, in his study, believed that success led to interpersonal rejection and the loss of femininity. Men with a high fear of success feared the responsibility of being an achiever, while women did not demonstrate any fear of additional responsibilities.

Josselson (1987) did a long-term follow-up study of women who were assessed for identity status in their last year of college. Those with diffuse identities throughout college continued to live lives with patterns of psychological distress. Foreclosed women obtained their self-esteem through their families and were still living by the themes they chose earlier. They demonstrated little personal development, never entering a new identity status. Those who reflected moratorium status obtained self-definition through relationships. Most were troubled by self-doubt and regretted decisions they had not yet made. Ego identity status evolving during adolescence has long-lasting impact on adult development.

Autonomy, independence, and serious exploration of alternatives are typically considered desired characteristics in males, while similar traits may be devalued in females. When considering the results of the aforementioned studies, it is important to consider both the time period and context in which the investigations took place. Many females today have positive role models, particularly mothers who are professionals or career women, and who thus lead alternate lifestyles in comparison to traditional expectations. Over the past 20 years, a relatively short period of time from a sociological perspective, we have seen many major changes which have expanded women's roles, particularly in the workplace.

Blos' Identity Formation Theory

No review of psychodynamic theory would be complete without mention of Peter Blos' (1962) formulations. According to Blos, the development of autonomy consists of four basic challenges: separation/individuation, maintaining ego-continuity, coping with residual trauma, and solidifying sexual identity. Blos built on Mahler's (1963) position that the first separation takes place during the first two years of life, where the demarcation of the body image of the self from the image of the mother is the core process in identity formation.

Blos (1962) extends the concept of separation to the adolescent process, where puberty once again vividly calls attention to the body image and the need for congruence between psychic structure and maturational change. As the young woman matures, she must confront her relationship with her mother. Her identification and dependency are viewed in a different light. Separateness from mother is often reflected in the teenager dressing differently, denigrating her mother's appearance, and having a strong identification with her peer group. However, there is also a strong pull toward mother for affirmation, advice, and guidance. Separation from father also has consequences as the rules of interaction change because of the girl's emerging sexuality. This shift in relationship is underscored as fathers begin to play a more active role in co-parenting and take on a more nurturing and less advisory role.

Sustaining ego continuity is a real challenge for the young woman. Body continuity is an essential part of ego continuity. The disorganizing effect of rapid body growth can be sensed in terms of a disconnected body image. The body may appear as totally new, and those new parts (i.e., breasts) can be experienced as separate. Mastery of the body as well as integrating perceived imperfections and flaws are major challenges. The formation of a realistic and positive body image is essential to the ultimate development of self-image.

Blos also emphasizes the importance of the consolidation of sexual identity during adolescence (1962), where sexual functioning needs to become integrated with being a female. Core gender identity evolves during the first two years of life and becomes further developed through interpersonal interaction and experience. Sexuality becomes another aspect of gender identity that must be integrated.

Gender identity tends to be more stable in girls than boys, possibly because of the primary identification with mother. "Sexual activity *per se* is obviously no indication of adolescent closure and offers no assurance that sexual identity has been achieved. Obviously…neither is the experience of pregnancy or an abortion an indication of sexual maturity" (p. 45). For the female, sexual identity can be seen in relational terms and can be facilitated or inhibited by the choice of partner and types of sexual encounters. Gilligan (1982) concurs with the importance of relational issues in the development of identity.

Ego functioning, beyond its defensive role, must consolidate autonomy through the internalization of values, self-esteem, and identity. The specific task is to become free of dependence on external environmental controls, such as those of parents and peer groups, and to internalize personal self-control. Defense mechanisms involving projection transform into those involving introjection to contribute to the process of individuation as the individual incorporates responsibility for behavior and actions. Thus, at the close of adolescence, the ego is sufficiently consolidated to meet the challenges of adulthood (Josselson, 1987).

Blos (1962), in formulating the second separation/individuation stage, provides us with the "why" of the move toward identity development and indicates what critical issues need to be wrestled with; Erikson and Marcia provide the details of how it happens and indicate the implications of the changes.

Review of Theoretical Perspectives

Autonomy, personal control, and independence dynamics typically include the process of separation/individuation and the formation of an independent identity (Blos, 1962; Erikson, 1968a, 1968b; and Marcia, 1980). In contrast, Gilligan (Brown & Gilligan, 1992; Gilligan, 1982) presents the view that females consolidate their identity through connections and relationships, rather than through separation.

According to Gilligan, the crossroads between being a girl and being a woman is the hallmark of adolescence. The transition often involves the disconnection from previous relationships and the disassociation with previous expectations. This is quite comparable to Blos' concept of separation/individuation. The disconnection leaves girls psychologically at risk and involved in relational struggles. In fact, this may precipitate premature identity foreclosure and may also explain why young women become culturally connected and prematurely involved in relationships and too early mothering.

This area has not been subjected to systematic investigation and, therefore, there is no empirical support for such speculations. What is apparent, however, when incorporating Gilligan's formulations, is that one of the many paradoxes of adolescence is the necessity of giving up old relationships and connections that may be extremely important to the forming of relationships essential for development.

Other theoretical explanations of the development of autonomy and personal control emerge from the locus of control construct, and from related concepts, such as learned helplessness. Yet, since these constructs have not been systematically investigated in terms of adolescent behavior, we shall not examine them here. Instead, the relevance of locus of control and related constructs have been thoroughly examined among the elderly and will thus be explored in detail in Nadien and Denmark's chapter on aging women.

Whatever the theoretical approach, the essential elements of female dynamics in adolescence are the simultaneous discovery and creation of a self leading to a deepening self-understanding (Garrod, Smulyan, Powers, & Kilkenney, 1995).

Whether terms are similar or different, or the perspective comes from internal dynamics or external expectation and reinforcement, it is clear that the primary challenges of adolescence are the evolution of a personal identity, the development of a sense of autonomy, and the creation of feelings of personal control. All writers agree that the onset of adolescence is precipitated by biologically regulated physical change that, in turn, is the impetus for the creation of a new sense of self, new expectations, and new roles. Many changes occur in what is perceived to be a rather quick sequence and the female adopts strategies and defenses to preserve her sense of self-esteem, self-concept, and belonging.

EXPRESSIONS OF PERSONAL CONTROL

It is not surprising that adolescents engage in elaborate psychological efforts to create the illusion of control at a time when so many aspects of personal functioning are perceived as being out of control. Everyone engages in at-risk behaviors and those behaviors are readily apparent and particularly prevalent in adolescents. At-risk behaviors are considered to be different than clinical dysfunctions, but could lead to maladaptive behavior patterns.

Elkind (1967) discusses a kind of egocentrism which emerges during adolescence and involves a preoccupation with self. Adolescents develop an "imaginary audience," which is a tendency to think that they are at the center of everybody's world. This contributes to the self-consciousness noticed in early adolescence. Therefore, behaviors tend to be a performance for others. At the same time, adolescents are living the "personal fable" whereby they begin to form exaggerated beliefs about their uniqueness, characterized by a delusion of immortality and the belief that the emotional experiences they are having are unlike those of anyone else. The sense of invulnerability contributes significantly to risk-taking behavior (Elkind, 1967).

It has been empirically established that adolescents experience the negative consequences of some risk behaviors to a disproportionately high degree (Quedrel, Fischoff, & Davis, 1993). Given that information, a conflict arises as to whether to restrict the adolescent's autonomy, that is, to restrict freedom until safety messages are incorporated, such as raising the driving age and instituting restrictions and prohibitions against certain behaviors. However, the price paid for such an approach is the restriction of freedom and autonomy.

Whether behaviors are adaptive or dysfunctional may ultimately be determined by what strengths and limitations the young woman brings to adolescence based upon her earlier developmental history. Another consideration in determining the impact of risk-taking behavior is whether there is the absence of dysfunctional behavior or the presence of optimal prosocial function.

Risk behaviors can be modulated by adaptive strengths (Kazdin, 1995). Prior sections have detailed the many stressors that adolescents face on personal, interpersonal, and social levels. Coleman (1980), in his focal theory, discusses the impact of multiple stressors in development leading to increased vulnerability. Recent research examining stress and coping indicates that education and information, support networks, a sense of self-esteem, and feelings of competence and control can modify the negative consequences of stress.

Obviously, not all adolescents experience the "storm and stress" that G. Stanley Hall wrote about in 1904. And not all young women lose a sense of personal control. In fact, Offer et al. (1981) suggest that storm, turbulence, and distress in adolescence is the exception rather than the rule. What, then, makes for more adaptive behavior during this period of change and reintegration?

Factors Contributing to Positive Adaptation

The successful integration of gender-role orientation and a sense of mastery contribute to adaptive coping and problem solving during adolescence. Hobfoll, Dunahoo, Ben-Porath, & Monnier (1994) report that, in general, females appear to have a wider range of beneficial coping skills than do males. Men resort less to assertiveness and more to aggressive and antisocial strategies, whereas women tend to use more prosocial and interpersonal strategies.

Harter (1990) indicates that positive self-esteem can act as a major buffer against stress and is linked to enhanced motivation. A well-developed self-concept is typically associated with positive psychological well-being. Rosenberg's (1975) work delineates the characteristics of a good self-concept, which includes high self-esteem, feelings of worth, stability in self-concept, low vulnerability, sense of personal control, and low levels of public anxiety.

An adolescent with interpersonal problems does not necessarily have low self-esteem. However, someone with low self-esteem may have interpersonal problems. Walker and Green (1986) found that positive peer relationships for girls was indicative of higher self-esteem and the best overall predictor of self-esteem was the self-evaluation of popularity.

Self-understanding has been found to be critical in overcoming serious challenges, and has been demonstrated to be an important "protective factor" (Beardslee, 1989) in mitigating risk to healthy development from serious stressors. Insight typically contributes to action. If one has insight without action, it could lead to profound feelings of helplessness and, ultimately, serious depression (Seligman, 1993).

Positive family relationships contribute to self-esteem and therefore to adaptive coping. Positive parental perception contributes to self-esteem (Rosenberg, 1985). It has been demonstrated that the more "competent" a family feels, the more autonomous the children. A young woman from a "democratic" and autonomy-giving family is armed with tools for effective decision making (Baumrind, 1975; Martin, 1985).

Looney and Lewis (1983) conducted an extensive study, evaluating adolescents judged to be of good psychological health. The population included middle-class white and lower-class black teenagers. They found that the competent adolescents were

1. more secure in their sense of self
2. able to talk about complex needs, although the black youngsters described their needs more in relation to their parents' expectations
3. active and assertive in their orientation, in other words, they were doers
4. good students, although the white adolescents took for granted that they would be attending college, whereas the black youngsters did not
5. active in extracurricular activities, however the black females were more involved in athletics than their white counterparts
6. future-oriented, while aspiring to be greater than their parents. However, the white students tended to see themselves more in professional roles
7. involved in wide circles of acquaintances with one or two close friends. The black women were more discriminating in their choice of close friends and wanted friends headed in the same positive direction as themselves
8. involved in good relationships with parents, but closer to mother. Father was seen as more of a disciplinarian. All perceived authoritarianism in parenting as assuredness and as a source of their own strength as well as their families' strength

These two groups were from different racial backgrounds and significantly different social classes, but their responses were more similar than different. Although the study is limited in that only two groups were used for comparison and all of the children were from intact families, the focus of the study on positive adaptation and the results are important to our understanding of adolescent development.

Typically, research has focused on adolescents with significant mental-health problems. However, there is an emerging body of research focusing on those who are resilient or seemingly invulnerable to serious risks and stresses that tend to have negative mental health consequences. We are somewhat clear on what causes risk: physical and sexual abuse, poverty, emotionally unsupportive relationships, family crisis, and loss of loved ones to name a few (Rutter, 1975; Werner, 1989). We are somewhat less certain as to what may be the protective factors that mitigate against risk. However, recent research seems to support Coleman's (1980) focal theory perspective; that is, when a single risk factor is present, the adolescent is no more vulnerable than individuals without that risk factor. Adolescents are more likely to succumb to the negative consequences of stress when there are multiple risk factors (Rutter, 1975).

The factors that protect the adolescent from the negative consequences of stress include positive self-esteem, family cohesion, a lack of discord, and the external support systems that encourage and reinforce the young women's efforts to cope (Garmezy, 1985). Cowan (1994) strongly believes in the critical need to focus on "wellness" rather than on illness in order to develop preventive intervention strategies and provide a positive mental health environment.

Research focusing on competence and resiliency is critical. Many of the environments in which our young women live, work, and play need to be further humanized in order to support the changing psychological needs, particularly those of autonomy and control. This is important, specifically, in the school environment, which becomes a microcosm of society in terms of social and personal relationships. Schools may provide the skills and coping strategies for life, or can prove to be destructive environments using shame and isolation as negative reinforcers, and exerting strict authoritarian control that does not leave room for autonomy, choice, and self-esteem. School-based intervention paradigms can be a vehicle for empowerment of adolescents (Robinson, Ruch-Ross, Watkins-Ferrel, & Lightfoot, 1993). There is a real need for more empirical research at the middle-school and high-school level to determine how these institutions make active contributions to positive mental health.

Factors Contributing to Negative Adaptation

What often appears to be dysfunctional by "normative" standards may be perceived as rational and adaptive in the adolescent's judgment. Strategies and patterns are adopted in order to preserve self-esteem, to protect against isolation and rejection, to feel attractive, to "matter" and to belong, to feel loved and worthwhile, and most importantly, to feel in control. Patterns of behavior are adopted which serve to elaborate, exaggerate, or maintain illusions of personal control. These maladaptive patterns become natural extensions of the risk factors in development. The most important considerations in labeling behavior as "dysfunctional" are whether the behaviors cause physical and psychological harm to the individual, and whether the pattern of behavior inhibits positive growth in meeting the developmental tasks of adolescence. We will focus primarily on those dysfunctional patterns in which the incidence is higher in young women or is exclusive to young women. These patterns include teenage depression and suicide, eating disorders, and teenage pregnancy.

Suicide

In general, the rate for attempted suicide increases in the 15- to 19-year-old age group and has increased 300% since 1956. The death rate for males is five times that of females (Davis & Sandoval, 1991). However, females have a significantly higher rate of suicide attempts and suicidal ideation.

A headline appearing in the June 28, 1995 *New York Times,* read "Town Tries to Comprehend Suicide Attempts by Eight Girls—a plea to parents to take a larger part in teenagers lives." The article reports that a minimum of eight high school girls, ages 12–17, in a suburban middle-class community had been involved in a suicide pact and that none of the parents were aware of what was happening. They were all rushed to the emergency room over a five-day period, having swallowed mixes of illegal drugs, alcohol, or over-the-counter drugs. It was commented that "the girls were crying for attention, but they don't understand how final it [suicide] could be" (B8). One attempter indicated that she was experiencing personal pain and needed a way to control it, which she did by swallowing 40 aspirins. Another said that she knew it could harm her, but she wasn't concerned; she was experiencing conflicts with her parents over her friends, the loss of a grandmother, and her family's recent move.

Recent events in New Milford, Connecticut, are not atypical. At least twice a year such accounts appear in the newspaper or on television, highlighting the fact that teenagers feel out of control and attempt to take control in a maladaptive, and sometimes, permanent manner.

Precipitating factors for suicidal behavior include a perception of humiliating life events, a sense of hopelessness, and the feeling that problems are unsolvable or uncontrollable (Eichenbaum & Orbach, 1983). Rubenstein, Heeren, Houseman, Rubin, and Stechler (1989) highlighted four areas in which stress might occur that would increase the probability of suicide for adolescent females. They include sexual pressures, achievement pressure, an exposure to suicide within the expanded family network, and the experience of personal loss. Ninety-two percent of the teenagers who score high on all four factors are expected to be suicidal (Pfeffer, 1988).

The suicidal act in adolescence can be looked at as an impulsive reaction to actual or anticipated failures in dealing with conflicts and crises. The impassivity suggests no control over life events, but also over fantasies and thoughts. This autonomy of inner impulses sometimes results in self-destructive behavior as an imagined method of gaining control (Pfeffer, 1986). Many adolescents deny that there are permanent consequences to such impulsive or planned decisions to end their own life because of feelings of invulnerability and omnipotence (Elkind, 1967), and therefore do not consider the implications of the outcome of their choice of "coping" behavior. They just want to get away from the pain. Research findings underscore the importance of considering Coleman's (1980) multiple-stressor approach. What is highlighted is that for the adolescent, the solution to a problem becomes paradoxical in that the choice of dealing with loss is the possible loss of one's own life.

Depression

While suicide and suicide attempts can be considered as the externalizing of the loss of control, depression can be considered as the internalizing of those same feelings. A clear picture of the prevalence of depression in adolescence is hard to obtain. Studies of nonclinical populations report rates of depression ranging from 18 to 28%. Studies of clinical populations report much higher numbers (Ehrenberg, Cox, & Koopman, 1990). Reynolds (1995) reported that depression was the primary problem for over 40% of adolescents who were referred to mental health centers. Many depressed adolescents remain hidden from adults and mental health professionals due to their struggle to protect both their own self-esteem and the adult expectations that "adolescents are like this" (Weiner, 1980).

Depressed moods are more frequently self-reported by females than males (Peterson et al., 1993). Females are particularly prone to depression in the middle adolescent years when rates continue to rise to three times that of men, and they continue to be more vulnerable than men through their adult years. Such gender differences emerge at about age 15. Longitudinal studies demonstrated that depression in boys decreased with age, but the level of depression remained the same over time for girls.

All studies indicate that increases in depressive disorders and depressed mood are greater for girls than boys. Gender differences may be reflective of stylistic differences, where women tend to be more open, self-reflective, and emotionally reactive. Conger (1981) suggests that gender intensification accounts for the difference between men and women and suggests that increased flexibility in roles for women could produce a decline in female depression.

African American and Hispanic youths tend to have lower measured rates of depression than European American and Asian American youths. It is hypothesized that these teenagers tend to act out their feelings rather than becoming self-reflective. Rural teenagers demonstrate greater depression than do urban youngsters, attributed to greater feelings of isolation and a sense of limited opportunities (Patterson, 1991).

Gay, lesbian, and bisexual youths are at two to three times greater risk of suicide than heterosexual adolescents, and feelings of depression are expressed at five times a greater rate. DiAugelli and Hersberger (1993) report that 42% of identified lesbian, gay, and bisexual youths had made suicide attempts, far more than typical for this age group.

Adolescents with non-stereotypical gender preference are at greater risk because of low self-esteem, depression, and fears of rejection by family and friendship networks. Whereas integrating sexual preference into the concept of identity is a challenging task, the greatest difficulty expressed (Di Augelli & Hersberger, 1993) is revealing their orientation first to family and second to friends. Common feelings among depressed adolescents are a harsh conscience and painful feelings of guilt, as well as a sense of a loss of self-esteem, negative thoughts, and despondency (White, 1989).

The ongoing stress from expected development tasks, such as forging an identity, developing intimate friendships, and deciding on a vocation, present further complications. Adolescents become depressed when faced with feelings of incompetence and of being unlovable. Dependency on adults may also lead to depression as the adolescent both fights against and demands such dependence.

Particularly prevalent during the middle and late adolescent periods are the feelings of anxiety and alienation associated with depression (White, 1989). Signs of anxiety include excessive concerns about past behavior, difficulties relaxing, extreme need for reassurance from others, and conspicuous self-consciousness (Strauss & Lahey, 1987). The associated alienation manifests itself in a withdrawal from planning for the future, lack of connection to the values of one's society, and cynicism that nothing really matters (Conger, 1981). Alienated late adolescents are primarily concerned with escaping from feelings of loneliness, insignificance, or incompetency (Weiner, 1980).

Feelings of learned helplessness or the perception of life as a pattern of uncontrollable events has direct consequences on feelings of depression. If an internalized attributional mode becomes part of a personality style, such individuals are particularly prone to depression (Peterson, Maier, & Seligman, 1993).

In summary, female adolescents are particularly vulnerable to chronic depression and are at high risk for suicide. These young women engage in withdrawal and escape behavior as coping strategies when faced with feelings of loss of control and isolation. Abdication of control ironically becomes the solution in order to feel "in control."

Eating Disorders

Feeling attractive or having a positive physical self-concept is the greatest contributor to overall self-concept for females. The majority of specifically female adolescent disturbances emerge around body issues such as anorexia, bulimia, and overeating.

A glance through any typical teen magazine or sitcom featuring adolescents gives visual evidence of the standards and expectations of body image for adolescents. Most African American women in mainstream magazines, for example, tend to have lighter coloring and "white features" like straight hair. What impact can that have on African American females in terms of their own features over which they have no control?

Despite the multiplicity of roles women play, our society still evaluates women on the basis of physical attractiveness. There are few ways available for women to compensate for the culturally determined lack of beauty. Self-esteem and self-confidence as well as level of anxiety fluctuate with the state of the body image, which clearly has a greater impact for women than men. During adolescence, the evaluation of self and other is particularly dependent on superficial characteristics; there is an acute awareness of how attractive each individual is in relation to others.

Some females, in their struggle with issues of control and autonomy, develop eating disorders as a means of coping with demands that are unacceptable to them (Bruch, 1991). Although different in their consequences, obesity and anorexia share some of the same dynamics when eating is used to solve or camouflage problems of living that otherwise appear insoluble. In both conditions, severe disturbances in body image and self-concept are prevalent. Youngsters perceive their bodies as separate from themselves. They view their bodies as externalized objects over which rigid control needs to be exerted, or else feelings of helplessness will prevail.

The presented clinical picture is that of young women who are stubborn and negative. However, such women are actually concealing a devastating sense of ineffectiveness. They feel powerless to direct their lives and to control their bodies. They actually lack a sense of ownership over their own bodies, and thus lack discriminatory awareness of their body needs. These young women are inaccurate in identifying hunger, bodily discomfort and bodily tensions, anxiety, depression, or other psychological stress (Bruch, 1991).

Deficits in the sense of control of the body affect other areas, particularly relationships with others, that are important to identity formation and personal development (Gilligan, 1982). Therefore, young women with eating disorders are poorly equipped to become self-sufficient and emancipated from dependency on mother and family, a critical task for successful adolescent development (Blos, 1962; Erikson, 1968a, 1968b). They also feel deprived of the support and recognition of their peers that facilitate the adolescent liberation process.

Developmental histories of those with eating disorders suggest that they were generally lacking in initiative and autonomy, although parents report, "my child was never any trouble." These young women demonstrate patterns of rigidly sticking to rules, enmeshment with the mother, and limited opportunity for engaging in self-reliant behavior. Early separation experiences can be characterized by significant elements of enmeshment, where the mother needs the child to feel complete and limits opportunities for autonomous behavior. As a consequence, there is evidence of early disturbance in the child's inner representation of self, which interferes with emotional and conceptual development.

Friendship patterns mirror the mother–daughter relationship where the young woman displays over-compliant behavior and becomes what the friend wants her to be, without expressing her own needs. Social isolation also becomes part of the pattern. A girl growing up compliant and enmeshed with her mother leaves her ill-prepared for the adolescent body changes that signal sexuality and independence. Feelings of being out of control of one's body are reinforced, often precipitating the need to take charge through regulating eating behavior. Anorexia represents a desperate striving to regain control over the body in order to attain a sense of personal identity and autonomy (Kaplan, 1984). Controlling food intake gives the illusion of power and control.

Ascetism is a defense mechanism unique to adolescence (Freud, 1958). Anna Freud suggests that the female uses ascetism to establish a sense of independence from parents. The adolescent body image ideal is thinness. There is, also, almost a phobic concern about what and how she eats. Taken together with ascetism as a defense, the rigid rules associated with taking control of the body may be one of the first ways that the young woman exerts independence. However, what initially appears to be adaptive becomes pathological when the defense becomes an end in itself, as with anorexia.

There is a high correlation between women characterized as "superwomen" and the presence of eating disorders. Superwomen are those who have succeeded on the same level as men, incorporating "traditional male values." Gilligan (1982) suggests that vulnerability to eating disorders occurs when young women focus on issues of perfection and control and are unable to recognize the importance of interpersonal connections, thus incorporating male values.

The etiology of eating disorders reflect dependency and a lack of control over the body, together with enmeshment in the mother–daughter relationship. Engaging in the excessive control of food intake gives the illusion of control and feelings of separating and moving towards total independence. However, as the outcome of eating disorders, we often find a young woman so weak and malnourished that she needs to be fed and taken care of. Again, as with depression and suicide, there is a paradox. The adolescent strives to achieve control and independence, while the outcome yields an abdication of control and, often, total dependency on others in order to survive. What may appear to be adaptive coping for the adolescent may yield dysfunctional consequences.

Adolescent Sexuality and Early Motherhood

For many young women, sexual activity and premature motherhood are often perceived as synonymous with autonomy, maturity, and the exertion of personal control (Blos, 1962). Lacking in a positive sense of self, many young women use their bodies to find ways to relate to others and to belong. By engaging in sexual activity, they attempt to compensate for lack of a positive self-image, feelings of isolation, and feelings of non-control. However, as with much dysfunctional behavior, the outcome serves to exacerbate those initial negative feelings rather than change them.

Teenage pregnancy continues to be on the rise, with the birthrate among adolescents in the United States exceeding that of all developed countries. More than one million teenagers become pregnant each year, with over half of those becoming mothers.

Early sexual behavior has become normative for most adolescents. By age 19, 80% of young women have had sexual intercourse. Daughters in single-parent families are more likely to engage in early sexual activity than in dual-parent families. The question may no longer be whether or not adolescents engage in sexual behavior, but which behaviors are psychologically healthy. Many young women engage in sexual behavior so as to belong, to satisfy a boyfriend, or to measure up to the expectations of others. All such motives are consistent with feelings of low self-esteem.

Low self-esteem has been correlated with infrequent use of contraceptives by females, whereas high self-esteem females rely on contraception. Adolescents who choose not to use contraceptives and who later become teenage mothers are significantly more likely to report self-devaluing experiences and are less likely to perceive themselves as competent, which is ironic as the motivation to become a parent might be to increase competence and autonomy.

Early parenting may have major consequences, creating a situation whereby premature foreclosure in identity development occurs (Marcia, 1976). The adolescent is cast into the role of parent before role experimentation and role clarification typical of middle adolescence occurs. The teenage mother is forced to cope with multiple stressors of reality and survival while coping with the normative stressors of adolescence. All of the stressors increase the vulnerability for serious mental health problems.

Musick (1993) speculates that many of the young women at risk for premature motherhood grow up without adequate nurturance and protection. There also may be experiences of early and traumatic sexualization.

Through pregnancy and childbearing, the young woman tends to reconcile her contradictory needs for autonomy and security. She may be able to draw close to her mother and to place claim on maternal affection through the grandchild. Early sexual activity and maternity may offer a way to retrieve childhood and enter adulthood simultaneously. The initial thrill of mothering, the need to be needed, the feeling of control and responsibility for another's life, and being fussed over and admired, all substantively meet the developmental needs of the adolescent.

Teenage pregnancy does not necessarily have only negative consequences. Recent research demonstrates that the African American teenage mother becomes somewhat more independent after motherhood, returning to school and developing a real future orientation. However, the Puerto Rican young woman is more likely to withdraw from responsibility after motherhood and become increasingly more dependent on her own mother (Hilton, 1983).

In the dynamics of teenage motherhood we find another paradox. There is a perception of control, independence, and achievement of adult identity status, but the consequences of too-early parenting may be restricted independence because of the need to care for the infant.

Conclusion

Offer and Sabshin (1984), in their most recent studies, indicated that only about 20% of adolescents are psychologically disturbed, with no gender differences emerging. Yet there is an increasing incidence of suicide, adolescent depression, teenage parenthood, delinquency, homicide, and personal violence. Feeling out of control, experiences of personal loss and the more generalized feelings of anomie and isolation are problems inherent in contemporary society. In view of such findings, adolescents' ability to survive so many challenges testifies to their great resilience.

The need to escape from adolescence and its problems is not uncommon and takes many forms. Passivity could be a normal reaction for some. For others, the feeling that the pressures and demands are too much may change the meaning of their experiences and create a different reality for them. Others use drugs or stimulants to change the way the mind experiences reality. Others, in a counter-phobic declaration of independence, make social demands, fight openly, break rules and mores, and become delinquent (Bruch, 1988).

The processes of denying, modifying, manipulating, and reconstructing reality all could be viewed as attempts by the adolescent to gain personal control over inner and external worlds. However, for many, the chosen strategies may prove maladaptive and lead to lifelong patterns of dysfunctional involvement with the self, family, friends, and the world. For others, there are protective factors which have evolved through early development that permit the young woman to adaptively and productively cope with the challenges of the adolescent years, permitting her to evolve a positive sense of autonomy, identity, and personal control.

Does adolescence have to be a period of stress, turmoil, and feeling out of control? Is crisis necessary for growth as Blos maintains? Can our social systems and institutions provide more and better opportunities for adaptive behavior, choice, decision making, and support so that female adolescents can enter into a healthy, cooperative, and collaborative adulthood without the burden of gender and power stressors?

Numerous factors contribute to the development of autonomous functioning. The internal factors such as values, temperament, and ability, interact with the external factors over which we have more control. The latter include the range and variety of experiences available, the nature and quality of interpersonal interactions, and the humanity inherent in the social systems the adolescent interacts with. Creating competent family systems to produce autonomous children is fundamental. Creating a balance between challenge and stress is vital.

Our challenge, then, is to create a "wellness model" that would support the development of adaptive coping strategies to successfully deal with the risks associated with adolescent development. We must also provide and support opportunities which enhance self-esteem, develop competence, and create feelings of autonomy for the young women of today, so they can successfully meet the challenges of adulthood and a rapidly changing world.

REFERENCES

Adams, G., & Jones, R. (1983). Female adolescents' identity development: Age comparisons and perceived child-rearing experience. *Developmental Psychology 19,* 249–256.

Addato, C. P. (1991). Late adolescence to early adulthood. In S. I. Greenspan and G. H. Pollock (Eds.), *The course of life IV: Adolescence* (357–375). Madison, CT: International Universities Press.

Adelson, J. (1964). The mystique of adolescence. *Psychiatry, 17,* 1–6.

Adelson, J. (1975). The development of ideology in adolescence. In S. E. Dragastin & G. H. Elder, Jr. (Eds.), *Adolescence in the life cycle: Psychological change and social context* (pp. 63–78). New York: Wiley.

Allen, P. G. (1992). *The sacred hoop: Recovering the feminine in American Indian tradition.* Boston: Beacon Press.

Balk, D. E. (1995). *Adolescent development.* Pacific Grove, CA: Brooks/Cole.

Baumrind, D. (1975). Early socialization and adolescent competence. In S. E. Dragastin & G. H. Elder, Jr. (Eds.), *Adolescence and the life cycle: Psychological change and social context* (pp. 117–146). New York: Wiley.

Beardslee, W. R. (1989). The role of self understanding in resilient individuals: The development of a perspective. *American Journal of Orthopsychiatry, 59*(2), 266–278.

Bernard, J. (1975). Adolescence and socialization for motherhood. In S. E. Dragastin & G. H. Elder, Jr. (Eds.), *Adolescence and the life cycle: Psychological change and social context* (pp. 227–251). New York: Wiley.

Blos, P. (1962). *On adolescence.* New York: Macmillan.

Brown, L. M., & Gilligan, C. (1992). *Meeting at the crossroads: Women's psychology and girls' development.* Cambridge, MA: Harvard University Press.

Bruch, H. (1991). Escape from change. In S. I. Greenspan & G. H. Pollock (Eds.), *The course of life IV: Adolescence* (pp. 313–332). Madison, CT: International Universities Press.

Canino, I. A., & Spurlock, J. (1994). *Culturally diverse children and adolescents.* New York: Guilford Press.

Caspi, A., & Elder, G. H. (1986). Life satisfaction in old age: Linking social psychology and history. *Psychology and Aging, 1,* 18–26.

Chen, C. L., & Yang, D. C. (1986). The self-image of Chinese American adolescents. *International Journal of Social Psychiatry 32,* 29–26.

Coleman, J. (1978). Current contradictions in adolescent theory. *Journal of Youth and Adolescence 7,* 1–11.

Coleman, J. (1980). *The nature of adolescence.* London: Methuen.

Conger, J. J. (1981). Freedom and commitment: Families, youth and social change. *American Psychologist, 43,* 291–300.

Coopersmith, S. (1967). *The antecedents of self esteem.* San Francisco: W. H. Freeman & Co.

Cowan, E. L. (1994). The enhancement of psychological wellness: Challenges and opportunities. *American Journal of Community Psychology, 22*(2), 149–177.

Crockett, L., Losoff, M., & Peterson, A. C. (1984). Perceptions of the peer group and friendship in early adolescence. *Journal of Early Adolescence, 4*(2), 155–181.

Csikszentmihalyi, M., & Larson, R. (1984). *Being adolescent.* New York: Basic Books.

Davis, J. M., & Sandoval, J. (1991). *Suicidal youth: Schoolbased intervention and prevention.* San Francisco: Jossey-Bass.

Di Augelli, A. R., & Hersberger, S. L. (1993). Lesbian, gay and bisexual youth in community settings: Personal challenges and mental health problems. *American Journal of Community Psychology, 21*(4), 421–448.

Dorn, L. D., Crockett, L. J., & Peterson, A. C. (1988). The relations of pubertal status to interpersonal changes in young adolescents. *Journal of Early Adolescence, 8,* 405–419.

Ehrenberg, M. F., Cox, D. N., & Koopman, R. F. (1990). The prevalence of depression in high school students. *Adolescence XXV,* 905–912.

Eichenbaum, L., & Orbach, S. (1983). *Understanding women: A feminist psychoanalytic approach.* New York: Basic Books.

Eichorn, D. (1973). The Berkeley longitudinal studies: Continuities and correlates of behaviour. *Canadian Journal of Behavioral Sciences, 5,* 297–320.

Elkind, D. (1967). Egocentrism in adolescence. *Child Development, 38,* 1025–1034.

Erikson, E. H. (1968a). *Childhood and society* (2nd ed.). New York: Norton.

Erikson, E. H. (1968b). *Identity, youth and crisis.* New York: Norton.

Freud, A. (1958). Adolescence. In *Psychoanalytic study of the child* (Vol. 13, pp. 225–278). New York: International Universities Press.

Galotti, K. M. (1989). Approaches to studying formal and everyday reasoning. *Psychological Bulletin, 105,* 331–351.

Garmezy, N. (1985). Stress-resistant children: The search for protective factors. In T. Stevenson (Ed.), *Recent research in developmental psychopathology* (pp. 97–111). Oxford: Pergamon Press.

Garrod, A., Smulyan, L., Powers, S. I., & Kilkenny, R. (1995). *Adolescent portraits: Identity, relationships and challenges.* Boston: Allyn & Bacon.

Gay, G. (1985). Implications of selected models of ethnic identity development for educators. *The Journal of Negro Education, 54*(1), 43–52.

Gibbs, J. T. (1985). City girls: Psychosocial adjustment of urban black adolescent females. *SAGE: A Scholarly Journal on Black Women, 2,* 28–36.

Gilligan, C. (1982). *In a different voice: Psychological theory and women's development.* Cambridge: Harvard University Press.

Gold, S. N. (1980). Relations between level of ego development and adjustment patterns in adolescents. *Journal of Personality Assessment, 44,* 631–638.

Goodman, N., & Feldman, K. (1989). Expectations, ideals and reality: Youth enters college. In S. E. Dragastin & G. H. Elder, Jr. (Eds.), *Adolescence in the life cycle: Psychological change and social context* (pp. 147–167). New York: Wiley.

Grotevant, H., & Adams, G. (1984). Development of an objective measure to assess ego identity in adolescence, validation and replication. *Journal of Youth and Adolescence, 13,* 419–438.

Group for the Advancement of Psychiatry (1968). *Normal adolescence: Its dynamics and impact.* New York: Charles Scribner and Sons.

Gullotta, T. P., Adams, G. R., & Montemayor, R. (Eds.). (1990). *Developing social competency in adolescence.* Newbury Park, California: Sage.

Hall, G. S. (1904). *Adolescence: Its psychology and relation to physiology, anthropology, sociology, sex, crime, religion, and education.* New York: Appleton.

Hamburg, D. A., & Takanishi, R. (1989). The critical transition of adolescence. *American Psychologist, 44,* 825–827.

Harter, S. (1986). Processes underlying the construction, maintenance and enhancement of the self-concept of children. In J. Suls & A. Greenwald (Eds.). *Pyschological perspective on the self* (Vol. 3, pp. 145–167). Hillsdale, NJ: Erlbaum.

Harter, S. (1990). Self and identity development. In S. S. Feldman & G. R. Elliot (Eds.), *At the threshold: The developing adolescent.* Cambridge: Harvard University Press.

Hauser, St. T., Powers, S. I., Noam, G., Jacobson, A. M., Weiss, B., & Follansbee, D. (1984). Familial contexts of adolescent ego development. *Child Development, 55,* 195–213.

Helms, J. (1990). *Black and white racial identity.* New York: Greenwood Press.

Hill, J. P. (1987). Research on adolescents and their families: Past and prospect. In S. Irwin (Ed.), *Adolescent social behavior and health* (pp. 13–31). San Francisco: Jossey-Bass.

Hilton, I. (1983). Teenage pregnancy: Causes, effects and alternatives. Paper presented at American Psychological Association. Anaheim, CA.

Hobfoll, S. E., Dunahoo, C. I., Ben-Porath, Y., & Monnier, J. (1994). Gender and coping: The dual axis model of coping. *American Journal of Community Psychology, 22*(1), 49–82.

Jessor, R. (1993). Successful adolescent development among youth in high-risk settings. *American Psychologist, 48,* 117–126.

Josselson, J. (1987). *Finding herself: Pathways to identity development in women.* San Francisco: Jossey-Bass.

Kaplan, L. J. (1984). *Adolescence: The farewell to childhood.* New York: Simon and Schuster.

Kaufman, J. (1993/1994). Abstract of interviews conducted by students. Fairleigh Dickinson University, Teaneck, New Jersey.

Kaufman, J. (1996). Teenage parents and their offspring. In *Proceedings of New York Academy of Sciences Symposium, Women and Health* (pp. 17–30). New York: New York Academy of Sciences.

Kazdin, A. E. (1995). *Conduct disorders in children and adolescents* (2nd ed.). Newbury Park, CA: Sage.

Kerr, M. M., & Milliones, J. (1995). Suicide and suicidal behavior. In V. B. Van Hasselt & M. Hersen (Eds.), *Handbook of adolescent psychopathology* (pp. 653–664). New York: Lexington Books.

Lates, J. (1981). Early marriage and identity foreclosure. *Adolescence, 16,* 809–815.

Lewis, C. C. (1987). Minors' competence to consent to abortion. *American Psychologist, 42*(1), 84–88.

Looney, J. G., & Lewis J. M. (1983). Competent adolescents from different socioeconomic and ethnic contexts. In M. Sugar (Ed.), *Adolescent psychiatry Volume XI: Developmental and clinical studies* (pp. 64–74). Chicago: University of Chicago.

Maccoby, E. E. (1990). Gender and relationships. *American Psychologist, 45*(5), 513–520.

Mahler, M. (1963). Thoughts about development and individuation. In *The Psychoanalytic study of the child Vol. 18* (pp. 307–327). New York: International Universities Press.

Mahler, M., Pine, F., & Bergman, A. (1975). *The psychological birth of the human infant*. New York: Basic Books.

Marcia, J. (1976). Development and validation of ego identity status. *Journal of Personality and Social Psychology, 3,* 551–558.

Marcia, J. (1980). Identity in adolescence. In J. Adelson (Ed.), *Handbook of adolescent psychology* (pp. 159–187). New York: Wiley.

Martin, R. P. (1985). Review of the offer self-image questionnaire for adolescents. In J. V. Mitchell, Jr. (Ed.), *The ninth mental measurements yearbook Vol. I* (p. 1080). Lincoln, NE: The Buros Institute of Mental Measurements.

Masten, A. S. (1991). Development psychopathology and the adolescent. In R. M. Lerner, A. C. Peterson, & J. Brooks-Gunn (Eds.), *Encyclopedia of Adolescence* (pp. 221–227). New York: Garland Publishing.

Mead, M. (1950). *Coming of age in Samoa*. New York: Morrow.

Meece, J., & Eccles, C. (1993). Gender and education. *Educational Psychologist, 28*(4), 313–319.

Montemayor, R., & Van Kormer, R. (1985). The development of sex differences in friendship patterns and peer group structure during adolescence. *Journal of Early Adolescence, 5,* 285–294.

Musick, J. (1993). *Young, poor and pregnant: The psychology of teenage motherhood*. Chicago: University of Chicago Press.

Newton N. (1995). *Adolescence: Guiding youth through the perilous ordeal*. New York: W. W. Norton.

Offer, D., Ostrov, E., & Howard, K. I. (1981). *The adolescent: A psychological self-portrait*. New York: Basic Books.

Offer, D., & Sabshin, M. (1984). Adolescence: Empirical perspectives. In D. Offer & M. Sabshin (Eds.), *Normality and the life cycle* (pp. 76–107). New York: Basic Books.

Orenstein, P. (1994). *School girls, young women, self-esteem and the confidence gap*. New York: Anchor Books.

Orlofsky, J. L. (1978). Identity formation, achievement and fear of success in men and women. *Journal of Youth and Adolescence, 7,* 49–62.

Parke, R. D. (1988). Families in life-span perspective. A multilevel developmental approach. In E. M. Hetherington, R. M. Lerner, & M. Perlmutter (Eds.), *Child development in life-span perspective* (pp. 156–198). Hillsdale, NJ: Erlbaum.

Parker, J. G., & Gottman, J. M. (1989). Social and emotional development in a relational context: Friendship interaction from early childhood to adolescence. In T. J. Berndt & G. W. Ladd (Eds.), *Peer relations in child development* (pp. 95–131). New York: John Wiley.

Peterson, A. C. (1988). Adolescent development. *Annual Review of Psychology, 39,* 583–607.

Peterson, C., Maier, S. F., & Seligmen, M. E. P. (1993). *Learned helplessness: A theory for the age of personal control*. New York: Oxford University Press.

Peterson, C., & Stunkard, A. J. (1989). Personal control and health promotion. *Social Science and Medicine, 28,* 819–828.

Pfeffer, C. R. (1986). *The suicidal child*. New York: Guilford Press.

Pfeffer, C. R. (1988). Child and adolescent suicide risk. In C. J. Kestenbaum & D. T. Williams (Eds.), *Handbook of clinical assessment of children and adolescents* (pp. 673–688). New York: New York University Press.

Phinney, J. (1989). Stages of ethnic identity development in minority group adolescents. *Journal of Early Adolescence, 9,* 34–49.

Piaget, J. (1965/1932). *The moral judgment of the child*. New York: Free Press.

Pipher, M. (1994). *Reviving Ophelia: Saving the selves of adolescent girls*. Ballantine Books: New York.

Quedrel, M. J., Fischoff, B., & Davis, W. (1993). Adolescent (in) vulnerability. *American Pyschologist, 48,* 102–116.

Raphael, D. (1979). Sequencing in female adolescents' consideration of occupational, religious and political alternatives. *Adolescence, 14,* 73–80.

Reynolds, W. M. (1995). Depression. In V. B. Van Hasselt & M. Hersen (Eds.), *Handbook of adolescent psychopathology* (pp. 297–348). New York: Lexington Books.

Robinson, B. (1988). *Teenage fathers.* Lexington, MA: D. C. Heath.

Robinson, W. L., Ruch-Ross, H. S., Watkins-Ferrel, P., & Lightfoot, S. (1993). Risk behavior in adolescence: Methodological challenges in school-based research. *School Psychology Quarterly, 8*(4), 241–254.

Rosenbaum, M. (1993). Changing body image of the adolescent girl. In M. Sugar (Ed.), *Female adolescent development* (2nd ed., pp. 62–80). New York: Brunner/Mazel.

Rosenberg, M. (1975). The dissonant context and the adolescent self-concept. In S. E. Dragastin & G. H. Elder, Jr. (Eds.), *Adolescence in the life cycle: Psychological change and social context* (pp. 97–116). New York: Wiley.

Rotter, J. (1966). Generalized expectancies for internal vs. external control of reinforcement. *Psychological Monographs, 81*(1), Whole No. 609.

Rubenstein, J., Heeren, T., Houseman, D., Rubin, C., & Stechler, G. (1989). Suicidal behavior in "normal" adolescents: Risk and protective factors. *American Journal of Orthopsychiatry, 59,* 59–71.

Rutter, M. (1975). Attainment and adjustment in two geographical areas I: The prevalence of psychiatric disorder. *British Journal of Psychiatry, 126,* 493–509.

Rutter, M., Graham, P., Chadwick, O., & Yule, W. (1976). Adolescent turmoil: Fact or fiction? *Journal of Child Psychology and Psychiatry, 17,* 35–56.

Santrock, J. W. (1990). *Adolescence* (4th ed.). Dubuque, IA: W. C. Brown.

Schlossberg, N. K., Waters, E. B., & Goodman, J. (1995). *Counseling adults in transition* (2nd. ed.). New York: Springer.

Seligman, M. E. P. (1991). *Learned optimism.* New York: Knopf.

Selman, R. (1980). *The growth of interpersonal understanding.* New York: Academic Press.

Shain, L., & Farber, B. (1989). Female identity development and self-reflection in late adolescence. *Adolescence, 24,* 381–392.

Strauss, C. C., & Lahey, B. B. (1987). Anxiety. In V. B. Von Hasselt & M. Hersen (Eds.), *Handbook of adolescent psychology* (pp. 332–350). New York: Pergamon Press.

Tanner, J. M. (1962). *Growth at adolescence.* Oxford, England: Blackwell Scientific Publications.

Taylor, J. M., Gilligan, C., & Sullivan, A. M. (1995). *Between voice and silence: Women and girls, race and relationship.* Cambridge, MA: Harvard University Press.

Town Tries To Comprehend Suicide Attempts by Eight Girls. (1995, June 28). *The New York Times,* p. B8.

Wagner, B. M., & Compas, B. E. (1990). Gender, instrumentality and expressivity: Moderators of the relation between stress and psychological symptoms during adolescence. *American Journal of Community Psychology, 18*(3), 221–236.

Wasserstein, W. (1993). Educating women. *New York Woman,* Spring, 1993, 68–70.

Waterman, A. S. (1985). Identity in the context of adolescent psychology. In A. S. Waterman (Ed.), *Identity in adolescence: Process and psychology* (pp. 5–24). San Francisco.

Weiner, I. B. (1980). Psychopathology in adolescence. In J. Adelson (Ed.), *Handbook of adolescent psychology* (pp. 288–312). New York: Pergamon Press.

Werner, E. (1989). High risk children in young adulthood: A longitudinal study from birth to 32 years. *American Journal of Orthopsychiatry, 59*(1), 72–81.

White, J. L. (1989). *The troubled adolescent.* New York: Pergammon Press.

Worell, J., & Danner, F. (1989). Adolescents in contemporary context. In J. Worell & F. Danner (Eds.), *The adolescent as decision maker* (pp. 3–12). New York: Academic Press.

Youniss, J., & Smollar, J. (1985). *Adolescent relations with mothers, fathers and friends.* Chicago: University of Chicago Press.

5

YOUNG WOMEN AND THEIR STRUGGLE TO BALANCE AUTONOMY AND AFFILIATION

VIRGINIA SMITH HARVEY[1]
University of Massachusetts at Boston

Finding a balance between autonomy and affiliation is a central theme in young women's lives. Autonomy affects every domain, including abortion, birth control, and fertility; civil, economic, and educational parity; cultural identity; parental relations; physical health and well-being; psychological health and well-being; spousal relations; and work and career development.

Autonomy was first clearly articulated by Immanual Kant, who believed that each person has two underlying traits: a passionate, irrational self and a rational, autonomous self. Kant's notion of the autonomous, rational side of humans influenced the thinking of philosophers and social thinkers including Hegel and Hume (Stainton, 1994). In turn, these authors influenced the authors of the Declaration of Independence, Emerson (1950), Mill (1859/1947), and others who describe autonomy as necessary for an effective democracy. Autonomous choice has become so closely identified with American culture that forswearing autonomy to embrace community, responsivity, and self-sacrifice can be considered "un-American" (Stack, 1986; Walum, 1977).

Thus, in the past several hundred years Westerners have come to value autonomy as a fundamental good and an appropriate life goal (Bornstein, 1994; Neki, 1976). Initially, autonomy was valued only for men; the idea that women should be autonomous is of very recent origin and is still not fully accepted in mainstream American culture and many non-Western cultures.

[1]Send correspondence to: Virginia Smith Harvey, Department of Counseling and School Psychology, Graduate College of Education, Wheatley Hall, University of Massachusetts at Boston, 100 Morrissey Blvd., Boston, MA 02125-3393.

Considering individual, familial, and societal perspectives illuminates the need to balance autonomy and community. Autonomy without community results in self-absorption and alienation, while community without autonomy smothers individual talents and energies (Kupfer, 1990). In many cultures, the sexes diverge in their perceptions and expressions of autonomy: as men take autonomous roles, women take affiliative roles and become responsible for maintaining community and familial relations. Social units have thus been dependent on women for their survival.

Individual women may avoid autonomous behaviors, particularly aggression and competition, because they fear abandonment, isolation, and loss of intimacy (Ullian, 1984). Indeed, dependency in adults is not necessarily maladaptive, for it correlates with both positive and negative outcomes (Bornstein, 1994). On the other hand, dependency is often equated with immaturity, flawed functioning, and maladjustment (Bornstein, 1994; Neki, 1976).

Because earlier chapters have explored differing views of autonomy, this chapter will merely touch on psychological theories regarding autonomy. A review of relevant research conducted with young women aged 18 to 30 will then be presented. This research explores manifestations of autonomy and demonstrates autonomy's effects on the expression of individual talents, on physical health, and the psychological well-being of young women.

DIFFERENT PERSPECTIVES ON AUTONOMY

Similar to other psychological terms, autonomy is not a precisely defined construct. One definition indicates that autonomy is self-determination, in opposition to being defined by external authorities. A person with autonomy acquires values, behaves independently, holds beliefs, and makes choices that reflect individual preferences and aspirations.

Several theorists indicate that individuals neither perceive nor express autonomy unidimensionally. Chickering (1969) describes autonomy as having two components: emotional autonomy (freedom from pressing needs for approval and reassurance), and instrumental autonomy (abilities to act upon the world, carry on activities, cope with problems, and take action to satisfy needs). Autonomy of thought is a prerequisite to autonomy of action (Kupfer, 1990). Schlenker and Weingold (1990) developed a scale to measure autonomy. They extracted three factors: autonomy (individualism and self-reliance), conformity (compliance and cooperation), and anti-conformity (disagreement regardless of actual beliefs).

Young adults perceive and express autonomy to different degrees in different life domains. That is, a young woman may be autonomous at work and simultaneously be dependent in her marriage or parental relationships.

The individual's struggle to balance autonomy and connectedness plays a central role in many psychological theories. The relative importance of individual autonomy for young women has not yet been determined. As Hartman (1989) describes, feminists in the 60s and 70s minimized the differences between the sexes to counteract explanations of gender differences as manifestations of inferiority. This minimization was considered necessary to free women from economic oppression, political suppression, and stereotypical role definitions. In contrast, recent feminists have expressed the opinion that women and men differ but that these differences, including choosing affiliation over autonomy, should be seen as strengths rather than weaknesses.

Psychological literature defines autonomy variously. Constructs as diverse as self-efficacy and locus of control are associated with autonomous thought and behaviors. A brief review follows of relevant theories, necessary to understand the underlying foci of research studies reported in the main body of the chapter.

Psychoanalytic and Neo-Psychoanalytic Approaches

Because earlier chapters have examined the influence of childhood and adolescent experiences in terms of the psychoanalytic views of Freud (Carvalho, 1992; Freud, 1953) and Blos (Blos, 1979; Gaskill, 1980), these theoretical positions will not be re-examined at this time. Instead, theories that focus on adult development will be presented, including those of Jung (1933), Erikson (1963), Loevinger and Wessler (1970), and Chodorow (1978).

Jung (1933) asserted that all mature men and women are able to demonstrate both masculine and feminine behaviors, including the capacities for autonomy, bonding, caring, and work. Heath (1980) and Bem (1983) support Jung's work, and advocate fostering androgyny, in which men and women both acquire the stereotypical male and female traits. Similarly, Kegan (1982) suggests that two human yearnings (to be distinct and separate, and to be included and attached) contribute equally to the psychological development of both men and women. An individual's balance between these two needs depends on individual differences, culture, and societal expectations. Women may be able to establish intimacy more easily than men, but have difficulty achieving autonomy (Rubin, 1983). Consequently, a major developmental task for adult women is to be able to learn to let go of others. In contrast, a major developmental task for adult men is to learn to be intimate. Not every adult accomplishes these tasks. Those who do are able to both foster individual talents and sustain mutual relationships (Forisha, 1978).

Erikson (1963) noted that the successful resolution of the crisis of young adulthood requires the ability to develop intimate, "fusing" relationships with others after having successfully forged an autonomous identity in adolescence. If an individual does not achieve the ability for intimate relationships, social isolation results. However, according to Erikson (1968), a young woman's identity could, and probably would, be incomplete until after marriage because of her need to reformulate her identity in response to her husband's characteristics. Thus, Erikson's theory suggests that identity, autonomy, and intimacy are enmeshed for young women.

In an attempt to clarify women's identity development, Dellas and Gaier (1975) describe three options available to young women. First, when assuming an identity based on the "traditional role and stereotype," young women delay identity formation until it can be embedded in family, home, and husband. The husband's vocational choice and achievement serve as the basis for the formation of the wife's identity, not her vocational choice or achievement. Second, when assuming an identity based on "achievement and role success," a young woman emphasizes fulfillment of potential and the development of the individual. Independence, activity, autonomy, aggression, and high achievement are characteristic. Third, the young woman with a "bi-modal sexual identity" blends both of the above and derives identity from two sources. The individual, autonomous identity and the relational, feminine identity are blended, resulting in simultaneous commitments to family and career.

Each of the above approaches provide young women with unique difficulties. The traditional role can lead to feelings of betrayal of the self, particularly since recent societal and scientific developments have eroded the centrality of reproducing and raising children. "Achievement and role success" might result in isolation, as well as hostility from males as their traditional territory is encroached. Adopting a "bi-modal sexual identity" will eventually require sex role revision within marriages for them to successfully endure (Dellas & Gaier, 1975).

Loevinger and Wessler (1970) describe the fifth stage of ego development, autonomy, as the modulation of an excessive sense of responsibility and the recognition that others have responsibility for themselves. Lemkau and Landau (1986) and McBride (1990) discuss the usefulness of Loevinger and Wessler's concept of ego development in therapeutic work with women, in which the healthy center of self is a midpoint between selflessness and self-absorption.

Chodorow (1978) proposed that women are more relational and empathic than men because they are both universally responsible for child care, and nurtured and cared for by the same-sex parent. Girls' separation from the female parent is less critical than boys', resulting in continued attachment for girls and increased autonomy for boys. Girls' development is characterized by increasingly differentiated levels of interpersonal relationships. Boys' development is characterized by separation, achievement, autonomy, and individuation in behavior, cognition, and morality.

Developmental Approaches

The perspective of developmental theorists is in marked contrast with the perspective of traditional psychoanalytic theorists. Current developmental models propose a balance between individuation and connectedness, in which the parent/child relationship is transformed rather than broken (Hill & Holmbeck, 1986; Kenny & Donaldson, 1992).

Miller (1976, 1984) proposed a "self-in-relation" theory of women's development in opposition to the traditionally male-based theories. She indicated that women develop their identity in the context of relationships, in contrast to men who develop their identity in the context of autonomy and mastery. She also indicated that to advocate women's autonomy would be to imply (and even threaten) that women "should be able to pay the price of giving up affiliation to become a separate and self-directed individual" (Miller, 1976, p. 94). Although often experienced from a subservient position, affiliation is also a source of strength and empowerment: relationships are a "natural" state and facilitate development (Miller, 1984).

Ethological theories developed by Ainsworth, Blehar, Walters, and Waly (1978) and Bowlby (1969) indicate that secure attachment is important to adaptive and psychological health. Through encouragement and assistance, attachment figures provide a secure base of support. Connections to others are the primary source of secure feelings that permit and promote exploration and mastery of the environment. Thus, secure affiliation is necessary before autonomy is possible.

In Kohlberg's (1973) theory of development, the highest level of moral behavior is allowing others to be autonomous, respecting other's rights, and simultaneously preventing others from limiting one's own autonomy. Gilligan (1982) extended Chodorow's theory into considerations of moral development and contrasted female-based morality with Kohlberg's male-based theory. She found that interpersonal contexts are critical in the determination of women's sense of self and morality. Women's moral values include caring, considering others' needs, being responsible for others, and maintaining interpersonal connections. Women express moral values in the "different voice" of an ethic of care. According to Gilligan, women's concern with relationships is a strength rather than a weakness. She believes that the traditional concept of adulthood is deficient, because it equates autonomy with maturity and does not consider the importance of affiliative connections.

Surrey (1984) extended Gilligan's theory, and discussed the emergence of the self in daughters as they alternated in the roles of caretaker and recipients of care, thereby accentuating the development of empathy. In contrast, both mothers and fathers encourage sons to separate from the mother and achieve individualization and independence. Kaplan and Klein (1985) assert that individuals can develop a differentiated sense of self while maintaining emotional relationships.

In sum, recent developmental theorists indicate that women develop, forge their identities, and express their moral judgments within the context of relationships and affiliation rather than through autonomy and separation. This theory has been criticized, as some feel that it will lead to a perception of greater differences between the sexes than actually exists. Critics also indicate that highlighting differences will encourage continued subjugation of women (Hartman, 1989).

Family Therapists

Similar to psychoanalytic theorists, family therapists define health and maturity in terms of autonomy, differentiation, independence, individuation, and rational decision making. Bowen (1978) defined a pathological person as one who is undifferentiated, who "negotiates away from the self" in relationships, and orients life goals around love, happiness, security, and relationships with others. According to this perspective, family therapy assessments and interventions use constructs of separateness (disengagement) and connectedness (enmeshment). Boundaries, hierarchies, and separations are critical for healthy functioning (Bowen, 1978; Minuchin, 1974; Minuchin, Rosman, & Baker, 1978).

Further, as Lang-Takac and Osterweil (1992) indicate, although family theorists do not specifically address gender differences, they do tend to describe females as connected (enmeshed) and males as separate (disengaged). Even when men and women are acknowledged as different, developmental goals are not reshaped accordingly. Disengagement from parents is seen as a major task for both sexes, for it defines an important phase of the family life cycle, the period during which young adults are "launched" into autonomous lives.

According to family therapists, a conflict-free relationship with parents may lead to a fear of separation and independence (Silverberg & Steinberg, 1987). During early adolescence a moderate degree of conflict is thought necessary for the development of autonomy, although if the conflict becomes severe and pervasive, benefits are lost. In late adolescence the drive toward autonomy creates disequilibrium in the family, culminating in the launching of the adult child (Pardeck & Pardeck, 1990). Families that are controlling, enmeshed, hostile toward self-control, and over-protective intrude on the child's development of autonomy and often result in pathology in the child (Bruch, 1978; Minuchin et al., 1978).

Social–Cultural Theorists

Social–cultural theorists maintain that cultural expectations are critical determinants of behavior: concepts of self cannot exist independent of social context (Miller, 1993). Vygotsky (1978), for example, indicated that appreciating the dynamic interaction of the individual with the environment is critical to understanding human development.

Social Learning Theorists

Social learning theorists focus on the individual's behavioral expression of self-efficacy and personal control. An internal locus of control, or the attribution of outcomes to internal factors, results in autonomy. An external locus of control, or the attribution of outcomes to outside forces or to chance, results in a lack of autonomy (Rotter, 1966).

As noted in earlier chapters, Bandura (1982) held that a sense of self-efficacy is critical for successful autonomous functioning. Without a sense of self-efficacy, the individual experiences life as stressful and depressing. Bandura perceived self-efficacy as resulting from individual experiences within social systems. Societal expectations that females will be non-achieving affect girls' perceptions of self-efficacy at early ages and throughout adulthood. Self-efficacy skills to be acquired by successful young adults include assuming responsibility for the self; dealing with heterosexual and marital relationships; choosing, establishing, and maintaining a career; and becoming a parent (Bandura, 1986).

MANIFESTATIONS OF AUTONOMY

To behave autonomously, the individual must be able to think independently and critically, and must have the confidence and strength of will to make and carry out decisions. Necessary prerequisites include education, knowledge of truth, privacy, and respect (Kupfer, 1990).

The autonomy/affiliation distinction is often a primary social method to manifest gender differences among young women and men (Rosenblum, 1986). American men are expected to display autonomy, achievement, and self-reliance while women are expected to display caring and service. This dichotomy becomes conflictual when individuals expect reciprocity, or expect to receive the same treatment they display.

A young woman achieving instrumental autonomy, as defined by Chickering (1969), counteracts centuries of custom and stereotype. Historically, women have been expected to suppress their instrumental strength and allow men to appear superior in thought, work, and action (Miller, 1976). Women are socialized to display expressiveness, sensitivity, and warmth. Women are discouraged from displaying the stereotypically male behaviors of assertiveness, competence, and independence. Women have been expected to be dependent on others in a number of domains including financial support and self-identity, that have resulted in a lack of fulfillment of individual potential and an increase in depression and anxiety.

Research on perceptions and manifestations of autonomy has been conducted in a wide variety of domains, and in response to the theoretical orientations previously described. Whether young men and young women differ in their perception and display of autonomy varies with the domain in question, the age of the women, and the context or culture. A few examples of general findings will illustrate this point.

Several studies have found minimal gender differences in autonomy. Macoby and Jacklin (1974) did not report significant gender differences for adults or children in various behaviors associated with autonomy, such as willingness to help others and independence. Cochran and Peplau (1985) did not find gender differences in attachment values, and found that women gave more importance to equality and maintaining autonomy than men. Similarly, Bar-Yam (1991) compared men and women's levels of self-evolution, expressions of autonomy, and emotional attachment. She found no gender differences, in contrast to both traditional psychoanalytic and more modern feminist theories. Instead, both genders expressed yearnings for both autonomy and community. Bar-Yam suggests from this data that the male stereotypic orientation toward individuation and increased autonomy, and the stereotypic female orientation toward attachment and dependence, are not innate characteristics but result from individual differences and social and cultural environments.

In contrast, several researchers have found that women scored higher than men in interpersonal relationships and lower on autonomy (Greeley & Tinsley, 1988; Pollard, Benton, & Hinz, 1983). Chiu (1990) found gender differences between Chinese men and women were similar to differences found between American men and women, with men in both cultures scoring significantly higher in autonomy. Lang-Takac and Osterweil (1992) studied Israelis of Western origin and found men more autonomous (self-other differentiated) and women more affiliative (empathic and desiring intimacy). In the opposite direction, Jordan-Cox (1987) found African American women to have significantly higher autonomy scores than African American men, contrary to studies using primarily European American respondents.

The following pages will relate relevant research results exploring autonomy, self-efficacy, and locus of control for young women. A wide variety of domains will be discussed including abortion, birth control, and fertility; civil, economic, and educational parity; cultural identity; parental relations; physical health and well-being; psychological health and well-being; spousal relations; and work.

Abortion, Birth Control, and Fertility

Perhaps nowhere is the struggle to balance young women's autonomy and affiliation more apparent than in issues of reproduction. Throughout their young adult years, women are constantly dealing with the related issues of abortion, birth control, and fertility treatment. The control of reproduction highlights and accentuates questions of autonomy, self-efficacy, and locus of control. Autonomy is relevant to these issues for two reasons. First, others within their cultures do not always grant young women autonomy regarding reproduction. Second, perceptions of autonomy and self-efficacy affect the choices young women make regarding abortion, birth control, and fertility treatment.

Some cultures foster autonomy in general, but specifically deny young women reproductive autonomy. For example, Nipa Island women have autonomy and authority in domestic, economic, and social domains and are decision makers, cultivators, labor organizers, and leaders. Yet young women are given little physical, reproductive, or sexual autonomy (Anderson & Anderson, 1986).

Establishing personal autonomy is an important cultural focus for both male and female Khmer, although in complementary domains. For women, however, the need to behave with propriety and "save face" for the family results in the suspension of autonomy during adolescence and young adulthood. Because Khmers expect women to be virgins at marriage and to agree to arranged marriages, young Khmer women (even those who have immigrated to the United States) often marry at young ages and subsequently drop out of school (Smith-Hefner, 1993).

The commonly used rhetoric in the ongoing controversy about abortion reflects the importance of autonomy in this issue. The "woman's right to choose" is pitted against the fetus's "right to life." Disagreement about whether parents and husbands have the right to take part in decisions about abortion highlights the precariousness of young women's autonomy. Despite the rhetoric, young women choosing abortion frequently cite reasons based on morality of care and concern for others, rather than reasons based on autonomy and self-interest (Gilligan, 1982).

Women with self-efficacy are most likely to report reliable use of birth-control measures (Gilcrest & Schinke, 1983). Increased self-efficacy also correlates with less negative adjustment after an abortion (Cozzarelli, 1993; Mueller & Major, 1989; Major, Cozzarelli, Sciacchitano, & Cooper, 1990).

Fouad and Fahje (1989) found young women with infertility displayed depression when they had an external locus of control, yet Mendola, Tennen, Affleck, McCann, and Fitzgerald (1990) did not find a relationship between perceived personal control and adaptation to impaired fertility. Women who had the poorest adaptation to failed *in vitro* fertilization (IVF) were more likely to report feelings of a general loss of control, feelings of depression before IVF, and a sense of responsibility for the IVF failure (Litt, Tennen, Affleck, & Klock, 1992).

Autonomy is also a factor in the decision to remain childless. According to one study, women who made the decision to remain childless later in life had parents who encouraged assertive autonomy. Women who made the decision to remain childless earlier in life were likely to have parents who encouraged high achievement (Houseknecht, 1979).

Thus, autonomy is necessary for positive adjustment to sexuality issues including abortion, birth control, and fertility, even though women's reasons for particular decisions are based on ethics of care and affiliation. However, young women's cultures often do not grant them autonomy in reproductive domains.

Civil, Economic, and Educational Parity

The lack of universal acceptance of young women's autonomy is also vividly demonstrated by continuing legal and social restrictions on enfranchisement, economic rights, and property ownership. Married women were legally unable to own property in the United States until the mid-19th century, and in many countries women still cannot own property. The ability to own property is critical to economic independence, and economic independence is a necessary prerequisite to autonomy (Bhutto, 1995). The 75th anniversary (1995) of women's suffrage in the United States reminds us of how very recently women, even in the West, gained fundamental civil rights. Further, the United Nations' Fourth World Conference on Women in Beijing, China (1995) reminds us of how very few women have attained civil autonomy throughout the world.

In most developed countries there is currently a discrepancy between physical maturity and economic independence (Starr, 1986), which results in a period during which individuals are legally adults (i.e., emancipated and enfranchised) yet still economically dependent on their parents. Paradoxically, young adults now have increased civil rights but decreased economic and social autonomy (Marks, 1975). That is, late adolescents and early adults are able to vote, be drafted, marry, and perform other civil adult functions, yet remain financially dependent for longer periods, often beyond their college years into their working careers.

Several factors affect a successful transition to adulthood: family support of autonomy, relevant skills and knowledge, the availability of part time jobs while in school to foster the development of work discipline and skills, and the availability of full-time jobs after the completion of schooling. The ability of young adults to achieve financial autonomy is severely compromised by insufficient jobs in the private sector (Starr, 1986).

Many of the preconditions for autonomy, including education, are not universally experienced by young women (Kupfer, 1990). Even in the United States, only very recently has society accepted the right of women to education and has female enrollment in college been in relatively the same proportions as men.

The perception of autonomy affects academic functioning. Abouserie (1994) investigated young adults' sources and levels of stress relative to locus of control and self-esteem, and found that females experienced more stress than men regarding academics and life events. According to this study, those students with external locus of control experience more stress than those with internal locus of control. In 1978, when women comprised only 3.5% of lawyers in the United States, and only 7.4% of law school applicants, Coplin and Williams (1978) found the self-confidence and autonomy of female law students was higher than that of female undergraduates. However, female law students described the ideal lawyer to be more masculine than themselves, which may have served to discourage women applicants. Since 1978, the percentage of women lawyers has increased to 22%, but the perceptions of autonomy experienced by current female law students is unknown.

Cultural Identity

Frequently, cultures are compared on the relative centrality of individualism and interdependence (Wainryb & Turiel, 1994). Western cultures are thought to afford centrality to autonomy, independence, and individualism. Cultures in the Middle East, Africa, and Asia are thought to afford centrality to connectedness and interdependence. Cultures that emphasize independence regard the individual as autonomous and sanctioned to meet personal needs. Cultures that emphasize interdependence define the individual within a social context. Moral precepts tend to be consistent with the culture, based on personal freedom and rights in the individualistic cultures and on the maintenance of social roles in interdependent cultures.

As Wainryb and Turiel (1994) point out, however, anthropological and psychological findings do not always support the proposition that actions are consistent with the patterns of culture. Context and group behaviors affect individuals' behaviors and beliefs. For example, United States citizens are more likely to support freedoms of assembly, press, religion, and speech when presented abstractly than when presented in conflict with considerations such as civic duties, custom, harm to others, maintenance of social order, and traditions. In Western society, patriarchy has always existed alongside cherished notions of autonomy and egalitarianism. Within the family context, men assert their own interests over women in sexual freedom and in distribution of household tasks, monies, and property.

Researchers have explored the relationship between autonomy and the development of cultural identity. However, empirical studies do not universally support the idea that autonomy and cultural identity are mutually exclusive. Robinson and Ward (1991) believe that when African American women focus on autonomy at the expense of the collective it is a short-term survival method that ultimately becomes destructive. They draw a parallel to other "quick fixes" such as food addictions, school failure, substance abuse, and unplanned pregnancy that provide short-term solutions to autonomy and affiliation needs, but that eventually erode self-confidence, impair positive identity formation, and lower self-esteem. Socializing African American women toward autonomy, competition, independence, and internal locus of control requires separating them from familial and racial allegiances. The resulting "racelessness" promotes separation from the African American community and is detrimental both to self-acceptance and the African American collective.

An investigation of autonomy and intimacy characteristics of black and white college women revealed no interracial autonomy differences, although autonomy did increase with increased age (Taub & McEwen, 1991). A subsequent study (Taub & McEwen, 1992) found that in black college students, the development of autonomy occurred in opposition to racial identity development.

In contrast, Rosenthal and Feldman (1992) found that parental warmth, control, and promotion of autonomy correlated with ethnic pride regardless of gender in Chinese American and Chinese Australian families. Martin, Nagayuma, and Gordon (1992) examined young women's racial identity, attitudes toward feminism, and locus of control, and found that as racial identity became more advanced, internal locus of control increased.

Parental Relations

Although a number of psychological theories (Blos, 1979; Freud, 1953) assert that gaining autonomy and restructuring relationships with parents are paramount and continue throughout young adulthood, research has been accumulating that indicates that many late adolescents and young adults have a need to stay close to and rely heavily on parents (Grayson, 1989; Hill & Holmbeck, 1986). Positive attachments to parents by college students is correlated with adjustment to college, career development, social competence, and positive psychological functioning (Armsden & Greenberg, 1987; Bell, Avery, Jenkins, Feld, & Schoenrock, 1985; Blustein, Walbridge, Friedlander, & Palladino, 1991; Friedlander & Siegel, 1990; Hoffman, 1984; Kenny, 1987; Kenny & Donaldson, 1992; Kobak & Sceery, 1988; Lapsley, Rice, & Fitzgerald, 1990; Lapsley, Rice, & Shadid, 1989; Lopez, 1991;

Lopez, Campbell, & Watkins, 1988; Ryan & Lynch, 1989). Close and emotionally support-ive relationships with parents, along with parental encouragement of individualism, appar-ently result in positive outcomes such as identity development (Grotevant & Cooper, 1986) and positive self-concept (Ryan & Lynch, 1989).

Attachment to parents is significant throughout adolescence and young adulthood. Epperson (1964) found that teenagers were more concerned with parental approval than younger children. Youniss and Smollar (1985) found that late adolescents seek parental assistance and hope to meet parental expectations. Frank, Pirsch, and Wright (1990) investigated relationships between college students and their parents. They found that de-idealization predicted greater autonomy and disengagement, but disengagement predicted greater insecurity and increased anxiety. Young adults continue to rely on parental support and encouragement until at least their late 20s (Gould, 1978).

As young adults leave families of origin, gender differences are evident. Young women are less likely than young men to be financially autonomous from parents (Peters, 1991). Fischer (1981) and Lurie (1974) found that young adults, particularly young women, expe-rience increased connectedness and hostility toward their mothers, and increased distance and hostility toward their fathers as they marry and have children. Baruch and Barnett (1983) found most women get along well with their mothers and Cohler (1988) argues that mother-daughter relationships improve with age.

Frank, Avery, and Laman (1988) interviewed men and women regarding autonomy and relatedness in their parental relationships. Analysis revealed three factors: connectedness versus separateness (concern, empathy, communication, closeness, and negative loading on separateness), competence (decision making and independence), and emotional autonomy (personal control, respect, and self-assertion). Their results indicated that young adult women contacted their families of origin more frequently, and felt more connected to their parents, than young adult men. In their relationships with their mothers, men felt greater emotional autonomy than women, and men were more competent than women in their rela-tionships with either parent. Marital status was unrelated to competence or women's feel-ings of emotional autonomy, although married men did tend to feel more emotionally autonomous from their fathers than unmarried men. Married women's emotional ties with their mothers were stronger than unmarried women's. Only in their late 20s did young men and women begin to feel confident they could be self-sufficient.

Schultheiss and Blustein (1994) found that women who were attitudinally dependent and emotionally attached to both parents progressed effectively in developing purpose and academic autonomy. Attitudinal dependence, not independence, positively correlated with development.

Individuation from parents increases throughout the college years for both men and women (Rice, 1992). As freshmen, individuation from parents correlated with adjustment for women but not for men: women who had disengaged relationships with their fathers and conflictual relationships with their mothers were at risk for adjustment difficulties. As jun-iors, both men and women were less emotionally dependent on parents, yet there was not an increase in attitudinal independence.

Most college women remain closely and positively attached to their parents. Secure attachment (including positive affect, support for autonomy, and emotional support) corre-lated with positive academic and personal adjustment. Anxious and conflictual parental relationships were the strongest predictors of adjustment problems in college (Kenny & Donaldson, 1992).

There are some populations for which individuation from parents appears to be important. For example, Sheridan and Green (1993) explored characteristics of adult children of alcoholics. Individuation from parents was one of the variables that discriminated between young adults receiving recovery services and young adults not receiving recovery services.

Young women who perceived that their parents encouraged autonomy while maintaining emotional closeness tended to more appropriately explore choices in friendships and dating relationships (Fullwinder-Bush & Jacobvitz, 1993). When parent-child boundary dissolutions (enmeshment, over-involvement, and role-reversal) characterized relationships, young women did not develop an independent identity. Instead, they limited their commitments without exploring alternatives. Late adolescents with a history of suicidal behavior were the least individuated from their parents and had the least autonomy. They also had the lowest security of parental attachment and were more likely than the control group to remember parental (especially maternal) unavailability during childhood (DeJong, 1992). Less well-adjusted young women had high levels of familial enmeshment and separation anxiety. This suggests that when connectedness is extreme, it is not helpful to an individual's well-being (Holmbeck & Wandrei, 1993).

These results support several theories discussed previously, including the attachment theories of Ainsworth et al. (1978) and Bowlby (1969), which indicate that secure attachment correlates with psychological health. In addition, results support the theories of Gilligan (1982) and Surrey (1984) which suggest that women can have close parental relationships simultaneously with a well-developed sense of "self-in-relation," and that interdependence is more adaptive to psychological functioning than complete autonomy and separation. The results do not support the theories of Freud (1953) and Blos (1979), who indicate that autonomy and independence are critical for psychological well-being and successful adult adjustment.

Physical Health and Well-Being

Most health-related research has explored the specific concept of self-efficacy rather than the general concept of autonomy. A substantial body of literature associates skill-specific self-efficacy with behaviors that foster health for both sexes including arthritis treatment, birth control, smoking cessation, and weight control (Bandura, 1991; Bernier & Avard, 1986; Desharnais, Bouillon, & Godin, 1986; DiClemente, 1986; Gilcrist & Schinke, 1983; Gonzalez & Gonzalez, 1990; Kaplan, Atkins, & Reinsch, 1984; Maibech, Flora, & Nass, 1991; Strecher, DeVellis, Becker, & Rosenstock, 1986). Further, dependency correlates with (although does not necessarily cause) a variety of physical disorders including asthma, arthritis, cancer, colitis, diabetes, epilepsy, heart disease, and tuberculosis (Bornstein, 1993).

The following pages summarize studies associating autonomy with young women's physical health and well-being. In general, internal locus of control is more predictive of good health in women than hardiness, reactivity, stress, or Type A behavior (Lawler & Schmied, 1992).

A number of studies have investigated young women's locus of control, or feelings of self-efficacy, and the successful treatment of eating disorders and weight control. According to Shannon, Bagby, Wang, and Trenkner (1990), self-efficacy correlates with success in weight control programs. Mills (1991) investigated locus of control in adults (aged 21–72) and adolescents (aged 13–18) attending obesity treatment programs. He found that adults were more likely to exhibit internal locus of control than anticipated, whereas adolescents were likely to exhibit external locus of control as predicted. The adults did not express feelings of control about their weight and eating behavior, but did express feeling control over other aspects of their lives. Nir and Neumann (1991) conducted a study that assessed the self-esteem and locus of control of young women in a weight loss program. Self-esteem, but not locus of control, was predictive of successful weight loss.

Williams, Chamove, and Millar (1990) found that young women with anorexia and bulimia reported significantly more external control and less self-assertion than women who were dieting (but not more than psychiatric patients). The women felt that their families were not more controlling, yet encouraged less independence. Friedlander and Siegel (1990) also investigated the link between a lack of individuation and eating disorders, and found dependency conflicts associated with bulimia. Young women with bulimia exhibited more external locus of control, lower sense of personal effectiveness, lower self-esteem, and more psychopathology than women without bulimia (Shisslak, Pazda, & Crago, 1990). Similarly, young women with bulimia and anorexia were substantially more likely to exhibit external locus of control than young women without these conditions (Williams & Manaster, 1990). Baell and Wertheim (1992) found that feelings of ineffectiveness, as well as feelings of low self-esteem and binge frequency, predicted beneficial treatment outcome for young women with bulimia nervosa.

Poag and McAuley (1992) assessed the perception of self-efficacy in women participating in an exercise program. Self-efficacy correlates with intensity, but not frequency, of exercise. Mariano, Donovan, Walker, and Mariano (1989) explored the locus of control of young adult Native Americans who were problem drinkers, non-problem drinkers, and recovered alcoholics. Male problem drinkers had more of an external locus of control than females.

A woman's chances of surviving the onset of breast cancer depends on the disease stage at diagnosis, and is thus directly related to whether the woman practices breast self-examination (BSE). In an attempt to encourage BSE, Rassaby, Hirst, Hill, and Bennett (1991) implemented a training program for young women designed to increase self-efficacy. Because women of color and low socioeconomic status have high rates of death from breast cancer, Gonzalez and Gonzalez (1990) validated a scale measuring self-efficacy of BSE among low-income Mexican American women.

Women, particularly minority women, are at increasing risk of contracting HIV infection. In exploring the effects of improved self-efficacy on increased risk prevention, Maibech and Flora (1993) found that self-efficacy regarding AIDS preventive behaviors improved when young women viewed videos that included information, modeling, and cognitive rehearsal. The self-efficacy issue most likely to change in this case was the ability to discuss preventive issues with partners, particularly for participants who rehearsed these practices in the context of their own lives.

Thus, the research on physical health and well-being provides support for Bandura's theory, in that increased self-efficacy results in increased health-promoting behaviors. However, the mixed results suggest that variables other than autonomy and self-efficacy play important roles in these behaviors.

Psychological Health and Well-Being

Research regularly finds that the general population of the United States believes the traits associated with psychological health, such as autonomy, are traits associated with masculinity (Rosenblum, 1986). In Europe and the United States, males perceive themselves as superior to females in psychological health, particularly in autonomy and industry (McClain, 1975). To explore the definition of "health" as it applies to women, Crowley-Long and Long (1992) surveyed feminists on the qualities associated with the "psychologically fully functioning woman." Respondents suggested a woman with psychological health balances independence and interdependence. Neither reliant on others nor passive, a psychologically healthy woman is assertive, confident, financially autonomous, and self-directed. A fully functioning woman meets her own needs in the context of relationships, without either sacrificing or isolating herself.

Autonomy has been found to correlate with higher self-esteem, ability, self-acceptance, and self-fulfillment (DeMan, 1981; Sacks & Einstein, 1979; Swenson, 1980), increased adult life satisfaction (Morgan, 1980), and the gaining of life control (Heath, 1980). Women with autonomous role orientations have greater self-esteem (Jones & Lamke, 1985) and a greater sense of personal control (Frank, Towell, & Huyck, 1985). Greater internal locus of control correlates with happiness and self-esteem when young women maintain the multiple roles of employee, mother, and partner (Kopp & Ruzicka, 1993).

Munro and Adams (1977) did not find stronger ego-identity development among students with instrumental, autonomous value systems. Ryff (1989) explored various dimensions of happiness and found that men had significantly higher measures on internal locus of control and morale, and significantly lower incidence of depression than women. There were no sex differences in balance, self-esteem, and self-control. Women, on the other hand, had more positive relations with others and higher scores in personal growth. Demographic variables, including age, education, ethnicity, marital status, and social class, accounted for little variance in this study of well-being.

Studies demonstrate some sex differences in autonomy and self-esteem. Josephs, Markus, and Tafarodi (1992) found men's self-esteem tied to individuation and achievement, and women's self-esteem tied to interpersonal connections and relationships. However, Baruch, Barnett, and Rivers (1983) found women who have feelings of mastery have greater feelings of well-being and are better able to overcome depression and lead rich lives. Dissatisfied women try to think of ways to improve relationships, rather than focus on improving their own sense of mastery and achievement.

Dien (1992) explored issues of Chinese gender and individuation. In China, as in the West, mothers are the primary caregivers and the culture is traditionally patriarchal. According to many psychological theories such as those of Freud and Chodorow, these factors lead to traditional male/female gender differences. Yet, according to Dien, Chinese men and women both define themselves through relationships, and feminine traits are valued in both sexes. Mothers pay less attention to girls than boys. Further, girls are given substantial responsibilities at an early age, resulting in increased independence and self-reliance. In contrast to the West, Chinese men are highly psychologically dependent on their mothers while women are independent within the context of the family. However,

Stander and Jensen (1993) contrasted American and Chinese students and found that regardless of ethnicity, women favored a caring orientation.

The expression of autonomy can be unique to a particular culture. In Nepal, the high value placed upon interrelatedness does not preclude a well-defined concept of the individual (McHugh, 1989). Some Muslim women are returning to wearing the veil as a coping strategy to maintain self-esteem and a small degree of autonomy in highly conservative, patriarchal settings (Mule & Barthel, 1992). Although Westerners see the veil as a public expression of subjugation, in Islamic societies a woman wearing a veil is more autonomous in that she is freer to walk in the streets and converse with men than a woman who does not wear a veil.

Over a 20-year period, Gatz and Karel (1993) studied four generations' (1,267 individuals) perceptions of personal control. Respondents expressed increased perception of internal control over time. In particular, young adults expressed increased internal loci of control as they progressed into middle age, and women and men in the younger generations perceived equally internal loci of control. In contrast, the group perceiving the least internal loci of control were older women, probably due to their sociohistorical context. Houts and Warland (1989) also found older women to have a relatively external loci of control.

The relationship of dependency to psychopathology and depression has been of considerable interest. Lemkau and Landau (1986) indicate that selfless giving, and obtaining identity through others, results in the ablation (i.e., removal) of the self, difficulty expressing emotions, low self-esteem, and poor self-expression.

As Stiver (1991) and Kaplan (1983) point out, however, excessive dependency is considered pathological, yet there is no pathological label for the corresponding male presentation of excessive autonomy, despite their shorter life span and higher alcoholism and suicide rates. Interestingly, the only forms of psychopathology actually associated with excessive dependency are depression and eating disorders (Bornstein, 1994).

Perceived stress is predictive of depression (Franks & Faux, 1990), as is high external locus of control (Benassi, Sweeney, & Dufour, 1988). Beck's cognitive theory of depression suggests that either sociotropy (placing a high value on interpersonal relations and having a strong desire to be loved and accepted) or excessive autonomy (investment in personal independence, achievement, and freedom of choice) predispose individuals toward depression. Excessive sociotropy frequently correlates with depression, but excessive autonomy has had mixed results (Clark, Beck, & Brown, 1992). Nietzel and Harris (1990) conducted a meta analysis of the studies relating depression, autonomy, and dependency. Of the 11 studies reporting gender effects, depression correlated with both ends of the autonomy/ dependency continuum for both men and women although it appeared to be more problematic when associated with dependency.

However, predictors of depression vary among recent immigrants to the United States. Among Chinese women, perceived stress was the best predictor of depression. Among Vietnamese women, the best predictor was a lack of social supports. For Portuguese women, social support and English language skills were most significant, and employment and financial status were most critical for Latin American women (Franks & Faux, 1990).

Depressed women were found to have greater fears of attachment and individuation than non-depressed women, suggesting fear of establishing a clear identity and of getting involved with others (Lester, 1991). In contrast to the above studies, Goodman, Cooley,

Sewell, and Leavitt (1994) found a diagnosis of schizophrenia, but not depression, associated with more external locus of control in low income African American women.

In general, psychological health requires some degree of autonomy. However, excessive autonomy and individuation preclude healthy adjustment as well. Thus it appears that a balance between autonomy and affiliation is most closely associated with psychological health and well-being.

Spousal Relations

The division of labor by gender is pervasive in most cultures (Rosaldo, 1974). Women are usually responsible for child care and "inside" work. Cultures do not encourage women to explore, act on, or meet their individual needs (Miller, 1976). Because women have been raised to be other-centered and to provide for the physical and emotional needs of family members, obtaining emotional autonomy has been difficult (Heath, 1980; McBride, 1990).

Division of labor by gender continues to exist even in countries touched by "women's liberation." Calasanti and Bailey (1991) found similar gender inequities in the division of household labor in Sweden and the United States despite the two countries' differing economic, philosophical, and social orientations.

Stiver (1991) suggests that when men develop qualities that facilitate close relationships, these qualities conflict with their sense of masculinity. This conflict is particularly evident in the aspect of masculinity associated with self-sufficiency and independence. Women, on the other hand, are reared in a context that facilitates close interpersonal relationships, even though these close relationships are not socially valued.

The stereotypic definitions of masculinity and femininity interfere with optimal functioning in both sexes. Men experience personal affiliations as threatening, which results in relational difficulties. Women perceive isolation as threatening, which results in their having difficulty choosing autonomous achievement over affiliation.

If a man does not develop a capacity for intimate relationships, he may depend on his wife to provide these feelings vicariously (Vannoy, 1991). Similarly, a woman may depend on her husband for autonomy, assertiveness, and financial support. Traditional marriages formalize such mutual dependency. Current societal changes may result in marriages in which both partners are autonomous, assertive, and financially independent. In turn, it is necessary for both partners to be supportive and nurturing. The current high divorce rate may be a result of a lag between social and workplace changes toward gender equity, and the lack of a concomitant change in marriage roles. Thus, traditional marriage roles are incongruent with the needs of post-industrial societies. Strong capacities in both partners for autonomy and intimacy (along with less adherence to traditional gender-role identities and behaviors) will be essential to achieve stable marriages in the post-modern world (Vannoy, 1991).

Stiver (1991) questions the common assumptions that women are more dependent than men, and suggests that men are actually better taken care of psychologically and physically than women. Women are traditionally the caretakers, not the ones receiving care within the family. Women hesitate to ask to have their own needs met for fear of appearing selfish or non-nurturing. Further, in many marriages women experience substantial physical, emotional, and sexual abuse. Consequently women, particularly married women, often experience anger, depression, and despair. In contrast, men are more depressed than women following marital separation, and have more difficulty with reduced attention received following the birth of a child.

Peterson (1990) investigated marital fairness by having partners assess their subjective perceptions at each of five phases of family life cycles. More than 50% of the surveyed women perceived their marriages as equitable, regardless of the family life cycle. In contrast, men perceived their marriages as most equitable before children were born and after children left the home. Both sexes agreed that if marriages were inequitable, the inequality benefited the husband.

Wainryb and Turiel (1994) compared the social judgments of persons in more (Arabian Druze) and less (secular Jews) hierarchical cultures in Israel. They found that entitlement was evident in both groups, although the Druze allowed men to have more power over women than did the secular Jews. Druze women accepted men's autonomy and power over them, but regarded this arrangement as unfair.

The development of intrapsychic autonomy, or the ability to maintain enduring mental representations of self-esteem and comfort (Hartmann, 1964), is essential for a Pakistani woman to form necessary relationships with her husband and his extended family (Ewing, 1991). Women who have not developed intrapsychic autonomy are likely to become psychologically disturbed. Interpersonal autonomy, however, is neither necessary nor expected. Family elders make all decisions, including career choice, spousal selection, and the frequency of sexual encounters among young married couples. Individuals are intensely interconnected: one person's anger can cause illness in another family member. Disturbed family relationships are thought to be caused by a failure of elders to love and protect the younger generation, or the younger generation's failing to respect or provide service for the elders, not by "enmeshed" relationships as described by Western family therapists. Family functioning depends on members' realistically perceiving and responding to the needs and interests of others, and simultaneously separating their own needs. Thus, middle class North Americans may value interpersonal autonomy in adult relationships, but other cultures may not.

For various economic, physiological, and psychological reasons, young women frequently experience a period of diminished autonomy following the birth of a child (Terry, 1991). How this lack of autonomy affects the psychological well-being of the individual woman depends upon various factors, including her satisfaction with social and instrumental support and the stress of her context (Hobfoll, Shoham, & Ritter, 1991).

Both in history and in the present, women have not experienced autonomy in Western spousal relationships. At this point it is not possible to draw conclusions about the effect of autonomy within spousal relationships because the data are minimal and inconclusive.

Work and Career Choice

Given that occupational sex segregation is a leading source of gender differences prohibiting economic parity, how women decide upon a career is of considerable interest. Self-efficacy and independence correlate with career choice and attainment (Betz & Hackett, 1986; Miller, Rzonca, & Snider, 1991).

Gender differences in goal orientations result from different socialization experiences regarding the importance of being attached to family and occupational goals (Langan-Fox,

1991). An early study by Rossi (1972) indicated that young adult women defined success for themselves as being the wife and mother of a prominent husband and accomplished children, and Eccles (1987) found that young women described parenting as more important than a professional career.

These results led to the speculation that women might choose female-dominated professions requiring less education and providing more flexible work conditions, to meet the needs of others including their children, parents, and partners (Dukstein & O'Brien, 1995). Relevant research is contradictory. Stickel and Bonett (1991) found that women employed in traditional female occupations felt more self-efficacy in their family responsibilities than women employed in traditionally male occupations. On the other hand, Lefcourt and Harmon (1992) found that women in female-dominated programs anticipated greater self-efficacy combining worker and family roles than those in non-female dominated professions. Dukstein and O'Brien (1995) explored the relationship of self-efficacy and gender role attitudes with women's career development, and found that young women had confidence in their ability to balance effectively the multiple roles of parent, partner, and worker. Older women were less confident in their ability to balance multiple roles. Further, women who had strong self-efficacy expectations had high career expectations.

Zuckerman (1985) found that men and women did not differ significantly in their career, education, or family goals. Similarly, Langan-Fox (1991) found no significant differences between young men and women in their degree of family or occupation-centered goals. Over time, young women had more persisting goals than men.

Research regarding the autonomy of women in the workplace has explored the impact of autonomy in various occupations. Mortimer and Lorence (1989) found that job satisfaction affects job involvement through autonomy. Active, independent, and competitive women adapted more easily to success and failure and were better able to attribute success to internal causes. Women without these traits attributed failure to poor ability and responded to failure by assumptions of incompetence (Welch, Gerrard, & Huston, 1986).

Pearson and Hall (1993) assert that autonomy is necessary for creativity and successful professional functioning. They developed an instrument to measure teachers' autonomy, and found two important factors: teaching autonomy and curricular autonomy. No gender or credential differences were found, and autonomy was not correlated with age or years of experience. However, middle school teachers had greater autonomy than teachers at elementary or high schools.

Despite previous studies indicating traits attributed to females were incongruous with traits associated with managers, Hatcher (1991) found female managers to be more autonomous than men. St. Yves, Contant, Freeston, and Huard (1989) examined the relationships between women's locus of control and occupational status. Locus of control did not significantly differentiate whether a woman was in middle management or non-management positions, although external locus of control correlated with lack of education. Long (1989) found that perceptions of increased self-efficacy resulted in decreased strain for women in non-traditional occupations, regardless of their masculine or feminine characteristics. Female business proprietors have higher internal locus of control than the general population (Nelson & Sharp, 1989).

Mandelbaum (1978) found that female medical students scored higher on autonomy, self-confidence, and aggression, and lower in deference and affiliation than their male counterparts. Leserman (1980) found gender differences in the professional orientation of medical students, with women less concerned about issues of autonomy, social status, and income and more expressive of humanitarian concerns. Seymour and Buscherhof (1991) explored sources of nurses' satisfaction and dissatisfaction. Altruism was a primary source of satisfaction, and perceived lack of autonomy, independence, and control were primary sources of dissatisfaction.

In general, autonomy correlates with greater job satisfaction and recent studies reveal few gender differences in autonomy needs relating to careers and work. Yet women earn considerably less than men because they are occupationally segregated and have unequal access to the higher paying positions characterized by authority and autonomy. Unexpectedly, this segregation does not result from "capital" or gender-related factors such as continuous work experience, education, household responsibilities, and job experience or training (Jaffee, 1989).

IMPLICATIONS FOR THERAPY

As discussed throughout this chapter, young women's struggles to balance autonomy and affiliation affect every domain of their personal and public lives. When they feel unable to satisfactorily balance autonomy and affiliation on their own, young women seek various forms of support, including therapy. For example, young women seek therapy when depressed because they feel frustrated and unhappy, yet are unable to decide to meet their own needs rather than the needs of others.

Traditional psychoanalytic therapy indicates that individual autonomy is the therapeutic goal of choice. However, the preceding review of literature indicates that young women's struggles to balance autonomy and affiliation is complicated by several factors, including the multifaceted nature of autonomy and cultural expectations.

Both dependency and autonomy have positive and negative aspects and are deficits in some contexts and strengths in others. Bornstein (1994) suggests that dependency has some adaptive aspects, including greater treatment adherence and higher levels of academic achievement, as well as greater interpersonal skills (Masling, Johnson, & Saturansky, 1974).

Miller (1976) indicates that women should not be castigated for putting relationships first, but McBride (1990) points out that "when women put relationships first, they often wind up putting others first with disastrous results" (p. 25). According to McBride, clients can choose autonomy, define themselves, and support themselves, much as they support others, without closing off relationships. Alberti and Emmons (1978) similarly suggest that to maintain relationships, women commonly yield to external pressure to conform to others' expectations and refrain from adequate self-expression.

Thus, a fundamental therapeutic dilemma is finding techniques to encourage young women to be appropriately autonomous, without giving up the strength they find through affiliation. Therapists should refrain from assuming young women need emancipation from relationships, for they may be simply seeking assistance in maturing within existing relationships.

Even when a young woman desires the traditional therapeutic goal of autonomy, individual psychotherapy may be counter-indicated. When a woman is in need of an increased sense of control, an additional dependent relationship is not appropriate, and in psychotherapy, the client is in a dependent position (Weitz, 1982). To help control this factor, a number of less traditional techniques have been successfully implemented. These include the following:

- cognitive behavioral approaches to raise self-esteem and increase autonomy (McBride, 1990; Phelps & Austin, 1987)
- using community resources and maximization of individual autonomy while keeping the client in the family context (Ingram, Katz, & Katz, 1991)
- fostering the improvement of physical self-defense skills (Ozer & Bandura, 1990)
- using group treatment to increase sense of control, externalize blame attribution, and decrease feelings of depression, helplessness, and worthlessness (Weitz, 1982)
- working within the context of relationships including family of origin and spousal relations rather than conducting individual therapy (Hartman, 1989)
- using family of origin therapy to discuss issues of identity formation and leaving home (Bowen, 1978)
- and using family therapy to define individuation, designate adulthood, foster positive dyadic relationships, and replace dysfunctional triangulation (Hartman, 1989)

Research on the adjustment of young adults and their parental relationships suggests that working through conflicted feelings toward parents can have positive effects. Fostering increased separation and distance from parents is not always the therapeutic course of choice (Kenny & Donaldson, 1992; Rice, 1992). Instead, helping clients resolve conflictual parental relationships is most likely to promote positive identity development and psychological health (Lopez, Watkins, Manus, & Hunton-Shoup, 1992).

In choosing a therapeutic approach for use with young women, therapists are wise to consider cultural factors. According to Ewing (1991) a principal difficulty in applying Western psychoanalytic or family therapy orientations to non-Western cultures is the confusion between interpersonal and intrapsychic autonomy. Intrapsychic autonomy is integral to positive functioning, but the desirability of interpersonal autonomy is situational. Leichter and Mitchell (1978/1967) found that New York social workers were ineffectual in working with their Eastern European Jewish clients because they consistently attempted to help them achieve distance from their parents, even though the clients felt they should maintain close relationships.

According to Robinson and Ward (1991), therapists should encourage African American women to resist individualism and separation from their families and their traditional African American beliefs, practices, and values. Instead, the clinician should encourage clients to act as leaders within the African American community rather than attempt to achieve autonomy and success within European American society.

Clinicians should be aware that different factors contribute to depression in different immigrant populations (Franks & Faux, 1990). For example, recently arrived women need interventions to address practical issues, but established immigrants need help dealing with stress and social relations. Adaptive outcomes for internal locus of control among homeless and drug abusing Hispanic women correlate with becoming economically autonomous and adequate providers for the health and well-being of their children (Nyamathi & Vasquez, 1989).

Conclusion

This chapter has reviewed theories and research relevant to young women's struggles to balance autonomy and affiliation. Intrapsychic autonomy and feelings of self-efficacy correlate with a lack of depression, the practice of health-promoting activities, issues of sexuality, and work and career success. However, affiliation and interdependence also correlate with successful functioning and are integral to women's development.

Dependency is a strength in some contexts and a deficit in others (Bornstein, 1994). Similarly, autonomy is a strength in some contexts and a deficit in others. Optimal functioning therefore requires both men and women to be able to balance autonomy and affiliation. For this to occur, private and public domains must expand options for both men and women, and decrease polarization of the sexes (Hartman, 1989). Men's opportunities for connection, intimacy, and caretaking in the home must be expanded, as should women's opportunities for autonomy, mastery, and goal-seeking activities outside the home. To maximize the expression of individual talents without excessive self-absorption and alienation, increased flexibility for both sexes would appear to be the avenue of choice.

It is interesting to speculate, however, on the lack of support such increased flexibility might encounter. The near universality of dichotomies between the genders on issues of affiliation and autonomy suggests that a number of economic, social, and psychological variables maintain the status quo.

On the societal level, meaningful expansion of these options requires a number of economic and social changes, as well as an increase in men's ability to seek emotional and problem-focused social support (Barbee, Cunningham, Winstead, Derlega, Gulley, Yankeelov, & Druen, 1993). These changes counteract many centuries of economic and societal traditions. If women universally increase the development of individual talents and reduce the energy they expend on supporting the community, men will need to correspondingly increase family and community support. Because this does not now occur, women tend to step in and try to "do it all." One sex cannot maintain overfunctioning indefinitely, and for marriages, families, and communities to survive, both sexes need to participate fully in both functions.

On an individual level, young men may not welcome a shift in the division of labor and the attendant loss of autonomy and status. Further, young women may not welcome a shift in the division of labor and the attendant loss of intense and intimate connections with others, particularly their children. Because young men have traditionally found their strength through autonomy and achievement, and young women have traditionally found their strength through affiliation and relationships, both sexes will need to develop the capacity to find strength in the non-traditional domains for gender role flexibility to be possible.

REFERENCES

Abouserie, R. (1994). Sources and levels of stress in relation to locus of control and self-esteem in university students. *Educational Psychology, 14*(3), 323–330.

Ainsworth, M. D. S., Blehar, M. C., Walters, E., & Waly, S. (1978). *Patterns of attachment: A psychological study of the strange situation.* Hillsdale, NJ: Erlbaum.

Alberti, R. E., & Emmons, M. L. (1978). *Your perfect right.* San Luis Obispo, CA: Impact Publishers.

Anderson, W. W., & Anderson, D. D. (1986). Thai Muslim adolescents' self, sexuality, and autonomy. *Ethos, 14*(4), 368–3954.

Armsden, G. C., & Greenberg, M. T. (1987). The inventory of parent and peer attachment: Individual differences and their relationship to psychological well-being in adolescence. *Journal of Youth and Adolescence, 16,* 427–454.

Baell, W. K., & Wertheim, E. H. (1992). Predictors of outcome in the treatment of bulimia nervosa. *British Journal of Clinical Psychology, 31,* 330–332.

Bandura, A. (1982). Self efficacy mechanism in human agency. *American Psychologist, 37,* 122–147.

Bandura, A. (1986). *Social foundations of thought and action.* Englewood Cliffs, NJ: Prentice-Hall.

Bandura, A. (1991). Self-efficacy mechanism in physiological activation and health-promoting behavior. In J. Madden, S. Matthyse & J. Barters (Eds.), *Adaptation, learning, and affect* (pp. 226–269). New York: Raven.

Barbee, A. P., Cunningham, M. R., Winstead, B. A., Darlega, V. J., Gulley, M. R., Yankeelov, P. A., & Druen, P. B. (1993). Effects of gender role expectations on the social support process. *Journal of Social Issues, 49*(3), 175–190.

Baruch, C., & Barnett, R. (1983). Adult daughter's relationships with their mothers. *Journal of Marriage and Family, 45,* 601–606.

Baruch, C., Barnett, R., & Rivers, C. (1983). *Life prints: New patterns of love and work for today's woman.* New York: McGraw Hill.

Bar-Yam, M. (1991). Do women and men speak in different voices? A comparative study of self-evolvement. *International Journal of Aging and Development, 32*(4), 247–259.

Bell, N. J., Avery, A. W., Jenkins, D., Feld, J., & Schoenrock, C. J. (1985). Family relationships and social competence during late adolescence. *Journal of Youth and Adolescence, 14,* 109–119.

Bem, S. L. (1983). Gender schema theory and its implications for child development: Raising gender-aschematic children in a gender-schematic society. *Signs: Journal of Women in Culture and Society, 8,* 598–616.

Benassi, V. A., Sweeney, P. D., & Dufour, C. L. (1988). Is there a relationship between locus of control orientation and depression? *Journal of Abnormal Psychology, 97,* 357–367.

Bernier, M., & Avard, J. (1986). Self-efficacy outcomes and attrition in a weight-reduction program. *Cognitive Therapy and Research, 10,* 319–338.

Betz, N. E., & Hackett, G. (1986). Applications of self-efficacy theory to understanding career choice behavior. *Journal of Social and Clinical Psychology, 4,* 279–289.

Bhutto, B. (1995). Address. United Nations' Fourth World Conference on Women. Beijing, China. Reported by Radin, C. A. (1995, September 5). *Boston Globe,* pp. 1, 18.

Blos, P. (1979). *The adolescent passage.* Madison, CT: International Universities Press.

Blustein, D., Walbridge, M., Friedlander, M., & Palladino, D. (1991). Contributions of psychological separation and parental attachment to the career development process. *Journal of Counseling Psychology, 38,* 39–50.

Bornstein, R. F. (1993). *The dependent personality.* New York: Guilford Press.

Bornstein, R. F. (1994). Adaptive and maladaptive aspects of dependency: An integrative review. *American Journal of Orthopsychiatry, 64*(4), 622–635.

Bowen, M. (1978). *Family therapy in clinical practice.* New York: Jason Aronson.

Bowlby, J. (1969). *Attachment and loss: Vol. I Attachment.* New York: Basic Books.

Bruch, H. (1978). *The golden cage: The enigma of anorexia nervosa.* Shepton Mallet, Somerset: Open Books.

Calasanti, T. M., & Bailey, C. A. (1991). Gender inequality and the division of household labor in the United States and Sweden: A socialist-feminist approach. *Social Problems, 38*(1), 34–53.

Carvalho, R. (1992). Some functions of the self personified by the father. *Journal of Analytical Psychology, 37*(4), 395–410.

Chickering, A. W. (1969). *Education and identity.* San Francisco: Jossey-Bass.

Chiu, L. H. (1990). Comparison of responses to Edward's personal preference schedule by Chinese and American college students. *Psychological Reports, 67,* 1296–1298.

Chodorow, N. (1978). *The reproduction of mothering: Psychoanalysis and the sociology of gender.* Berkeley, CA: University of California Press.

Clark, D. A., Beck, A. T., & Brown, G. K. (1992). Sociotropy, autonomy, and life event perceptions in dysphoric and nondysphoric individuals. *Cognitive Therapy and Research, 16*(6), 635–652.

Cochran, S. D., & Peplau, L. A. (1985). Value orientations in heterosexual relationships. *Psychology of Women Quarterly, 9,* 477–488.

Cohler, B. J. (1988). The adult daughter-mother relationship: Perspectives from life course family study and psychoanalysis. *Journal of Geriatric Psychiatry, 21,* 51–72.

Coplin, J. W., & Williams, J. E. (1978). Women law students' descriptions of self and the ideal lawyer. *Psychology of Women Quarterly, 2*(4), 323–333.

Cozzarelli, C. (1993). Personality and self-efficacy as predictors of coping with abortion. *Journal of Personality and Social Psychology, 65*(6), 1224–1236.

Crowley-Long, K., & Long, K. J. (1992). Searching for models of fully functioning women. *Women and Therapy, 12*(1/2), 213–225.

DeJong, M. L. (1992). Attachment, individuation, and risk of suicide in late adolescence. *Journal of Youth and Adolescence, 21*(3), 357–373.

Dellas, M., & Gaier, E. L. (1975). The self and adolescent identity in women: Options and implications. *Adolescence, 10*(39), 399–407.

DeMan, A. F. (1981). Autonomy-control variation in child rearing and level of self-acceptance in young adults. *Journal of Psychology, 107,* 137–140.

Desharnais, R., Bouillon, J., & Godin, G. (1986). Self-efficacy and outcome expectation as determinants of exercise adherence. *Psychological Reports, 59,* 1155–1159.

DiClemente, C. C. (1986). Self-efficacy and the addictive behaviors. *Journal of Social and Clinical Psychology, 4,* 302–315.

Dien, D. (1992). Gender and individuation: China and the West. *Psychoanalytic Review, 79*(1), 105–119.

Dukstein, R. D., & O'Brien, K. M. (1995). *The contribution of multiple role self-efficacy and gender role attitudes to women's career development.* Paper presented at the 104th Annual Convention of the American Psychological Association, New York.

Eccles, J. (1987). Gender roles and women's achievement-related decisions. *Psychology of Women Quarterly, 11*(2), 135–171.

Emerson, R. W. (1950). Self-reliance. In B. Atkinson (Ed.), *The Selected Writings of Ralph Waldo Emerson* (pp. 145–169). New York: Modern Library. (Original work published in 1841).

Epperson, D. C. (1964). A reassessment of indices of parental influence in "the adolescent society." *American Sociological Review, 29,* 93–96.

Erikson, E. H. (1963). *Childhood and society* (2nd ed.). New York: Norton.

Erikson, E. H. (1968). *Identity, youth, and culture.* New York: Norton.

Ewing, K. P. (1991). Can psychoanalytic theories explain the Pakistani woman? Intrapsychic autonomy and interpersonal engagement in the extended family. *Ethos, 19*(2), 131–160.

Fischer, L. R. (1981). Transitions in the mother-daughter relationship. *Journal of Marriage and the Family, 43,* 613–622.

Forisha, B. L. (1978). *Sex roles and personal awareness.* Morristown, NJ: General Learning Press.

Fouad, N. A., & Fahje, K. K. (1989). An exploratory study of the psychological correlates of infertility on women. *Journal of Counseling and Development, 68*(1), 97–101.

Frank, S. F., Towell, P. A., & Huyck, M. (1985). The effects of sex-role traits on three aspects of psychological well-being in a sample of middle-aged women. *Sex Roles, 12*(9/10), 1073–1087.

Frank, S. J., Avery, C. B., & Laman, M. S. (1988). Young adults' perceptions of their relationships with their parents: Individual differences in connectedness, competence, and emotional autonomy. *Developmental Psychology, 24*(5), 729–737.

Frank, S. J., Pirsch, L. A., & Wright, V. C. (1990). Late adolescents' perceptions of the relationships with their parents: Relationships among deidealization, autonomy, relatedness, and insecurity and implications for adolescent adjustment and ego identity status. *Journal of Youth and Adolescence, 19*(6), 571–588.

Franks, F., & Faux, S. A. (1990). Depression, stress, mastery, and social resources in four ethnocultural women's groups. *Research in Nursing and Health, 13,* 283–292.

Freud, S. (1953/1905). Three essays on the theory of sexuality. In J. Strachey (Ed. and Trans.), *The standard edition of the complete psychological works of Sigmund Freud* (Vol. 7, pp. 136–248). London: Hogarth Press.

Friedlander, M. L., & Siegel, S. M. (1990). Separation individuation difficulties and cognitive-behavioral indicators of eating disorders among college women. *Journal of Counseling Psychology, 37*(1), 74–78.

Fullwinder-Bush, N., & Jacobvitz, D. B. (1993). The transition to young adulthood: Generational boundary dissolution and female identity development. *Family Process, 32,* 87–103.

Gaskill, H. S. (1980). The closing phase of the psycho-analytic treatment of adults and the goals of psycho-analysis: "The myth of perfectibility." *International Journal of Psycho-Analysis, 61*(1), 11–23.

Gatz, M., & Karel, M. J. (1993). Individual change in perceived control over 20 years. *International Journal of Behavioral Development, 16*(2), 305–322.

Gilcrest, L. D., & Schinke, S. P. (1983). Coping with contraception: Cognitive and behavioral methods with adolescents. *Cognitive Therapy and Research, 7*(5), 379–388.

Gilligan, C. (1982). *In a different voice: Psychological theory and women's development.* Cambridge, MA: Harvard University Press.

Gonzalez, J. T., & Gonzalez, V. M. (1990). Initial validation of a scale measuring self-efficacy of breast self-examination among low-income Mexican-American women. *Hispanic Journal of Behavioral Sciences, 12*(3), 277–291.

Goodman, S. H., Cooley, E. L., Sewell, D. R., & Leavitt, N. (1994). Locus of control and self-esteem in depressed, low-income African American women. *Community Mental Health Journal, 30*(3), 259–269.

Gould, R. L. (1978). *Transformations: Growth and change in adult life.* New York: Simon and Schuster.

Grayson, P. A. (1989). The college psychotherapy client: An overview. In P. A. Grayson and K. Cauley (Eds.), *College Psychotherapy* (pp. 8–28). New York: Guilford Press.

Greeley, A. T., & Tinsley, H. E. A. (1988). Autonomy and intimacy development in college students: Sex differences and predictors. *Journal of College Student Development, 29,* 512–520.

Grotevant, H. D., & Cooper, C. R. (1986). Individuation in family relationships. *Human Development, 29,* 82–100.

Hartman, A. (1989). Growing up female: A different route? *Smith College Studies in Social Work, 59*(3), 252–266.

Hartmann, H. (1964). *Essays in ego psychology.* New York: International Universities Press.

Hatcher, M. A. (1991). The corporate woman of the 1990s: Maverick or innovator? *Psychology of Women Quarterly, 15,* 251–259.

Heath, D. H. (1980). Wanted: A comprehensive model of health development. *The Personnel and Guidance Journal, 58,* 391–399.

Hill, J. P., & Holmbeck, G. N. (1986). Attachment and autonomy during adolescence. *Annals of Child Development, 3,* 145–189.

Hobfoll, S. E., Shoham, S. B., & Ritter, C. (1991). Women's satisfaction with social support and their receipt of aid. *Journal of Personality and Social Psychology, 61*(2), 332–341.

Hoffman, J. (1984). Psychological separation of late adolescents from their parents. *Journal of Counseling Psychology, 31,* 170–178.

Holmbeck, G. N., & Wandrei, M. L. (1993). Individual and relational predictors of adjustment in first-year college students. *Journal of Counseling Psychology, 40*(1), 73–78.

Houseknecht, S. K. (1979). Timing of the decision to remain voluntarily childless: Evidence for continuous socialization. *Psychology of Women Quarterly, 4*(1), 81–97.

Houts, S. S., & Warland, R. H. (1989). Age and locus of control among women food preparers. *Psychological Reports, 65*(1), 227–233.

Ingram, B. L., Katz, E., & Katz, E., (1991). A comprehensive alternative to residential treatment for adolescents and young adults. *Psychiatric Quarterly, 62*(1), 9–18.

Jaffee, D. (1989). Gender inequality in the workplace: Autonomy and authority. *Social Science Quarterly, 70*(2), 373–390.

Jones, S. L., & Lamke, L. K. (1985). The relationship between sex role orientation, self-esteem, and sex-typed occupational choice of college women. *Psychology of Women Quarterly, 9,* 145–153.

Jordan-Cox, C. A. (1987). Psychosocial development of students in traditionally black institutions. *Journal of College Student Personnel, 28,* 504–512.

Josephs, R. A., Markus, H. R., & Tafarodi, R. W. (1992). Gender and self-esteem. *Journal of Personality and Social Psychology, 63*(3), 391–402.

Jung, C. (1933). *Modern man in search of a soul.* New York: Harcourt, Brace, and World.

Kaplan, A. G., & Klein, R. (1985). The relational self in late adolescent women. *Works in Progress, 17.* Wellesley, MA: Wellesley College Stone Center.

Kaplan, M. (1983). A woman's view of DSM-III. *American Psychologist, 38,* 786–792.

Kaplan, R. M., Atkins, C. J., & Reinsch, S. (1984). Specific efficacy expectations mediate exercise compliance in patients with COPD. *Health Psychology, 3,* 223–242.

Kegan, R. (1982). *The evolving self.* Cambridge, MA: Harvard University Press.

Kenny, M. (1987). The extent and function of parental attachment among first year college students. *Journal of Youth and Adolescence, 16,* 17–27.

Kenny, M. E., & Donaldson, G. A. (1992). The relationship of parental attachment and psychological separation to the adjustment of first-year college women. *Journal of College Student Development, 33,* 431–438.

Kobak, R. R., & Sceery, A. (1988). Attachment in late adolescence: Working models, affect regulation, and representation of self and others. *Child Development, 59,* 135–146.

Kohlberg, L. (1973). *The philosophy of moral development.* San Francisco: Harper and Row.

Kopp, R. G., & Ruzicka, M. F. (1993). Women's multiple roles and psychological well-being. *Psychological Reports, 72*(3, Pt. 2), 1351–1354.

Kupfer, J. H. (1990). *Autonomy and social interaction.* Albany, NY: State University of New York Press.

Langan-Fox, J. (1991). Motivation and the self-concept: Persisting goals of young women and men. *International Journal of Psychology, 26*(4), 409–427.

Lang-Takac, E., & Osterweil, Z. (1992). Separateness and connectedness: Differences between the genders. *Sex Roles, 27*(5/6), 277–289.

Lapsley, D. K., Rice, K. G., & Fitzgerald, D. P. (1990). Adolescent attachment, identity, and adjustment to college: Implication for the continuity of adaptation hypothesis. *Journal of Counseling and Development, 68,* 561–565.

Lapsley, D. K., Rice, K. G., & Shadid, G. E. (1989). Psychological separation and adjustment to college. *Journal of Counseling Psychology, 36,* 286–294.

Lawler, K. A., & Schmied, L. A. (1992). A prospective study of women's health: The effects of stress, hardiness, locus of control, Type A behavior, and physiological reactivity. *Women and Health, 19*(1), 27–41.

Lefcourt, L. A., & Harmon, L. W. (1992). *Self-efficacy expectation for role management (SEERM): Measures of development.* Paper presented at the 101st Annual Convention of the American Psychological Association, Toronto, Canada.

Leichter, H., & Mitchell, W. (1978/1967). *Kinship and casework: Family networks and social intervention.* New York: Teachers College Press.

Lemkau, J. P., & Landau, C. (1986). The "self-less syndrome": Assessment and treatment considerations. *Psychotherapy, 23,* 2276–2302.

Leserman, J. (1980). Sex differences in the professional orientation of first-year medical students. *Sex Roles, 6*(4), 645–660.

Lester, D. (1991). Depression and fears of individuation and attachment. *Transactional Analysis Journal, 21*(4), 218–219.

Litt, M. D., Tennen, H., Affleck, G., Klock, S. (1992). Coping and cognitive factors in adaptation to in vitro fertilization failure. *Journal of Behavioral Medicine, 15*(2), 171–187.

Loevinger, J., & Wessler, R. (1970). *Measuring ego development.* San Francisco: Jossey-Bass.

Long, B. C. (1989). Sex-role orientation, coping strategies, and self-efficacy of women in traditional and nontraditional occupations. *Psychology of Women Quarterly, 13,* 307–324.

Lopez, F. G. (1991). Patterns of family conflict and their relation to college student adjustment. *Journal of Counseling and Development, 69*(3), 257–260.

Lopez, F. G., Campbell, V. L. & Watkins, C. E., Jr. (1988). Constructions of current family functioning among depressed and non-depressed college students. *Journal of College Student Development, 30,* 221–228.

Lopez, F. G., Watkins, C. E., Manus, M., & Hunton-Shoup, J. (1992). Conflictual independence, mood regulation, and generalized self-efficacy: Test of a model of late-adolescent identity. *Journal of Counseling Psychology, 39*(3), 375–381.

Lurie, E. E. (1974). Sex and stage differences in perceptions of marital and family relationships. *Journal of Marriage and the Family, 36,* 260–269.

Macoby, E., & Jacklin, C. N. (1974). *The psychology of sex differences.* Stanford, CA: Stanford University Press.

Maibech, E., & Flora, J. A. (1993). Symbolic modeling and cognitive rehearsal: Using video to promote AIDS prevention self-efficacy. *Communication Research, 20*(4), 517–545.

Maibech, E., Flora, J. A., & Nass, C. (1991). Changes in self-efficacy and health behavior in response to a minimal contact community health campaign. *Health Communication, 3,* 1–15.

Major, B., Cozzarelli, C., Sciacchitano, A. M., Cooper, M. L. (1990). Perceived social support, self-efficacy, and adjustment to abortion. *Journal of Personality and Social Psychology, 59*(3), 452–463.

Mandelbaum, D. R. (1978). Women in medicine. *Signs, 4*(1), 136–145.

Mariano, A. J., Donovan, D. M., Walker, P. S., & Mariano, M. J. (1989). Drinking related locus of control and the drinking status of urban Native Americans. *Journal of Studies on Alcohol, 50*(4), 331–338.

Marks, F. R. (1975). Detours on the road to maturity: A view of the legal conception of growing up and letting go. *Law and Contemporary Problems, 39*(23), 78–92.

Martin, J. K., Nagayuma, H., & Gordon, C. (1992). Thinking black, thinking internal, thinking feminist. *Journal of Counseling Psychology, 39*(4), 509–514.

Masling, J. M., Johnson, C., & Saturansky, C. (1974). Oral imagery, accuracy of perceiving others and performance in Peace Corps training. *Journal of Personality and Social Psychology, 30,* 414–419.

McBride, M. C. (1990). Autonomy and the struggle for female identity: Implications for counseling women. *Journal of Counseling and Development, 69,* 22–26.

McClain, E. W. (1975). An Eriksonian cross-cultural study of adolescent development. *Adolescence, 10*(40), 527–541.

McHugh, E. L. (1989). Concepts of the person among the Gurungs of Nepal. *American Ethnologist, 16,* 75–86.

Mendola, R., Tennen, H., Affleck, G., McCann, L., & Fitzgerald, T. (1990). Appraisal and adaptation among women with impaired fertility. *Cognitive Therapy and Research, 14*(1), 79–93.

Mill, J. S. (1859/1947). *On liberty.* New York: Appleton Century Crofts.

Miller, J. B. (1976). *Toward a new psychology of women.* Boston: Beacon Press.

Miller, J. B. (1984). The development of a woman's sense of self. *Work in Progress, 84–01.* Wellesley, MA: Wellesley College Stone Center.

Miller, P. H. (1993). *Theories of developmental psychology* (3rd ed.). New York: W. H. Freeman.

Miller, R. J., Rzonca, C., & Snider, B. (1991). Variables related to the type of post secondary education experience chosen by young adults with learning disabilities. *Journal of Learning Disabilities, 24*(3), 188–191.

Mills, J. K. (1991). Differences in locus of control between obese adult and adolescent females undergoing weight reduction. *Journal of Psychology, 125*(2), 195–197.

Minuchin, S. (1974). *Families and family therapy.* Cambridge, MA: Harvard University Press.

Minuchin, S., Rosman, B., & Baker, L. (1978). *Psychosomatic families—Anorexia nervosa in context.* Cambridge, MA: Harvard University Press.

Morgan, C. S. (1980). Female and male attitudes toward life: Implications for theories of mental health. *Sex Roles, 6,* 367–380.

Mortimer, J. T., & Lorence, J. (1989). Satisfaction and involvement: Disentangling a deceptively simple relationship. *Social Psychology Quarterly, 57*(4), 249–265.

Mueller, P., & Major, B. (1989). Self-blame, self-efficacy, and adjustment to abortion. *Journal of Personality and Social Psychology, 57*(6), 1059–1068.

Mule, P., & Barthel, D. (1992). The return to the veil: Individual autonomy vs. social esteem. *Sociological Forum, 7*(2), 1992.

Munro, G., & Adams, G. R. (1977). Adolescent values: Measuring instrumental and expressive orientations. *Adolescence, 12*(47), 329–337.

Neki, J. S. (1976). An examination of the cultural relativism of dependence as a dynamic of social and therapeutic relationships. *British Journal of Medical Psychology, 49,* 1–10.

Nelson, G. W., & Sharp, W. H. (1989). Locus of control and achievement of female proprietors of small businesses. *Psychological Reports, 65,* 890.

Nietzel, M. T., & Harris, M. J. (1990). Relationship of dependency and achievement/autonomy to depression. *Clinical Psychology Review, 19,* 279–297.

Nir, Z., & Neumann, L. (1991). Self-esteem, internal-external locus of control, and their relationship to weight reduction. *Journal of Clinical Psychology, 47*(4), 568–575.

Nyamathi, A., & Vasquez, R. (1989). Impact of poverty, homelessness, and drugs on Hispanic women at risk for HIV infection. *Hispanic Journal of Behavioral Science, 11*(4), 299–314.

Ozer, E. M., & Bandura, A. (1990). Mechanisms governing empowerment effects: A self-efficacy analysis. *Journal of Personality and Social Psychology, 58*(3), 472–486.

Pardeck, J. A., & Pardeck, J. T. (1990). Family factors related to adolescent autonomy. *Adolescence, 25*(98), 311–319.

Pearson, L. C., & Hall, B. W. (1993). Initial construct validation of the Teaching Autonomy Scale. *Journal of Educational Research, 86*(3), 172–178.

Peters, J. F. (1991). Parental contributions to adolescents' possessions and educational expenses: Gender difference. *Adolescence, 26*(103), 649–657.

Peterson, C. C. (1990). Husbands' and wives' perceptions of marital fairness across the family life cycle. *International Journal of Aging and Human Development, 31*(3), 179–188.

Phelps, S., & Austin, N. (1987). *The assertive woman: A new look.* San Luis Obispo, CA: Impact Publishers.

Poag, K., & McAuley, E. (1992). Goal setting, self-efficacy, and exercise behavior. *Journal of Sport and Exercise Psychology, 14*(4), 352–360.

Pollard, K. D., Benton, S. E., & Hinz, K. (1983). The assessment of developmental tasks of students in remedial and regular programs. *Journal of College Student Personnel, 24,* 20–23.

Rassaby, J., Hirst, S., Hill, D. J., & Bennett, R. (1991). Introduction of a breast self-examination teaching program in Victoria, Australia. *Health Education Research, 6*(3), 291–296.

Rice, K. G. (1992). Separation-individuation and adjustment to college: A longitudinal study. *Journal of Counseling Psychology, 39*(3), 298.

Robinson, T., & Ward, J. V. (1991). A belief in self far greater than anyone's disbelief: Cultivating resistance among African-American female adolescents. *Women in Therapy, 11*(3–4), 87–103.

Rosaldo, M. Z. (1974). Women, culture, and society: A theoretical overview. In M. Z. Rosaldo and L. Lamphere (Eds.), *Women, culture, and society* (pp. 17–42). Stanford, CA: Stanford University Press.

Rosenblum, K. E. (1986). The conflict between and within genders: An appraisal of contemporary American femininity and masculinity. *Sociological Inquiry, 56*(1), 93–104.

Rosenthal, D. A., & Feldman, S. S. (1992). The relationship between parenting behavior and ethnic identity in Chinese-American and Chinese-Australian adolescents. *International Journal of Psychology, 27*(1), 19–31.

Rossi, A. S. (1972). Barriers to the career choice of engineering, medical and science among American women. In J. M. Bardwick (Ed.), *Readings on the psychology of women* (pp. 72–82). New York: Harper and Row.

Rotter, J. B. (1966). Generalized expectancies for internal versus external locus of control reinforcement. *Psychological Monographs, 80*(1), 609.

Rubin, L. (1983). *Intimate strangers: Men and women together.* New York: Harper and Row.

Ryan, R. M., & Lynch, J. H. (1989). Emotional autonomy versus detachment: Revising the vicissitudes of adolescence and young adulthood. *Child Development, 60,* 340–356.

Ryff, C. D. (1989). Happiness is everything, or is it? Explorations on the meaning of psychological well-being. *Journal of Personality and Social Psychology, 57*(6), 1069–1081.

Sacks, S. R., & Einstein, H. (1979). Feminism and psychological autonomy: A study in decision-making. *The Personnel and Guidance Journal, 57,* 419–423.

Schlenker, B. R., & Weingold, M. F. (1990). Self-consciousness and self-presentation: Being autonomous versus appearing autonomous. *Journal of Personality and Social Psychology, 59*(4), 820–828.

Schultheiss, D. E. P., & Blustein, D. L. (1994). *Journal of Counseling Psychology, 41*(2), 248–255.

Seymour, E., & Buscherhof, J. R. (1991). Sources and consequences of satisfaction and dissatisfaction in nursing: Findings from a national sample. *International Journal of Nursing Studies, 28*(2), 109–124.

Shannon, B., Bagby, R., Wang, M. Q., & Trenkner, L. L. (1990). Self-efficacy: A contributor to the explanation of eating behavior. *Health Education Research, 5*(4), 395–407.

Sheridan, M. J., & Green, R. G. (1993). Family dynamics and individual characteristics of adult children of alcoholics: An empirical analysis. *Journal of Social Science Research, 17*(1–2), 73–97.

Shisslak, C. M., Pazda, S. L., & Crago, M. (1990). Body weight and bulimia as discriminators of psychological characteristics among anorexia, bulimic, and obese women. *Journal of Abnormal Psychology, 99*(4), 380–384.

Silverberg, B., & Steinberg, L. (1987). Adolescent autonomy, parent-adolescent conflict, and parental well-being. *Journal of Youth and Adolescence, 16*(3), 293–311.

Smith-Hefner, N. J. (1993). Education, gender, and generational conflict among Khmer refugees. *Anthropology and Education Quarterly, 24*(2), 135–158.

Stack, C. B. (1986). The culture of gender: Women and men of color. *Signs, 11,* 321–324.

Stainton, T. (1994). *Autonomy and social policy.* Bookfield, VT: Avebury.

Stander, V., & Jensen, L. (1993). The relationship of value orientation to moral cognition: Gender and cultural differences in the United States and China explored. *Journal of cross-cultural psychology, 24*(1), 42–52.

Starr, J. M. (1986). American youth in the 1980's. *Youth and Society, 17*(4), 323–345.

Stickel, S. A., & Bonett, R. M. (1991). Gender differences in career self-efficacy: Combining a career with home and family. *Journal of College Student Development, 32,* 297–301.

Stiver, I. P. (1991). The meaning of dependency in female-male relationships. In J. Jordan, A. Kaplan, J. B. Miller, I. P. Stiver, and J. L. Surrey, *Women's growth in connection* (pp. 143–161). New York: Guilford Press.

Strecher, V., DeVellis, B. M., Becker, M. H., & Rosenstock, I. M. (1986). The role of self-efficacy in achieving health behavior change. *Health Education Quarterly, 13,* 73–91.

St. Yves, A., Contant, F., Freeston, M. H., & Huard, J. (1989). Locus of control in women occupying middle-management and nonmanagement positions. *Psychological Reports, 65*(2), 483–486.

Surrey, J. (1984). The self-in-relation: A theory of women's development. *Works in progress, 13.* Wellesley, MA: Wellesley College Stone Center.

Swenson, C. H. (1980). Ego development and a general model for counseling and psychotherapy. *The Personnel and Guidance Journal, 58,* 382–388.

Taub, D. J., & McEwen, M. K. (1991). Patterns of development of autonomy and mature interpersonal relationships in black and white undergraduate women. *Journal of College Student Development, 32,* 502–508.

Taub, D. J., & McEwen, M. K. (1992). The relationship of racial identity attitudes to autonomy and mature

interpersonal relationships in black and white undergraduate women. *Journal of College Student Development, 33,* 439–446.

Terry, D. J. (1991). Stress, coping, and adaptation to new parenthood. *Journal of Social and Personal Relationships, 8*(4), 527–547.

Ullian, D. (1984). Why girls are good: A constructivist view. *American Journal of Orthopsychiatry, 54,* 71–82.

Vannoy, D. (1991). Social differentiation, contemporary marriage, and human development. *Journal of Family Issues, 12*(3), 251–267.

Vygotsky, L. S. (1978). *Mind in society: The development of higher psychological processes.* In M. Cole, V. John-Steiner, S. Scribner, and E. Souberman (Eds.), Cambridge, MA: Harvard University Press. (Original work published 1930, 1935).

Wainryb, C., & Turiel, E. (1994). Dominance, subordination, and concepts of personal entitlements in cultural contexts. *Child Development, 65*(6), 1701–1722.

Walum, L. (1977). *The dynamics of sex and gender: A sociological perspective.* Chicago: Rand McNally.

Weitz, R. (1982). Feminist consciousness raising, self-concept, and depression. *Sex Roles, 8*(3), 231–241.

Welch, R., Gerrard, M., & Huston, A. (1986). Gender-related personality attributes and reaction to success/failure: An examination of mediating variables. *Psychology of Women Quarterly, 10,* 221–233.

Williams, E. L., & Manaster, G. J. (1990). Restricter anorexia, bulimic anorexia, and bulimic women's early recollection and Thematic Apperception Test response. *Individual Psychology Journal of Adlerian Theory Research and Practice, 46*(1), 93–107.

Williams, G. J., Chamove, A. S., Millar, H. R. (1990). Eating disorders, perceived control, assertiveness and hostility. *British Journal of Clinical Psychology, 29*(3), 327–335.

Youniss, J., & Smollar, J. (1985). *Adolescent relations with mothers, fathers, and friends.* Chicago: University of Chicago Press.

Zuckerman, D. M. (1985). Confidence and aspirations: Self-esteem and self-concepts as predictors of students' life goals. *Journal of Personality, 53*(4).

6

AUTONOMY IN THE MIDDLE YEARS

GEORGIA BABLADELIS[1]
California State University at Hayward

The particular focus of this chapter is the perceived achievement and implementation of autonomy in the middle-aged woman. Middle age is generally seen as encompassing the time between 40 and 65 years of age. The meaning of autonomy and the behaviors associated with it have been discussed earlier in this book. In much of the world, but particularly in Western culture, autonomy is synonymous with personhood. Its Greek roots suggest the idea of embodying one's own laws, or more loosely put, being a law unto oneself. It is commonplace to observe that it is not only the right but also the expectation that an individual will be "one's own man." Does it include the right and the expectation that one also may be "one's own woman?"

Following an overview of the theoretical perspectives of Jung, Erikson, and Henry, this chapter will examine the research literature pertaining to a perceived sense of autonomy in the middle years of adulthood. This will be undertaken through studies of a mature woman's sense of generativity, integrity, and inner-directedness, as well as her experiences arising from her multiple roles (e.g., those of wife, mother, and worker), her physical and psychosocial changes (e.g., changes in reproductive concerns, parental concerns, and work status), and her altered sense of personal power owing to the multiple roles, changes, and concerns. This chapter will conclude with the author's own recent survey of a group of middle-aged women.

[1]A portion of this work was completed under a grant for professional release time from the School of Science, CSUH. I gratefully acknowledge that support. I thank the students who helped collect and score protocols: Emma Martins, Yvonne Sanchez Laschak, Jeanne Randolph, Monica Roberts, and Patricia Sharp. Special thanks to Yvonne Sanchez Laschak and Jeanne Randolph for their help in drafting portions of an earlier version of this chapter and to Suzanne Adams for her helpful comments on the final version.

Address correspondence and reprint requests to Georgia Babladelis, Professor Emeritus, Department of Psychology, California State University at Hayward, Hayward, CA 94545.

Let us look briefly at the implications for middle age that inhere in some theoretical views addressing autonomy either explicitly or implicitly. From among the several well known theorists who have made important contributions to our understanding of middle age in the total life span, I have chosen to discuss selected contributions from Jung, Erikson, and Henry because I think they represent the general body of theoretical influence on our understanding of autonomy in middle age.

THEORETICAL PERSPECTIVES

Jung's View

In Carl Jung's (1960) theory of personality development, many systems interact to produce a total psyche or personality. Among these, the relationship between the ego and the persona is important to the development of autonomy. If the ego (i.e., one's conscious mind—perceptions, memories, thoughts, feelings, identity, and sense of continuity) identifies with the persona (i.e., the mask worn by the individual in response to the demands of social conventions—the role assigned by society), as it frequently does in Jung's opinion, one becomes more conscious of the part one is playing than of genuine feelings. One becomes a mere semblance of a person, a reflection of society instead of an autonomous human being.

At the center of personality is the self, holding all the other systems together and providing the personality with unity, equilibrium, and stability. Before a self can emerge it is necessary for the various components of the personality to become fully developed and individuated. For this reason, the archetype of the self does not become evident until the person has reached middle age. For Jung, all the separate systems must develop and ultimately be coordinated and integrated into a total system called self. Premature identity of one system with another (the ego and the persona in this case) precludes the development of autonomy. Such development, individuation, and coordination cannot be seen until middle age.

It is important to note that in Jung's view the nucleus from which the persona develops is an archetype. The relevant archetypes in this discussion are those of anima and animus, gender-related concepts, reflecting a view of human beings as bisexual animals. Both men and women must develop their archetypical nucleus from which their persona springs and avoid identifying their persona with their ego if they are to emerge as an autonomous human being in middle age. An implicit directive for us stemming from Jung's theory, therefore, is to examine the research literature for signs of androgyny and its correlates in the middle-aged woman's perception of herself as an *autonomous* person. Progress to middle age by aging alone, therefore, will not result in that integrative system—the self. It is at middle age, however, that such integration, if achieved, can be manifested.

Erikson's View

It is in Erikson's (1950) theory that we find a clear, explicit emphasis on autonomy as an important achievement at a relatively early stage of human development. Personality theorists who discriminate stages in human development recognize that an individual's failure to realize the potential inherent at one stage of development will impair that person's ability to fully integrate the next stage of development; similarly, effective mastery at one stage facilitates effective mastery at the next. In Erikson's view, failure to resolve conflicts at an early stage of development in favor of autonomy (as opposed to shame and doubt) will impair the personal development of that person at subsequent stages. At the later stage labeled "adulthood" the important conflict which must be resolved is that between generativity (e.g., doing, creating) as opposed to stagnation (e.g., being fearful, resentful). It is reasonable to expect that successful achievement of autonomy at an earlier stage should, in part, contribute to the manifestation of generativity (versus stagnation) at the later stage of adulthood. Our review of the literature, therefore, must look for clues that middle-aged women are "doing" or "creating"—that they are learning, contributing, and growing as ways of combatting fear of change, resentment of losses, and inability or unwillingness to extend and express themselves. If we were to adopt Erikson's descriptions of healthy development at middle age, the presence of those factors would lead us to conclude that autonomy must have been achieved else generativity would not have been likely. Our continued examination of the research literature, therefore, should inform us about the successful (or unsuccessful) attainment of autonomy as it is manifested at the middle-aged stage of development in generativity (or stagnation).

Henry's View

Henry (1968) claims that middle age is a time of engagement. By this he means that persons at this stage of life are highly engaged in achieving consonance with social norms and forms. According to Henry, one of the important changes occurring in adulthood may very well be the attainment of stability so that the duality in human nature is stabilized in accordance with the possibilities inherent in life situations. People become more responsive to social values which are used to direct their lives at work and in the family situation, as well as in their attitudes toward friends and neighbors (communal). Henry also thinks that adults take stances toward themselves and others that are active and instrumental (agentic). The major attainment of adulthood, says Henry, is the degree to which identity is established. Both agency and communion, terms borrowed from Bakan (1996), are important in adult identity. The individual is not merely bound to social norms but is vigorously individualistic in expressing social continuity. Therefore, in our review of the research findings, we will look for signs of individuality, a sense of identity or self that incorporates both agency (as expressed in instrumentality; doing) and communion (as expressed in social responsibility; relationships).

THE RESEARCH EVIDENCE

Definitions of autonomy suggest that we examine the research literature pertaining to a middle-aged woman for evidence that she is aggressive, adventurous, hard-headed, unconventional, opinionated, individualistic, self-confident, gets things done, has high self-esteem, and so forth. From various theoretical perspectives, it is suggested that we look also for evidence of androgyny, generativity, instrumentality, and community. Additionally, it is reasonable to include in our list Rotter's (1966) locus of control concept of personal control and Bandura's (1982) concepts of self-efficacy and competence. I will call all these indicators the "vital signs" of autonomy.

The Vital Signs

It is important to note that almost all of the studies reviewed were based on European American, middle-class, fairly well-educated women. Additionally, many of the studies that included more than one age group were cross-sectional studies, making it difficult to interpret findings as necessarily being developmentally based. However, we can at least see whether or not certain vital signs of autonomy are present at middle age for women even if we cannot determine their developmental history.

Instrumentality
Studying how women perceive their own personality functioning, Ryff (1982) found that middle-aged women gave higher priority to instrumental functions. Ryff studied 160 middle-aged and older people of varied educational levels but of a similar middle-class socioeconomic level. Participants included 80 middle-aged (40–55) people and 80 old-agers (over 60) with an equal number of women and men in each group. Ryff identified the unique personality dimensions of middle and old age with derivations from theoretical frameworks that were used in an earlier study. Empirical measures were made of value systems and personality characteristics using a modified version of the *Rokeach Value Survey* and *Jackson's Personality Research Form.* Concurrent, retrospective, or prospective instructions preceded the testing, and participants of each age and sex group were randomly assigned to the instruction conditions. Of particular interest to us is that women gave higher priority to instrumental values when focusing on middle age (both concurrently and retrospectively) than when focusing on old age (both concurrently and prospectively).

Generativity and Complexity
Subsequently, Ryff & Heincke (1983) examined personality from a developmental perspective; in other words, how individuals perceived that their personality had or would change across the major phases of adult life. Again, we are interested here on the data about middle-aged women participants. Participants in this study were 90 young adults, 90 middle-aged persons, and 90 old-agers with equal numbers of males and females in each group. The same age categories were employed except that now a younger group (undergraduates) was included. The other participants were recruited from religious organizations (Catholic, Protestant, Jewish) in suburban New York City. They had, on the average, three years of college, and 90% of them were married. On the whole, then, we have a more highly educated group than the national average and a group for the most part European American and middle-class in socioeconomic status.

The developmental scales used were derived from theoretical formulations. *Generativity* and *integrity* were drawn from Erikson's psychosocial stage theory of development; the dimension of *complexity* was drawn from Neugarten's discussion of adult personality; the dimension of *interiority* came from discussions by Jung, Buhler, and others. Generativity, important to middle-aged development, referred to having a concern for guiding the next generation and a sense of responsibility to younger persons. Integrity, important to old age, was defined as adapting to the triumphs and disappointments of life and finding one's past to have been meaningful. Complexity, appropriate to middle age, referred to being actively engaged in a complex environment and to selectively manipulating and controlling activities in multiple spheres. Interiority, a dimension characterizing old age, described a greater turning inward or becoming more reflective, contemplative, and individuated, characteristics that several theorists have ascribed to old age. Therefore, the study showed that both generativity and complexity are important personality issues for middle-aged persons and, in our particular scrutiny, for middle-aged women.

Instructions to the participants established present, retrospective, and prospective data; in other words, the self-reports included middle-aged individuals assessing themselves in the present, as well as the past and the future. Similarly, young adults assessed what they thought they would be like in middle and old age as well as how they perceived themselves in the present. Older adults assessed themselves in the present as well as recalling what they were like in their youth and middle age.

All groups of women rated themselves higher on generativity and complexity at the stage called middle age. That is, young women (prospective views) and older women (retrospective views) as well as current middle-aged women all characterized middle age as a time of instrumentality or complexity (i.e., being actively engaged in a complex environment and selectively manipulating and controlling activities in multiple spheres) and generativity (i.e., having a concern for guiding the next generation and a sense of responsibility to younger women).

Leadership—An Unconventional Role

Astin & Leland (1991) reported an ambitious and informative study in a book titled *Women of Influence, Women of Vision.* This work was based on a cross-generational study of women leaders active in bringing about social change. Previous meetings with women leaders led the authors to design a study of (women's) leadership. In 1984 they began to profile and compare women who provided leadership in the period from the 1960s to the 1980s. Their initial focus was on women they called "Instigators" whose leadership activity in the 1960s and 1970s resulted in significant societal changes for women. Two other generational groups were added: "Predecessors" and "Inheritors." Predecessors were identified as those women who played visible leadership roles as early as the 1950s (i.e., prior to the most recent flowering of the women's movement). They occupied positions of leadership most often available to women in that era (e.g., presidents of women's colleges or deans with special concerns for student affairs and women's issues). Inheritors were identified as women then in leadership roles and thought of as having inherited the challenges, changes, programs, or organizations brought into existence through the women's movement of the 1960s and 1970s.

The total sample of 77 women (17 Predecessors, 31 Instigators, and 29 Inheritors) were selected from four broad categories: educational institutions, foundations, and governmental agencies; national educational and professional associations and independent agencies; special programs for and about women and founders or publishers of educational publications about women; and scholars and researchers. Predecessors, Instigators, and Inheritors were identified within each of these four categories. No claim is made that this sample is inclusive.

From their various contacts, knowledge, and experience, the authors generated names of women leaders who also became an important source of additional names for Instigators and Predecessors. Instigators were the primary source of names for the Inheritors, that is, the younger women who took on leadership roles in the same or similar settings as the Instigators and some of whom were mentored by the Instigators themselves. The authors define empowerment as "an expandable resource that is produced and shared through interaction by leader and followers alike" (p. 1). Leadership was exercised through empowerment and collective action, and was conceptualized as "the actions and behaviors of women who worked toward changing social institutions in order to improve women's lives" (p. 7).

Findings were based on separate case study data sets for each of the participants plus an in-depth personal interview, a background questionnaire, and supporting materials (e.g., relevant publications, speeches, etc.). These women saw themselves as confident of their abilities and their knowledge—saw as good at what they do. They were independent and sure of their opinions. They were assiduous (aggressive?) in their pursuit and mastery of information so that they knew what they were doing and felt confident in their knowledge. They were conscientious, persistent, and serious in approaching the task of leadership. Identified as generative were leadership behaviors that empowered others. Women involved in scholarship and teaching also taught and mentored students and junior faculty. These women perceived themselves as intelligent, assertive, and determined. They had a high level of self-esteem, and, unconventionally, were not averse to acknowledging it.

Although specific information about the age range of these women was not provided, it can be safely inferred that the ages of those women in the leadership roles described fall within our middle-aged range. In this highly select sample of leaders—an unconventional role—are found many of the characteristics of autonomy including self-confidence, unconventionality, aggressiveness, independence, sense of mastery and ability, personal locus of control, ability to be critical of authority, adventurousness, generativity, and creativity. Undesirable characteristics of autonomy such as being autocratic, cynical, opinionated, and avoiding responsibility and obligation, were not found.

Inner-Direction

Noting that some theorists view personal development as continuous and others view it in terms of stages, Hyman (1988) designed research to build and test a theory of adult developmental stages, stressing that the study was exploratory in nature. She explored the growth patterns of autonomy and orientation in time over four stages of development, using the *Personal Orientation Inventory* (POI) to measure these dimensions.

Four developmental stages were examined in reference to changes in inner-direction (autonomy) and time-competence (orientation in time), the operational variables of adult growth. The four stages employed were

- *Stage 1,* ages 19–27—the research cited regards this as a time when people are mastering what they are supposed to be. It is a time characterized by lack of introspection and self-understanding and by an orientation toward future goals. Hyman expects both autonomy and time-orientation to be low during this stage.

- *Stage 2,* ages 28–34—this is seen as a transitional period when people devote themselves to what they want to be. Previously omitted inner aspects are emerging. Hyman expects to see an increase in scores on autonomy and little change in present time orientation.
- *Stage 3,* ages 35–45—this period is recognized as that of the middle-aged transition. Major shifts in the psyche are expected to occur at this time with a growing awareness of the reality of death. A reassessment of life goals occurs and the person tries harder to incorporate previously omitted aspects of life. In this stage Hyman expects to see continued increase in inner-direction (autonomy) along with aberrations in time-orientation.
- *Stage 4,* ages 46–55—this period is referred to as true middle age, marking an end to the transition. Changes from the transition are consolidated, resulting in integrity. Introspection without middle-aged pressures is possible and as depression lifts, guilt and resentment diminish. Inner-direction (autonomy) should level off and time-competence (present orientation in time) should increase.

Hyman studied a non-representative sample of 343 female helping professionals of above average education. She dropped persons who did not complete the POI, resulting in the following numbers per stage: Stage 1, N = 99; Stage 2, N = 88; Stage 3, N = 86; Stage 4, N = 70. Polynomial regression was used to study the two dependent variables (inner-direction and time-competence) against age, followed by separate analyses for each of the four developmental stages for each dependent variable. Finally, Hyman performed a trend analysis of each dependent variable. Again, for our purposes, the focus is on middle-aged women, and therefore on the findings regarding stages 3 and 4.

Separate polynomial regression analyses of inner-direction (autonomy) and time-competence for each stage were non-significant. Time-competence increased through stages 1 and 2, decreased markedly in stage 3 before rising again, and leveled off in stage 4, suggesting a crisis in time perspective. The trend analysis showed a significant linear relationship for both variables (inner-direction or autonomy and time-competence or orientation) to increases with the stage of development. Although time-competence also increased with age, the findings suggest a crisis period at stage 4, and the time breaks suggest distinct stages in the lifespan. Hyman discussed the failure of this study to find evidence of crisis in inner-direction as reported in biographical studies, suggesting several explanations but pointing out the need for longitudinal studies. Changes in society obscure findings from cross-sectional studies. Also unanswered are the causes of fluctuations in one's orientation in time during the middle-aged transition. She speculates that women's change in time-orientation might be related to children leaving home, re-entry into the world of work, and so forth. Whatever the explanation, the findings in this study indicate the presence of autonomy in middle-aged women.

Creativity

Wink (1991) found that the majority of middle-aged women with successful careers scored high on autonomy, which, in turn, was in strong positive correlation with several measures of creativity. Wink studied 103 adult women, using data from the Mills College longitudinal sample described in detail below (Helson, Elliot, & Leigh, 1990). He was interested in studying the personality configurations of those women in terms of narcissism and object-directedness. Persons in whom issues of self-concern and self-esteem predominate have been labeled as narcissistic. Persons whose dominant issues are those of relations with others have been labeled as object-directed. The narcissistic person is concerned with issues of self-definition, self-worth, identity, and autonomy. Narcissistic development may be either healthy or pathological. Appropriate levels of concern lead to a healthy self-concept and to the optimal use of one's talents. Similarly, the development of object-directedness may result in healthy or pathological outcomes. The healthy person with this personality configuration is characterized by warm, unconflicted relations with others—this person upholds the rules of social conduct.

Narcissism and object-directedness were measured with five subsets of scores derived from a prototype of narcissism based on Q sorts and the Q-sort descriptions of the women at age 43. Wink was interested in finding the relationship of those two personality configurations to other personality characteristics of the middle-aged woman, as well as to their psychological health, work patterns, relationships, and creativity. Factor analysis of the scores permitted the investigator to identify individual scores for each woman on factors that summarized items indicative of the prototype. Wink assessed data for each woman in terms of healthy or unhealthy narcissism or object-directedness. The data covered the lives of the women since college, including marital and family relations, work history, and so forth. Selected scales from the *California Personality Inventory* (CPI) and the *Adjective Checklist* (ACL) obtained at age 43 were used to compare with narcissism and object-directed factors. Satisfied with the correlates to the two factors of narcissism and object-directed factors, Wink discussed autonomy (a factor in narcissism). Autonomy showed no relation to ratings on pathology and was interpreted as a healthy variant in narcissism. The autonomy factor showed a strong correlation with measures of achievement, satisfaction, and work status. In this study, the majority of women with successful careers had high autonomy scores. Moreover, autonomy showed a strong correlation with all the measures of creativity used in this study. In an earlier study, Helson (1987) found that those women who were identified at age 21 as having a potential to be creative were fulfilling that potential by age 43.

Multiple Roles: Confidence, Control, and Competence

The idea that many of the attributes associated with autonomy are developed as a result of the enactment of multiple roles has received some attention. Here we will examine the findings about some of those attributes (e.g., self-esteem, confidence, personal control, and the like) pertaining to middle-aged women, followed by an examination of the quality of those roles.

Locus of Control

Mellinger and Erdwins (1985) investigated personality correlates of adult women in certain roles. They studied 80 young adult (29–31) women, 80 middle-aged (40–55) women, and 60 older (over 60) women. The participants in this study were well-educated, and middle-class, and were divided into role groups based on marital status, children's ages, and career. There were 20 participants in each of the four role groups designated for young and middle-aged women and in each of the three role groups designated for older women. The four groups used for the assignment of younger women were

1. Homemakers: married women with one or more children under 15 years of age, and currently working in the home with no plans for outside employment.
2. Students: married women with one or more children under 15 who were currently attending the university.
3. Married Career: women who were employed on a full-time basis outside the home and who had one or more children under 15.
4. Single Career: women who were employed full-time, had never married, and had no children.

For the 80 middle-aged participants, the group designations were the same except that their children were all 15 years or older. The 60 older participants were assigned to three role groups.

1. Homemakers: women who had spent most of their adult years working in the home with little or no outside employment, and who were currently married (or widowed) with one or more grown children.
2. Married Career: women who were retired after a substantial number of years spent in full-time employment outside the home, had one or more grown children, and were either married or widowed.
3. Single Career: women who were retired after many years of outside employment, had never married, and were childless.

Several psychological measures of personality were administered, including the *California Psychological Inventory* (CPI), a shortened form of the *Edwards Personal Preference Schedule* (EPPS), the *Tennessee Self-concept Scale* (TSCS), the *Bem Sex Role Inventory* (BSRI), and the *Rotter Internal-External Control Scale*. A brief questionnaire was administered as well in order to obtain personal and demographic data.

Multivariate analysis of variance was performed testing age, role, and age by role effects. We will focus on the findings regarding middle-aged women. On the basis of age alone, middle-aged women did not show significant differences from the other two age groups on the variables studied. When role was examined, it was found that the career women (single and married) showed more internal locus of control than did students and homemakers. Within that career group, single career women scored highest on need for autonomy and married career women scored lowest. Although the differences were not large, interaction effects (between age and role) revealed that middle-aged career women, both married and single, had higher internal locus of control and less of the characteristics traditionally associated with femininity than the other groups. Student groups (both young and middle-aged) scored as more independent and less stereotypically feminine than did their peers in other role groups. Of course, no conclusion about cause can be drawn from a cross-sectional study such as this. For instance, we do not know if personality determines role choice or vice versa, but we do know that middle-aged women in certain role groups exhibit some of the signs we have listed as indicators of autonomy. Until longitudinal studies can provide more definitive answers, the authors suggest that some aspects of personality (e.g., locus of control) appear to be related to life roles (e.g., employment, marital status) but not to age, while other characteristics, such as autonomy and femininity, show a complex relationship to both age and role variables.

Self-Esteem, Personal Control, and Well-Being

Research is generally limited to samples of middle-class European American women. Wishing to expand on the information about the influence of roles on the lives of women, Coleman, Antonucci, Adelmann, and Crohan (1987) studied 451 middle-aged (40–64) African American women and 215 older (65–101) African American women. The data was taken from the *National Survey of Black Americans*. The sample was interviewed from 1979 to 1980. Several criteria were used for sample selection, for example, geographical area of residence, individual dwelling occupant, high and low density areas, and income and educational levels. The researchers were satisfied that the data analyzed in this investigation fairly represented the experiences of middle-aged and older African American women. Among the dependent variables studied of interest to us here were self-esteem and perceived personal control. The self-esteem scale consisted of (sometimes adapted) items from the *Rosenberg Self-Esteem Scale*. Perceived control was measured by responses to one item inquiring about the ability to run one's own life. Variables such as income and level of education served as control variables. The roles studied were parental, marital, and occupational. Respondents were categorized on marital status as either married or unmarried (single, divorced, or widowed); on parental status as having or not having living children (not necessarily living at home); and on occupational status as having paid employment outside the home for 20 or more hours per week.

Coleman et al. found that few African American women enact all three roles simultaneously. The majority of the middle-aged women filled one or two of the roles studied (older women one or none). Most of the middle-aged women were employed. Among the middle-aged women, 26% were single working parents, 27% were single non-working parents, 19% were married working parents, and 16% were non-working married parents (homemakers). A multivariate analysis produced the following significant findings for middle-aged African American women: high-income working women had high self-esteem, while educated women had high perceived control. Thus, middle-aged African American women who worked and had high incomes and levels of education enjoyed high self-esteem and high perceived control in their lives, and reported higher levels of psychological well-being.

In general, the research evidence suggests the importance of multiple-role enactment for the manifestation of autonomy in middle-aged African American women. On the whole, such findings fit with general expectations from various theoretical views. In Jung's terms, the enactment of varied roles helps prevent the too-early equation of ego with a particular persona, thus enabling a woman to achieve autonomy. For Erikson, the enactment of many roles may aid in conflict resolution as well as provide the arena for manifesting generativity and creativity. Bandura links the development of self-efficacy with the opportunity to engage in varied (implicit and explicit) problem-solving experiences, much like the experiences involved in multiple-role enactment. Rotter's work would lead us to expect that varied experiences (e.g., varied roles) lead to a sense of being in control of one's life. Surely, how well one performs one's roles and other qualitative aspects of role behavior must have an important effect on the enhancement of the self. It is such speculation and claims about the salubrious effects of multiple roles that led Helson et al. (1990) to examine both the number and quality of roles.

The Quality of Roles

Different Roles, Different Gains

Using longitudinal data, Helson et al. (1990) found that the number of roles (partner, parent, worker) was not related to autonomy, individuality, and complexity as expected. Instead, they found that particular roles were associated with corresponding advantages.

The authors noted two weaknesses in most of the existing research. First, the research contained only a paucity of information about personality characteristics; in other words, did multiple role enactment result in women feeling more independent, confident, or individualistic than women with fewer roles? Second, it lacked longitudinal data since cross-sectional data cannot tell us whether or not particular personality characteristics lead women to take on multiple roles.

A representative two-thirds of the senior class (total N = 140) at Mills College, a prestigious private college on the West Coast, was studied in 1958 and again in 1960. Personality characteristics and plans for the future were assessed, and the women were between 42 and 45 years of age. Personality data used in this study is from the *California Personality Inventory* (CPI) assessed at ages 21 and 43; role data is from age 43. At age 43 personality data for 106 women was available and role data was available from all participants (N = 110). Where possible, antecedent data were used for these 110 women.

Role variables studied by these researchers included the number of roles and the quality of the roles. The possible roles were

1. Partner: if in a marriage or marriage-like relationship
2. Parents: having a child or stepchild in the household
3. Paid workers: if pay was received for more than 20% of the time during the previous year

Two measures of role quality were

1. Marital satisfaction: assessed on a five point scale, it is the sum of ratings of seven aspects of the relationship. The current or most recent relationship that had lasted for more than 5 years was scored
2. Status level: in the work force, rated on a seven point scale to reveal the amount of autonomy, responsibility, training, and talent required for the paid work

Measures of role quality and number of roles were not significantly correlated with each other, allowing independent assessment of their effects. Other measures, although very interesting, are not directly related to our current concerns. They included: psychological health, physical health, energy, and role strain.

Analysis of variance, specific comparisons, and correlation analyses were applied to the data. Our focus is on findings about these middle-aged women with regard to personality characteristics. This study found that the number of roles per se and the personality characteristics associated with autonomy were not significantly related. Examination of differences within the two role groups on measures of personality revealed that working mothers (N = 11) scored higher than the other two role groups on independence and self-acceptance. When the quality of roles was examined with regard to personality measures, significant relationships were found. Marital satisfaction was significantly related to respect for social rules, outgoing attitudes, desire to make a good impression, firm values, and individualism. Status level at work showed a significant relationship to achievement, independence, dominance, self-acceptance, responsibility, and several more aspects that were studied. Next, the relationships found were examined after taking antecedent individual differences into account. Personality variables at age 21 (e.g., social energy, tolerance, intellectual efficiency, and independence) were significantly good predictors of the number of roles a woman would undertake. The authors concluded that specific roles and role combinations showed the advantages predicted for them: independence for women who worked, contentment for women with partners, roots and generativity for women with children. As Helson et al. (1990, p. 84) observed

> *Working brings independence, marriage brings intimacy, having children brings a sense of roots and generativity, and the combination of these buffers the woman against unhappiness in any one of these areas, increases her control over her life, increases self-esteem, and adds facets to the self.*

Since categorization into the role groups included women with different life histories (e.g., women who had been married or remarried for one year were in the same group as those married for 20 years), the researchers concluded that it would not be informative to study the influence of antecedent individual personality differences on self-selection into roles nor the long-term effects of roles. Both measures of role quality were associated with achievement via independence (CPI), and status level in work was associated with indexes of autonomy, individuality, and complexity.

Complexity of Personal Identity

Taking issue with developmental models based on male experience, Hornstein (1986) sees middle age as a more central time for women to structure identity than the adolescent period suggested by Erikson. She cites evidence from a number of studies showing that middle-aged women have already made significant commitments to a number of roles. She suggests that the process of structuring one's identity and autonomy for middle-aged adults may well be different than is the case for adolescents who have yet to make such commitments. Hornstein believes we need a dynamic model of identity that incorporates multiple role commitments. She uses a concept termed "multiple worlds." Very briefly, the idea is that individuals are committed to a number of "experiential worlds" (e.g., work, family, community) and they organize their lives in terms of those commitments. The degree of involvement in any one "world" varies with the centrality of that world and the changing relations among "worlds." Therefore, middle-aged women are not a homogeneous group. Identity is derived from participation in diverse worlds (roles) of varying centrality and relatedness.

Hornstein chose to study the patterns of involvement in employment because "For many women, employment seems to offer an important source of self-esteem and autonomy, as well as opportunities for creativity and competence" (p. 553). Using longitudinal data from the work of Helson et al. (1990), Hornstein selected 96 women who had completed a sufficient number of questions in the 1981–82 assessment, allowing her to categorize their responses in terms of their level of involvement in employment from the time they graduated from college until their mid-40s. She cautioned that a high level of involvement should not be equated with high status in the work setting. The three categories of level of involvement in employment were

- *Group 1* (N = 44): Continuous Low Involvement—women who engaged in paid employment after marriage or after having children in their 20s, women who worked sporadically at part-time jobs, or women who worked continuously on a part-time or volunteer basis.
- *Group 2* (N = 20): Shift from Low to High Involvement—women who shifted to greater involvement in employment after a number of years of raising children or working in low-level or volunteer jobs.
- *Group 3* (N = 32): Continuous High Involvement—women who maintained a pattern of continuous, full-time paid work in a field studied in college or chosen soon afterward.

Participants were asked to rate their perceived level of involvement in each of several roles (worker, mother, wife, etc.) on a five point scale (as opposed to listing activities in which they engaged. The investigator was interested in psychological commitment, and also wanted to see if a woman's perceived degree of commitment in one role varied as a function of her perceived level of involvement in other roles). The participants plotted their ratings on graphs spanning ages 20–50 in 5 year intervals. This data allowed the experimenter to discern variations in patterns of commitment. The women were asked also to rate how they felt about their lives on a set of nine self-descriptive phrases. They rated themselves at two age points, retrospectively for their early 30s and currently for their early 40s. In addition, each woman indicated the degree to which a particular phrase was descriptive of her (e.g., very, somewhat, not at all) for each of the two age periods. The nine descriptive phrases rated were

1. "a sense of being my own person"
2. "feeling powerful"
3. "feeling confident"
4. "searching for a sense of who I am"
5. "worried about the children"
6. "having a wider perspective"
7. "looking old"
8. "feeling needed by people"
9. "rebelling against constriction"

The data were analyzed by analysis of variance with the following results.

- *Group 1* showed a pattern of high involvement in the mother role, steady and high involvement in the wife role, increasing involvement in the volunteer role, and low involvement in the work role. Both the decrease in the mother role and the increase in involvement in the volunteer role were statistically significant. *Group 1* had two main worlds: mother and wife. Ratings on the descriptive phrases showed that this group felt needed by others, felt confident, and had a sense of being their own person. By age 40 they reported feeling even more confident.

- *Group 2* showed a high but decreasing involvement in the roles of mother (significant) and wife, an increase then a striking decrease in involvement in the volunteer role, paralleled by the inverse (low then high; statistically significant) pattern of involvement in the work role. Hornstein interpreted the changes in this group's pattern of commitment in later years as a clear demonstration that significant reorganization of one's identity can occur in middle age. Descriptive phrases for this group included "worried about the children;" the lowest ratings on "feeling confident" and on "feeling powerful"; the lowest ratings on "sense of being my own person"; and the highest ratings on "searching for who I am." By age 40 they rated themselves as having gained a wider perspective and more of a sense of being one's own person.
- *Group 3* showed a consistently high level of involvement in the roles of mother, wife, worker, and an increased level of involvement in the volunteer role. In Hornstein's view, these women were able to integrate multiple worlds into their life structure without having to remove an existing world (role) in order to include a new one. Ratings on the descriptive phrases showed they possessed a clear sense of who they were and a broad perspective on their lives, plus a tendency to rebel against constriction (perhaps, the author suggests, because at that time such involvement in work roles was not wholly accepted by society). By their 40s, this group chose the same descriptive phrases but increased their ratings of confidence, sense of being their own person, and added sense of "feeling needed by others."

In general, women with low, medium, and high levels of commitment to employment reached middle age with feelings of confidence, power, and a sense of autonomy. Contrary to stereotypes, women with continued low levels of commitment to employment (e.g., homemakers in other studies) developed feelings of efficacy; women with continued high levels of commitment to employment reveal the capacity for involvement in others—"feeling needed." For the women in this study, it appears that middle age is a dynamic time, as postulated by Hornstein who stressed the need for models of identity that can do justice to the complexity of women's lives.

Gender Identity

Among the derivations from theory is the expectation that middle-aged women would move toward a more androgynous self-concept. Neugarten (1973) and Gutmann (1985) have reported that women incorporate more traditionally masculine characteristics (e.g., become more aggressive and domineering) in their self-concept at middle age. Levinson (1978) views middle age as the time when the integration of masculine and feminine characteristics takes place. Rossi (1980) sees middle age as a period of transition for women from relational concerns (family, kinships, friends) to becoming more independent, assertive, and work-oriented. Stroud (1981) suggests that career-committed women achieve personality organizations that integrate masculine and feminine traits.

Convergence

In this context, the notion of convergence requires that a significant increase in one sort of concept (e.g., masculinity) be accompanied by a significant decrease in some other concept (e.g., femininity). To test the notion that convergence in gender identity parallels increasing age, Puglisi (1983) studied three age groups of adults (male and female): young (17–29), middle-aged (30–59), and older (60–85). There were 21 males and 41 females in each group. The participants were asked to rate themselves on the *Bem Sex Role Inventory* (BSRI) for ages 20, 45, and 70. It was thought that using a prospective and retrospective method would reveal more information on the development of sex-role concepts in adulthood. In an earlier study, using cross-sectional data, no age-related convergence in sex roles was found, although middle-aged women did score higher on masculinity concepts than did the other groups.

Similarly, in this later study, the results of the multivariate analysis of variance failed to find evidence of sex-role convergence related to age. However, again it was found that middle-aged women showed an increased score on masculinity (significant) and a decreased score on femininity (non-significant). Because of the latter non-significant decrease in femininity and the lack of sustained masculinity concepts in older age, Puglisi concluded that the convergence hypothesis was not supported. However, research using common measures of gender identity suggests that it is an increase in masculinity (for women) that accounts for androgyny. The middle-aged women in this study showed such an increase. Moreover, the idea that any trait must be decreased or replaced to make room for another is viewed as faulty. Hornstein emphasized that women are capable of integrating several traits into the sense of self without the necessity of eliminating some in order to make room for others.

Ego Mastery

For many women the parental role is paramount in their self-concept and the loss of that role in middle age is expected to show consequences. Although for women this phenomenon has been referred to in pejorative terms such as the empty nest "syndrome," numerous researchers have reported that, in fact, many women look forward to their release from the parent role as an opportunity to develop other, often neglected, aspects of the self (e.g., Neugarten, 1976). Among the aspects of the self that heretofore have been suppressed are those associated with masculinity. Reflecting on his numerous cross-cultural studies, Gutmann (1985) hypothesized that middle-aged women would show a more active ego mastery style, usually associated with masculinity, than they previously used in the parenting role.

Cooper and Gutmann (1987) tested that hypothesis by comparing the gender identity and ego mastery styles of two groups of women of the same age: those actively parenting and those no longer actively parenting. In all, 50 women between the ages of 43 and 51 were studied, with 25 in each group. The post-parenting group (called post-empty nest in this study) was defined as those women who had no children under 19 and whose adult children resided away from the parental home and were financially independent. In an attempt to control for the effects of the work role, the investigators studied only women then employed as teachers. The two groups of women were similar in marital status (i.e., the number of women married, divorced, or widowed) but varied in the number and in the ages of their children. Previous employment was not assessed. There was no significant difference between the two groups in years of continuous current employment and all women worked during the child-rearing years.

This study assessed gender identity using the *PRF ANDRO* scale based on Murray's needs theory. It categorized gender identity as masculine, feminine, androgynous, or undifferentiated. Also, a self-report measure of gender identity was obtained using a specially designed Gender Identity Questionnaire. The women's self-descriptions in terms of traditionally masculine or feminine traits were used to assign them to the gender-identity categories. The study measured ego mastery style on five *Thematic Apperception Test* (TAT) cards based on a scoring system developed by Gutmann, and reported appropriate reliability and validity measures. The ego mastery categories were active mastery, active bimodal mastery, passive bimodal mastery, and passive mastery. Trained, independent raters scored the TAT responses.

Chi-square analysis revealed no significant relationship between parental status and gender identity as measured on the *PRF ANDRO* scale. Analysis of the self-descriptions revealed that post-empty nest women were significantly more likely to see themselves as self-confident, independent, assertive, capable of solving problems, and creative; they perceived themselves as significantly more competitive than did the pre-empty nest group. Chi-square analysis of scores on ego mastery style showed a significant relationship to parental status, with post-empty nest women scoring in the active or active bimodal mastery style categories. The investigators concluded that overall, post-empty nest women show the changes expected to occur in theory when the parental role changes: they are more free to express masculine traits of assertion, aggression, and executive capacity. In a conclusion reminiscent of Hornstein's view, they stated "Because the post-empty nest women still perceived themselves as nurturant, it appears that emerging masculine characteristics would be added to existing feminine characteristics rather than replacing them" (p. 352).

MENTAL HEALTH

The psychological well-being of middle-aged women is an important factor, albeit indirectly, in our discussion of autonomy. Both comprehensive and "mini" theories of personality state or imply that appropriate adult development hinges on good (or at least adequate) mental health at earlier stages. The discussion of the research literature about autonomy or one of its "vital signs" has hinted at the underlying importance of mental health. Many of the studies that provided us with evidence of autonomy in middle-aged women also frequently included measures of well-being. Sometimes these were commented on more explicitly. Possibly, much of the research reviewed here was undertaken to counter the pervasive view that middle-aged women are depressed, and not in control of their lives. I will digress briefly to give an overview of the work and thinking regarding adult women's mental health.

Biological and Psychosocial Changes

A common attitude is that poor mental health, especially depression, is to be expected in middle-aged women because of biological changes (Pillay, 1988). Such studies give the false impression that women more than men are found in mental health facilities (Amaro & Russo, 1987). Events such as menopause and the departure of children from the home are interpreted as the so-called empty nest syndrome—a view belied by the findings discussed. In a review essay, Raup and Myers (1989) called it a myth. Black and Hill (1984) suggest that studies reporting mental illness in middle age focus on women who have been hospitalized for mental illness, and that studies of non-hospitalized women report higher levels of satisfaction and happiness during the empty nest period than in other periods of life. Women who are better educated and employed or who return to employment fare quite well on mental health and self-esteem (Powell, 1977).

Research findings strongly suggest that women who experience a crisis during middle age are those who equate their identity with reproductive roles. When the role is gone the woman is gone. We have seen that this is not the case for many women; instead the post-parental period is often a positive time for middle-aged women. Freedom from child-rearing allows time for self-expansion, relationship growth, and leisure. Women in the post-parental period often have experienced a transition from a nurturing, other-oriented view of self to a more traditionally masculine self-oriented view. Women during this period still view themselves as nurturing, but with the added dimension of masculine gender identity. That is, they view themselves as having characteristics usually associated with males. They also score higher in tests of active ego mastery (active achievement) than do younger women.

Barnett and Baruch (1978) criticized most studies of middle-aged women because they focus on the reproductive role without considering other factors important in women's lives. Many researchers have established the importance of socioeconomic status, education, life stressors, menopause, labor force participation, family responsibilities, and husband's attitude toward the wife's working as some of the other factors important in women's lives. In general, middle-aged women who are well educated, relatively affluent, in intact marriages, have at least one child, and who are employed for pay and enjoy the support of their husbands in that employment activity, are reported to be happy and well-adjusted.

Houser, Berkman, and Beckman (1984) found that childless women reported more rewards or advantages and fewer costs or disadvantages from being childless than did women who were parents. The point is, each group of middle-aged women saw certain advantages to their status. This fits with other findings and speculations that coping strategies, whether life-long or newly minted, are weighty determinants of successful coping at middle age, whether with empty nests, no nests, or re-feathered nests. In short, there is no consistent pattern of panic, depression, neurosis, or psychosis that accompanies marital status, biological changes (e.g., menopause), and social changes (e.g., absent children) in the lives of middle-aged women. Among higher-status (middle-class, educated) women, middle-aged women in general and those who participate in the work force in particular demonstrate instrumentality, autonomy, assertiveness, higher self-esteem, a feeling of control over their lives, self-efficacy, generativity, and good mental and physical health (research on the latter was not reviewed here).

Middle Age as "Prime Time"

Mitchell and Helson (1990) explored the hypothesis that middle-aged women exhibit autonomy, enjoy secure relationships, are androgynous, and have good health. They studied women in their early 50s to determine if that period can be designated as the prime of life. The early 50s was selected as a good candidate for "prime time" because it encompasses an early or middle post-parental period. Despite popular negative descriptions of that time of life (e.g., crisis, depression, and poor mental and physical health as a result of physiological and role changes) as being the worst time for women, many scholars have found that, on the contrary, women look forward to physiological and family changes so that their energies can be directed to other activities and to the enhancement of self. This more positive view prompted the current study.

Both cross-sectional and longitudinal data for two samples of women were provided by the data obtained in the Mitchell and Helson (1990) study of women at Mills College (previously described). The cross-sectional sample was comprised of 700 women between young adulthood and old age, 60 of whom were in their early 50s. The longitudinal sample comprised 118 women studied in their early 40s and early 50s. Similarities and differences between the samples were examined so that findings could be placed in context. For example, at the time of the study in 1983, very few of the women in their early 50s said that when they were undergraduates they had expected to go on to graduate work; differences in the degree of participation in work were also noted. Description and discussion of the findings of each (cross-sectional and longitudinal) sample follows.

The Cross-Sectional Sample

A large mailing was made in 1983 to potential participants, and alumnae returned 700 questionnaires. The investigators were satisfied, on the basis of demographic information provided, that these women were generally representative of college educated women over the last 60 years. The 60 women in the "prime time" groups (average age 51 in 1983) were compared with the other groups: youngest, oldest, and two middle-aged groups—early middle age (41–46) and late middle age (56–61). Measures from the questionnaire included quality of life (first rate, good, poor, bad); conditions of life (financial security, health, etc.); importance of and satisfaction with seven areas of life rated on a 5 point scale; and concerns and interests including items dealing with people, problems, and feelings rated on a 3 point scale.

Analyses included chi-square analysis of the distribution of ratings and analysis of variance comparisons of characteristics of the prime group with other groups. Results of the chi-square analysis showed that significantly more "prime time" women rated their lives as "first rate" than did the youngest or the oldest groups and than did all the younger and older groups in the sample. Differences in ratings among the middle-aged groups were not significant but were in the expected direction. Therefore, all the other aspects of life were examined for differences among the middle-aged groups. The "prime time" middle-aged group showed more dramatic changes in household composition (for example, the nest became empty), slightly higher health ratings than the younger middle-aged group and significantly higher than the older middle-aged group, with fewer women working for pay, and enjoying more financial security than either of the other groups. There were no differences in how time was allotted between the groups, but there was greater concern for parents in the "prime time" than in the younger middle-aged group, no differences in marital satisfaction, and less concern with loneliness and with ethical or spiritual issues. Both "prime time" and older middle-aged women scored higher on interest in politics, social issues, the importance of and satisfaction in friendships, and joy in living. Ratings of the quality of life for the "prime time" group were significantly related to living alone with a partner, health, financial comfort, interest in sex, satisfaction in most areas of life. Quality of life was negatively related to a concern with loneliness.

The Longitudinal Sample

Data was used from the responses of 118 participants at ages 43 (in 1981) and 52 (in 1989). Personality inventory data were available also for 104 of the participants at age 52. The same measures were used with this sample as with the cross-sectional sample (e.g., quality of life, sense of well-being, conditions of life, status level of work, satisfactions and dissatisfactions, feelings about life). The question asking women to rate their quality of life as either first rate, good, fair, or not so good was not asked at age 43. Therefore, assessment of well-being at age 43 was based on scores from the *California Psychological Inventory* (CPI). Analyses included chi-squares, *t*-tests for repeated measures, correlations, and a hierarchical multiple regression analysis to take into account antecedent individual differences.

At age 52, 47% of the women rated their lives as first rate and 36% as good. The percentages are similar to those found for the cross-sectional group. Changes from age 43–52 showed dramatic change in household composition, higher ratings on health, increased responsibility for parents, no significant change in level of participation in work (which was lower than the cross-sectional group, as previously mentioned), an increase in income, no change in time allocations, and no change in marital satisfaction. Almost all women said they had developed more control over their lives, while a majority had increased their present-oriented contentment along with reductions in emotion and worry.

Quality of life ratings were significantly correlated with living with a partner, being an empty nest parent, health, satisfaction and status level in work, marital satisfaction, feeling secure and committed, intimacy, and optimism for the future. When the influence of subjective well-being at age 43 was taken into account, the relationships increased significantly. Only the strong influences of ratings on health and living with a partner were not changed by well-being levels at age 43.

Mitchell and Helson (1990) explain "prime time" of life as coming late enough in life to permit service to society and a sense of achievement. They chose the early post-parental period as a likely candidate for the prime of life because of the changes that occur at that time and the evidence that women gain in freedom, power, or status. They sought to find evidence that the "androgyny of later life" (Gutmann, 1987) was put to effective use. They found that both prime groups were characterized by engagement in the present, with little or no negative affect or need for change. In addition, the longitudinal group emphasized their increased sense of autonomy. These findings are seen by Mitchell and Helson as representing control over emotions and feelings of control over personal life—two aspects of control that are thought to be significant in the prediction of quality of life. They found, too, that the importance of intimacy in the lives of these women was not displaced or reduced by the growth in autonomy, suggesting a view of androgyny that we have come to characterize as adding or blending new self-concepts but not at the expense of already held self-concepts. The sustained interest in family, friends, community, care of parents, care of self, and in responsible careers can be seen as the mature care that Erikson associated with generativity. These findings support the view that in the specific life span of women, early middle age is a "prime time"—"…a time when various forces converge to support them—the formerly subordinate and adapting sex—in a sense of entitlement and self-efficacy in the real world. It is an opportunity for autonomy, androgyny, and generativity…" (Mitchell & Helson, 1990, p. 468).

The Story of Women's Development

In a thoughtful and compelling essay, "Finished at 40," Mary Gergen (1990) compared developmental theory to a regressive narrative in which the valuation of events (for women) steadily decreases. The woman's story, argues Gergen, is told with a negative downhill trajectory after a climactic high in early adulthood. Marriage and childbearing are the events that mark and define that achievement. After that, from age 40 on, a woman's life is basically downhill, according to this narrative. That attitude, Gergen said, is based on developmental theory biased by the "ideology of power," a patriarchal view of women as reproducers.

Women Are Rewriting Their Story

Scant attention has been given to how middle-aged women themselves account for times marked by stress and problems. Helson (1992) studied middle-aged women's descriptions of their difficult times and what aspects of life affected those difficult times. She saw a need for an empirical study in this area since women's development was typically portrayed in terms of an awakening to insurmountable limitations that sometimes culminated in madness or suicide. She acknowledged the large body of theoretical work calling for new perspectives on female development and the research aimed at addressing this need.

Her study is based on data from the Mills Longitudinal Study, in which women filled out questionnaires and personality inventories when they were seniors in college (in 1958 or 1960), again 4 or 5 years after graduation (in 1963–64), and subsequently in 1981 and 1989 when they were in their early 40s and early 50s, respectively. At the age of 52 most of the women were in stable relationships, had children, and worked at least part time in paid employment. The major variables in the current study were age at the difficult times, motherhood, and the self system. The first two variables are self-explanatory (i.e., the age that difficulties occurred and whether or not the woman was a mother). The self system is based on Erikson's view of ego-identity status. Four identity statuses were identified and assessed using the *California Adult Q Deck* (CAQ). Each identity status is described as follows.

1. Achieved: values own independence; clear, consistent personality; ethically consistent behavior; warm, compassionate; productive; possesses insight into own behavior
2. In moratorium: values own independence; philosophically concerned; anxious; rebellious and nonconforming; introspective; verbally fluent
3. Foreclosed: sex-appropriate behavior; satisfied with self; conventional; moralistic; guided by conservative values; represses conflicts; overcontrols impulses; self-defensive
4. Diffuse: unpredictable; avoids close relationships; brittle ego-defense system; reluctant to act; lacks personal meaning; withdraws from frustration (p. 335)

Trained raters (see Wink, 1991) sorted the Q cards for 105 women at age 43 on the basis of their responses to an open-ended questionnaire. Individual Q sorts were correlated with the Q sort for each ego-identity prototype, with the following results: 12 diffuse, 23 foreclosed, 24 in moratorium, and 46 achieved. The women in their early 50s were asked to respond to open-ended questions about the occurrence of difficult times. This technique presented problems (e.g., selective memory, recency effects, privacy concerns, etc.). Ninety-three women did write answers, five of whom reported no difficult times. The analysis is based on the remaining 88 participants. Scores on the CPI at ages 43 and 52 were available at each of the four times of testing. In addition, the sample rated a set of feelings about life on a 3 point scale.

Chi-square analysis revealed a non-significant trend: the 30s were generally bland, while the 40s were a time of turmoil. Women with children identified problems at a significantly earlier age (before 36) than women with no children (after 36). The two less adequate ego identities (diffuse and foreclosed) were combined as were the two more adequate ego identities (achieved and in moratorium). A significant difference between the two groups showed that women with more adequate self systems ascribed difficult times to the middle period (ages 36–46) whereas women with less adequate self systems reported their problems at early or late periods.

Raters were trained to use a coding system developed by Helson to detect themes of difficult times. Themes about an unhappy self came early, closely followed by themes of a bad partner (21–26); themes about independent identity came in two middle-aged periods (27–36, 36–46) with themes of abandonment and put-downs coming in the latter middle-aged period (36–46); themes of overload and unhappiness in bad relationships emerged in the last period (47–52). Women with no children, mainly single, wrote no bad partner stories but did write about put-downs in the work setting. Women with diffuse identities produced themes of unhappy selves in bad relationships; those with foreclosed identities wrote stories with bad partner and overload themes; those with in moratorium and achieved identities mostly gave stories coded as independent identity.

Changes in CPI measures showed women with feelings of vulnerability and self-criticism between ages 21–27, becoming more confident and independent from 27–43, and even more confident and independent between 43–52. A significant majority of women changed in the same direction. This analysis and the several prior analyses show that the early 40s was more difficult for these women than the early 50s. The feelings about life responses and the scores from the inventory measures show the 40s as a time of identity turmoil, gender-role conflict, a search for a sense of self-identity, and worry over unfulfilled potential. Helson interprets this combination of turmoil and confidence as suggesting that the search for independent identity arises as feelings of vulnerability lessen (about age 30); and the continued growth of confidence and independence combined with a sense of potential to be actualized leads to conflict with the partner and to the many difficult times reported in the next period (36–46). It appears that middle-aged women change to correct an illogical inequality between the self and other and to focus on issues of power. The women in the Mills study, generally able to take charge of their lives, considered middle age as the critical time for the affirmation of independence. Helson views this as evidence of a modest revision in the life story of many women.

POWER

The emergence of autonomy at middle age for women is reflected in growths in self-esteem, confidence, individualism, self-efficacy, independence, and a willingness to be unconventional and to incorporate traditionally masculine characteristics in the self system. Many middle-aged women are beginning to rewrite their life stories and to redress the inequalities between self and other. There appears to be a shift in interpersonal power for the middle-aged woman—a shift towards equality with men.

Todd, Friedman, and Kariuki (1990) studied participants drawn from urban groups: European Americans, African Americans, and two groups of Kenyans. The age range was 21 to 60. Each of the four groups included 15 women age 35 or younger and 15 women age 45 or older. The European Americans were middle-class students at an urban university. The African Americans came from working-class and lower-class neighborhoods near the university. The Kenyans, all of African descent, included both a middle-class group of women and a lower-class group of women.

The researchers used card 4 from the TAT to collect stories from the United States sample, and an adapted version was used to collect stories from the Kenyan sample. Trained raters scored the stories on several dimensions of interpersonal power on a five point scale. The dimensions scored were tone of the story (negative or positive), theme of the story (rejection, helping, etc.), character of the female (weak, powerful, etc.), success of the female, and influence strategies used by the female (reasoning, hinting, etc.). Similar ratings were made for the male participants in the study. The researchers reported satisfaction with the reliability of the ratings.

High inter-correlations among the power scales led the investigators to average the ratings for an average overall power score that served as the dependent variable in an analysis of variance. Significant effects for age, strategies, and their interaction were reported: stories by women of higher status showed greater power than those of lower-status; stories by older women showed greater power than stories by younger women; the interaction showed a shift in power with age for European Americans but not for African Americans, and for middle-class but not for lower-class Kenyan women.

This cross-sectional study does not permit the conclusion that increased age per se brings increased power. However, other evidence we have examined suggests that, though not universal, the increase in autonomy (and related concepts) does result in a shift in power, and it is a developmental phenomenon for many women. The changes that have been reported are associated with a post-parental freedom from constraint, financial security, and higher-than-average educational levels. The study by Todd et al. (1990), along with other studies (Brown & Kerns, 1985), suggests that this is a phenomenon not restricted to affluent women in the United States, although it might be restricted to higher-status women. In her preface to a special issue on women and power in *The Psychology of Women Quarterly,* Worell (1992, p. 379) observed "...gender and power form an intersect in which effects usually attributed to gender may better be explained by status differentials."

An increased attention to gender and power led Stewart and Chester (1982) to review several decades of work. They found that although power was stereotypically assigned to men, both men and women are interested in power and are likely to find different expressions of their interest. Sagrestano (1992a) reviewed the research on the effects of gender and power on the strategies chosen by men and women in interpersonal relationships. She found that people with power use strategies typically associated with men (for example, being direct in giving orders) whereas those without power choose strategies typically associated with women (for example, suggesting rather than directing). The stereotypes about gender differences, she conjectured, may reflect real power differences that exist in our society.

Sagrestano (1992b) examined the relationship between gender and status on the choice of strategy employed. She aimed to disentangle the effects of gender and power by studying them together and varying the amount of power a person has. Since her participants in the study were all undergraduates (not middle-aged women), the details of the study are not discussed here. She found that it is the amount of power an individual has (not gender) that underlies the selection of strategies used to influence others. When women are in a position of power, they use strategies typically associated with men in positions of power (for example, being more direct). We have noted that as middle-aged women grow in status, gender differences decrease and interpersonal power shifts. Sagrestano suggested that college students may reflect the changing trends in women's roles.

The growing consensus that middle age provides an opportunity for a shift in interpersonal power and the possibility that the phenomenon influences younger women's expression of power forms a picture that fits closely with Miller's (1976, p. 119) remarkable redefinition of power as "feeling effective and free along with feeling intense connections with others." In that redefinition she replaced the conventional (male) dualism of dependence/independence with a potent form of interdependence as the definition of power. A redefinition of power liberates it from the narrow constraints of having control over others to the wider arena of being able to get things done and to make changes. The latter sense of the meaning of power was underscored in the Astin and Leland work described early in this chapter. Those authors included the empowerment of others in their definition of power. The empowerment of others encompasses an aspect of generativity—to mentor others and to help others achieve. It is the nurturing (a feminine characteristic) of power.

It appears that middle-aged women shatter the conventional link between gender and strategies of influence; they dare not only to express power in typically masculine ways, but also to integrate it with relational concerns seen as typically feminine. Surely this achievement resembles the individuation and integration that Jung associated with mature, healthy adults; surely it resembles what Erikson meant by generativity at middle age; and surely it can be seen as an integration of agency and communion. We can thus claim that the evidence for the development of autonomy in (a specific sample of) middle-aged women is strong.

A Recent Survey

With the help of my students, I undertook to survey middle-aged women on the variables discussed in the research literature to see if a current (Spring, 1994) study revealed similar findings. Only middle-aged women (between the ages of 40 and the mid-60s) were studied. The questionnaire for this survey was based on the same areas of study reported in the literature: role enactment, satisfaction with home and/or work, self-esteem, health, masculinity concepts in the self-concept, attitude toward menopause and toward the absence of children from the home, and perceived feeling of being in control of one's life.

Our sample was by no means representative of middle-aged women and it was certainly not a random sample. Instead, I asked several students of varied ethnic backgrounds to solicit the cooperation of their mothers and their mother's friends as participants in our survey. In addition, I contacted friends and relatives (who, in turn, contacted other friends) in two other states. As a result, our participants were of varied ethnic backgrounds (although the majority of them were European Americans) from the upper peninsula of Michigan, central Indiana, and the San Francisco and East Bay area in northern California. Of the 85 questionnaires that were distributed, 75 were returned. One respondent failed to make any ratings, so that questionnaire was omitted, leaving a total of 74 participants between the ages of 40 and the mid-60s. There were 33 women in the 40s age group, 29 in the 50s age group, and 12 in the 60s age group.

A pilot study was conducted to refine the questionnaire. The resulting questionnaire comprised the usual requests for demographic information, including

- age
- marital status (married, divorced, remarried, never married, or widowed, and subsequently coded as partnered, unpartnered, and widowed)
- employment status (defined as working outside the home for pay, and including not employed, employed part-time, employed full-time, retired)
- salary
- level of education (high school, college, advanced degree)
- number of children (including each child's sex and age and which children, if any, lived at home)

In addition, the participants were asked to rate themselves (using a five point scale where 1 = lowest or very bad, and 5 = highest or excellent) on several variables

- satisfaction with home life
- satisfaction with presence or absence of children in the home
- satisfaction with work
- satisfaction with one's life on the whole
- evaluation of one's own personal health
- attitude toward menopause
- attitude toward meeting new challenges

Open-ended questions included

- What was your most rewarding time of life?
- What was the worst time of life?
- How do you account for your successes?
- How do you account for your failures?
- If you had it to do over, what would you change?
- What would you keep?

Participants were also requested to make evaluations about the quality of their lives at their current age and other ages (their 20s, 30s, 40s, and 50s), thus inviting retrospective and prospective (depending on respondent's age) as well as current assessments.

Finally, the participants were asked to respond to questions from standardized psychological tests: *Manifest Anxiety Scale* (MAS; Taylor, 1953), *Self-Esteem* (Rosenberg, 1965), *Locus of Control* (Rotter, 1966), and the *Personal Attributes Questionnaire* (PAQ; Spence, Helmretch, & Stapp, 1974; adapted by Broverman, Broverman, Clarkson, Rosenkrantz, & Vogel, 1974, for the assessment of three variables: instrumental, expressive, and sex-stereotyped).

The Participants

The majority (70%) of all the women were partnered as was the majority of women in each age group. Women in their 60s differed significantly from the other two age groups in that they were either partnered (75%) or widowed (25%); in other words, none of them were otherwise unpartnered. The majority of all women (73%) were educated beyond high school, and that was true for the educational level in each age group as well; the 60s age group had the highest proportion of women with college or higher education. The majority of all the women (53%) were employed full-time, and that also characterized the women in their 40s and 50s but not their 60s—a lower proportion of them worked full time. Employment status was affected by marital status in that a (not significant) higher proportion of unpartnered or widowed women worked full-time than did women who were currently partnered. Women with high-school educations and those with college or advanced degrees were equally represented in the full-time work force. A large majority of the women (84%) had children but women in their 60s had larger families than did the other two age groups. Compared to the other age groups, a larger proportion (60%) of women in their 40s had children living at home.

The Ratings

The majority of women (71%) in all age groups rated their lives as good or very good (the two higher ratings); the 60s group had more high ratings than did the other two groups. The majority (71%) rated their satisfaction with the status of the "nest" as very high. Both the 60s and the 50s age groups had higher ratings than the 40s group who had the highest proportion of children living at home. Only 48% of all the women rated satisfaction with work as good or very good, with the 50s age group giving higher ratings to work than did the other groups. As might be expected, attitudes toward menopause varied by age: women in their 40s were split between a relatively negative and a fairly positive anticipation of menopause; the majority of women in their 50s were very positive about menopause, with a minority reporting negative feelings. The overwhelming majority of women in their 60s (80%) were very positive about menopause and the other 20% were neutral; none of them reported any negative attitudes toward menopause. The majority of women (80%) representing all age groups rated their health as good or very good. The majority of women (77%) in all age groups rated themselves high or very high in welcoming the challenge of new experiences. Almost all women in their 60s (92%) rated looking forward to new experiences very high. In this sample, women in their 60s (N = 12) differed (not significantly) from women in their 40s and 50s as follows: they were in stable marital relationships, they reared larger families, participated less in the workforce, had a higher level of education, had higher ratings of satisfaction with their lives, were very satisfied with the "nest" status of their lives, were the most positive about menopause, and gave the highest ratings to welcoming new experiences.

Quality of Life at Different Ages

The 40s age group rated their 20s and 30s as being fairly poor but rated their current decade as acceptable or good and anticipated that their 50s would be very good. The 50s age group rated their 20s, 30s, and 40s as fairly poor, but felt good about their 50s. The 60s age group rated their 20s as good, their 30s and 40s as fairly poor, and their 50s as good. None of the age groups rated the 50s as excellent (or prime), and, as mentioned earlier, each age group had a generally positive feeling about the current decade of their lives. It is possible that a more precise question to elicit rankings of the decades might reveal a preference for the 50s, but that was not done here.

Most of the participants liked and would keep many aspects of their lives if given the opportunity to change. For example, they would keep their families, parental status (i.e., if they were parents they would like to keep on being parents and if they were not parents they would like to keep on not being parents), marital status (i.e., partnered or unpartnered), sense of humor, careers, love life, and self-esteem. They would change things such as getting more education, not marrying so young, starting their careers earlier, having more money, having more self-esteem at earlier ages, being more aggressive in their earlier years, and having more time for themselves. Evaluating their lives on the whole, they reported high satisfaction with children, marriage, education, work, and friends; and they reported high dissatisfaction with not getting enough education, not starting work early, and in some cases, with an unhappy marriage ending in divorce. In general, they saw themselves as more independent and financially comfortable now than at some earlier period, regardless of the age group, and as having been more energetic and enjoying more robust health at an earlier period (relative to the age group responding). The death of a loved one (child or mate) was rated as the worst time in life in all age groups. Divorce received mixed reviews with some women seeing it as devastating and others seeing it as liberating.

The Psychological Tests

I will refer to the score categories as low, moderate, and high. Women in their 40s and 50s had moderate levels of anxiety; women in their 60s scored significantly lower on anxiety than either of the other age groups. The women in all age groups scored high on locus of control (cutting across age groups, widows scored significantly lower than all others on locus of control). Women in all age groups scored high on self-esteem. Women in all groups scored high on instrumentality (getting things done, being in command, etc.) and on expressiveness (caring about others, expressing feelings, etc.). Women in their 50s scored significantly higher than the other age groups on expressiveness. All women achieved moderate scores on the sex-stereotype scale (scored for masculinity concepts), but women in their 50s did score significantly lower than the other two groups—perhaps being more sex-stereotyped only in comparison to them, not necessarily otherwise. It appears that this group of middle-aged women were able to integrate both feminine and masculine concepts in their self-concept, or, to put in Bakan's terms, they had achieved and integrated both agency and communion.

The results from this relatively current survey of middle-aged women reveal a good fit with the findings reported in the literature. This small sample of women did contain a wider range of income (about 20% were clearly not affluent) and of education (about 27% did not go beyond high school). We conclude that middle-aged women, who are generally middle class and above average in level of education, enact multiple roles (partner, parent, worker), enjoy their lives, feel good that the children are on their own, have high self-esteem, and perceive themselves to be in charge of their lives. There was no clear indication that the 50s are or were an exceptionally super time, but by and large it is a decade that received positive ratings.

GAPS AND CONCERNS

Obviously, research efforts must address the characteristics of other status groups of middle-aged women. There is now an impressive amount of consistent findings about relatively high status (middle-class, better-educated) women in both this and other cultures. (Our more recent study hints at the possibility that the findings reported might be more pervasive in middle-aged women). In addition to that obvious and much discussed need, we must refine variables. For example, in determining the duration of a partner relationship, we must settle on a gauge such as the number of years together, and we must distinguish among unpartnered persons such as life-long singles, as distinct from other unpartnered persons, and more conscientiously include retired women. Further, as so many people have pointed out, if we want to know anything about antecedent characteristics we must have longitudinal studies that address this issue. It is not an easy job, as Helson et al. (1990) pointed out in their longitudinal study of the number and quality of roles enacted by women.

Moreover, there has to be an integration of the body of information we have amassed with a scholarly examination of social–economic–political variables. Some scholars have begun such an undertaking (for example, Stewart & Platt, 1982; Kulka & Colten, 1982), and have alerted us to the importance of the changes in post-war society and their impact on this generation of middle-aged women. We are entering an era of social-political changes which appear to threaten the achievements of women. Will such changes eliminate or reduce opportunities for women and thus preclude the manifestation of autonomy for future generations of middle-aged women? Or will the (albeit small) group of higher-status middle-aged women we have studied prevail in keeping open the path to autonomy?

Conclusion

The evidence that many women develop more power and control in their lives, along with the gain in greater self-expression and the development of personal ambitions in new directions outside the home, suggest that middle-aged women have been able to increase their sense of power, autonomy, and self-efficacy through the perspective of a greater breadth of personality. It appears that feelings of efficacy in a particular role account for a positive view of self regardless of what that role may be. Certain roles are associated with certain advantages. Some women gain competencies in traditional roles, while others gain them in their careers. Moreover, many career women continue to be involved in traditional roles as well. The number of roles per se (wife, mother, worker) is not directly associated with self-enhancement, whereas factors related to role quality and involvement are.

Adler (1927) saw all women as perforce neurotic since they lived in a society of male dominance. He said (p. 135) "the whole history of civilization...shows us that the pressures exerted upon women…are not to be borne by any human being; they always give rise to revolt." Perhaps we dare suggest that the so-called "midlife-crisis" *is* that revolt, after which there is a shift in power, at least for women with higher levels of education.

REFERENCES

Adler, A. (1927). *Understanding human nature.* (W. B. Wolfe, Trans.). Garden City, NY: Garden City.

Amaro, H., & Russo, N. F. (1987). Hispanic women and mental health. An overview of contemporary issues in research and practice. *Psychology of Women Quarterly, 11,* 393–407.

Astin, H. S., & Leland, C. (1991). *Women of influence, women of vision.* San Francisco: Jossey-Bass.

Bakan, D. (1996). *Duality of human existence.* Chicago: Rand-McNally.

Bandura, A. (1982). Self-efficacy mechanisms in human agency. *American Psychologist, 37,* 122–147.

Barnett, R. C., & Baruch, G. K. (1978). Women in the middle years: A critique of research and theory. *Psychology of Women Quarterly, 3*(2), 187–197.

Black, S. M., & Hill, C. E. (1984). The psychological well-being of women in their middle years. *Psychology of Women Quarterly, 8*(3), 282–292.

Broverman, I. K., Broverman, D. M., Clarkson, F. E., Rosenkrantz, P. E., & Vogel, S. R. (1970). Sex role stereotypes and clinical judgments of mental health. *Journal of Consulting and Clinical Psychology, 34,* 1–7. (Shorter version adaptation, copyright 1974, Psychology Training & Research, Inc., University of Massachusetts).

Brown, J. K., & Kerns, V. (Eds.). (1985). *In her prime: A new view of middle-aged women.* South Hadley, MA.: Bergin & Garvey.

Coleman, L. A., Antonucci, T. C., Adelmann, P. K., & Crohan, S. E. (1987). Social roles in the lives of middle-aged and older black women. *Journal of Marriage and the Family, 49,* 761–771.

Cooper, K. L., & Gutmann, D. L. (1987). Gender identity and ego mastery style in middle-aged, pre- and post-empty nest women. *The Gerontologist, 27*(3), 347–352.

Erikson, E. (1950/1963). *Childhood and Society.* New York: W. W. Norton.

Gergen, M. M. (1990). Finished at 40: Women's development within the patriarchy. *Psychology of Women Quarterly, 14*(4), 471–493.

Gutmann, D. L. (1985). The parental imperative revisited. In J. Meachan (Ed.), *Family and individual development* (387–403). Basel: Krager.

Gutmann, D. L. (1987). *Reclaimed powers: Toward a new psychology of men and women in later life.* New York: Basic Books.

Helson, R. (1987). Which of these young women with creative potential became productive? Part II. In R. Hogan & G. H. Jones (Eds.), *Perspectives in Personality* (Vol. 2, pp. 51–92). Greenwich, CT: JAI.

Helson, R. (1992). Women's difficult times and the rewriting of the life story. *Psychology of Women Quarterly, 16*(3), 331–347.

Helson, R., Elliott, T., & Leigh, J. (1990). Number and quality of roles. *Psychology of Women Quarterly, 14*(1), 83–101.

Henry, W. E. (1968). Personality change in middle and old age. In E. Norbeck, D. Price-Williams, & W. M. McCord (Eds.), *The study of personality: An interdisciplinary appraisal* (pp. 161–174). New York: Holt, Rinehart & Winston.

Hornstein, G. A. (1986). The structuring of identity among mid-life women as a function of the degree of involvement in employment. *Journal of Personality, 54*(3), 551–575.

Houser, B. B., Berkman, S. L., & Beckman, L. J. (1984). The relative rewards and costs of childlessness for older women. *Psychology of Women Quarterly, 8*(4), 395–398.

Hyman, R. B. (1988). Four stages of adulthood: An exploratory study of growth patterns of inner-direction and time-competence in women. *Journal of Research in Personality, 223*(1), 117–127.

Jung, C. G. (1960). The Stages of Life. In *Collected Works* (Vol. 8, pp. 387–403). Princeton, NJ: Princeton University Press, (originally published 1931).

Kulka, R. A., & Colten, M. E. (1982). Secondary analysis of a longitudinal survey of educated women: A social psychological perspective. *Journal of Social Issues, 38*(1), 73–87.

Levinson, D. J. (1978). *The seasons of a man's life.* New York: Knopf.

Mellinger, J. C., & Erdwins, C. J. (1985). Personality correlates of age and life roles in adult women. *Psychology of Women Quarterly, 9*(4), 503–514.

Miller, J. B. (1976). *Toward a new psychology of women.* Boston: Beacon Press.

Mitchell, V., & Helson, R. (1990). Women's prime of life: Is it the 50s? *Psychology of Women Quarterly, 14*(4), 451–470.

Neugarten, B. L. (1973). Personality change in later life: A developmental perspective. In C. Eisdorfer & M. P. Lawton (Eds.), *The psychology of adult development and aging* (pp. 311–335). Washington, DC: American Psychological Association.

Neugarten, B. L. (1976). Adaptation and the life cycle. *Consulting Psychologist, 6,* 14–30.

Pillay, A. (1988). Midlife depression and the "empty nest" syndrome in Indian women. *Psychological Reports, 63,* 591–594.

Powell, B. (1977). The empty nest, employment, and psychiatric symptoms in college-educated women. *Psychology of Women Quarterly, 2*(1), 35–43.

Puglisi, J. T. (1983). Self-perceived age changes in sex role and self concept. *International Journal of Aging and Human Development, 16*(3), 183–191.

Raup, J. L., & Myers, J. E. (1989). The empty nest syndrome: Myth or reality? *Journal of Counseling and Development, 68,* 180–183.

Rosenberg, M. (1965). *Society and the adolescent self-image.* Princeton, NJ: Princeton University Press.

Rossi, A. S. (1981). Life span theories and women's lives. *Signs, 6,* 4–32.

Rotter, J. B. (1966). Generalized expectancies for internal versus external control of reinforcements. *Psychological Monographs, 80*(1), (whole no. 609).

Ryff, C. D. (1982). Self-perceived personality change in adulthood and aging. *Journal of Personality and Social Psychology, 42*(1), 108–115.

Ryff, C. D., & Heincke, S. (1983). Subjective organization of personality in adulthood and aging. *Journal of Personality and Social Psychology, 44*(4), 807–816.

Sagrestano, L. M. 1992a. Power strategies in interpersonal relationships. *Psychology of Women Quarterly, 16*(4), 481–495.

Sagrestano, L. M. 1992b. The use of power and influence in a gendered world. *Psychology of Women Quarterly, 16*(4), 439–447.

Spence, J. T., Helmreich, R. L., & Stapp, J. (1974). The personal attributes questionnaire: A measure of sex-role stereotypes and masculinity–femininity. *JSAS Catalog of Selected Documents in Psychology, 4,* 127.

Stewart, A. J., & Chester, N. L. (1982). Sex differences in human social motives: Achievement, affiliation, and power. In A. J. Stewart (Ed.), *Motivation and society* (pp. 172–218). San Francisco: Jossey-Bass.

Stewart, A. J., & Platt, M. B. (1982). Studying women in a changing world: An introduction. *Journal of Social Issues, 38*(1), 1–16.

Stroud, J. G. (1981). Women's careers: Work, family, and personality. In D. H. Eichorn, J. A. Clausen, N. Haan, M. P. Honzik, & P. H. Mussen (Eds.), *Present and past in middle life* (pp. 353–390). New York: Academic Press.

Taylor, J. A. (1953). A personality scale of manifest anxiety. *Journal of Abnormal and Social Psychology, 48,* 285–290.

Todd, J., Friedman, A., & Kariuki, P. W. (1990). Women growing stronger with age. *Psychology of Women Quarterly, 14*(4), 567–577.

Wink, P. (1991). Self- and object-directedness in adult women. *Journal of Personality, 59*(4), 769–791.

Worell, J. (1992). Preface to special issue: Women and Power. *Psychology of Women Quarterly, 16*(4), 379.

7

AGING WOMEN: STABILITY OR CHANGE IN PERCEPTIONS OF PERSONAL CONTROL

MARGOT B. NADIEN
Fordham University

FLORENCE L. DENMARK[1]
Pace University

We share with geropsychologists a preference for linking the onset of old age not with a specific chronological age, but rather with functional old age, which represents the specific age at which a given person becomes unable to function without assistance from other people. Nevertheless, so as to conform to the view held by society as well as many researchers, we shall regard the 65th year as the starting point of old age.

In the 1990s, the fastest growing age segment in the United States is composed of older persons. Those in the 65+ category, while composing over 25 million in 1987, are expected to reach 52 million by the year 2020, with persons aged 65+ projected to account for 13% of the population in the year 2000, and for almost 22% in 2030 (U.S. Bureau of the Census, 1988).

Among these elderly, women will continue to predominate over men. In the mid-1980s, life expectancy (the estimate at birth of how long a person is expected to live) was 78.2 years for females, but only 70.8 years for males, although the gap in female-male longevity decreased by four years for persons who reached age 65, at which point the average woman could expect to live until age 83, and the average man until age 79 (Bogue, 1985). By 1991, life expectancy had increased to 72 years for men and 79.2 years for women (Bronte, 1993). This trend of more women reaching old age, and of living longer as aging persons, is continuing. Hence, studies of the aged have particular applicability to women. Indeed, a study of old age is a study mainly of women, especially in the case of the "medium-old" (persons aged 75 through 84), and even more so among persons categorized

[1]Grateful thanks to Justine Adam of Pace University for her help in securing books and articles.

as the "old-old" (persons aged 85 and over) among whom there are 100 women for each 39 men (Moody, 1994).

A long life is customarily viewed as desirable. Yet the value of a prolonged old age may depend in part on whether it brings unwanted changes. For example, are there declines in physical health and cognitive functioning? Will the working elderly be subject to increasing pressure by organizations to retire at age 65 or 70 so as to open up opportunities for younger generations? And even if retirement seems to be an appealing prospect, might the termination of one's working career signal a loss of status, the end of social relationships enjoyed at work, and a reduced standard of living, especially if social security, personal savings, and private pensions fail to offset the weekly salary? Beyond these considerations, might not old age usher in the actual or threatened loss of significant others—family, peers, and those adult children who must work in distant places? More generally, might one or more of these inner biological and outer situational factors stir inner psychosocial change as well? Such possibilities raise concerns about adaptation in old age, especially if biopsychological declines and societal stereotypes militate against the continued exercise of personal autonomy during the last decades of life.

AUTONOMY

At each stage or phase of development, the sense of having an autonomous self is conceptualized in different terms. For toddlers, autonomy centers around self-control in daily activities such as feeding or dressing oneself and controlling the time and place of toileting. In childhood, autonomy deals with gaining psychomotor, cognitive, and social skills that permit personal decisions about problem solving and interacting with significant family members, peers, and teachers. In adolescence, autonomy includes a wish to gain independence from the family of origin in emotional, social, and economic terms. Then, during adulthood, a sense of autonomy is sought within one's career and close intimate relationships with a partner and offspring.

By old age, however, people's perceptions of autonomy or personal control may become vulnerable to the processes of aging (Brandtstadter & Rothermund, 1994). Many of the features of autonomous behavior so arduously acquired during childhood and adulthood may need to be reworked if declines in health or unfavorable life situations should reduce a person's self-reliance. Certainly, any one or a combination of events—for example, impaired hearing, vision, cognitive abilities, or psychomotor skills (often including a diminution of sphincter control)—could serve to undermine financial and mental self-reliance and might require a struggle to retain personal control over the basic psychomotor skills that had been slowly mastered in childhood and then taken for granted all through adulthood.

In other words, continuity in an older person's autonomy and sense of self tends to focus less on independence, and more on the continued exercise of personal (or internal) control over very fundamental life events. These include the *activities of everyday life* (ADL's), such as eating, eliminating waste, and feeding and dressing oneself. They also concern *the instrumental activities of daily life* (IADL's), such as shopping for food and other necessities, cleaning and cooking, and otherwise maintaining oneself in the home and community without having to rely on others for assistance.

Thus, in old age a sense of autonomy centers around a stable sense of personal control and a continuing sense of self in the face of the stress evoked by what Lieberman and Tobin (1983) call the three challenges to adaptation in the last decade or two of life. These writers define adaptation according to a dynamic equilibrium model. Such a model holds that, when confronted with new demands or conditions, the aged achieve equilibrium (adaptation) if their actions permit their continued stable functioning. Conversely, they are maladapted if, following change, they show physical and/or psychological decline, deterioration, or breakdown.

As to the three challenges to adaptation, they include

1. changes in life space, as occurs during relocation to a new residence or an institution
2. inner and outer losses (e.g., physical changes, retirement, widowhood)
3. the increasing realization that one's own personal life is coming to an end (Lieberman & Tobin, 1983)

The Purpose of This Chapter

Our aim in this chapter is to consider some personality factors that affect adaptation in old age, especially among aging females, whose greater longevity means that they make up a large proportion of the elderly population. Our chief concern is with the extent to which an altered sense of autonomy or personal control may undermine the sense of self and of adaptation.

Since self-perception is an essential feature of personality (Hubley & Hultsch, 1994), our analysis of stable or changing perceptions of personal control and of self in old age will be couched, initially, in terms of research and theories about "disengagement," "activity," and "continuity." We shall then examine the impact of stress on personality continuity or change. Thereafter, we shall consider adaptation within the framework of Erikson's Life Span Theory of development, noting how "basic trust" and "autonomy" help in mastering the ego tasks of later life stages, and then reviewing research suggesting that adjustment in old age may require the reworking of one's sense of basic trust and autonomy. Before concluding, we shall survey differing perspectives on personal control and shall then probe research that links the adjustment and continued sense of personal control of some old-agers to a revision in their concepts of self-efficacy.

RESPONSES TO AGING: THEORY AND RESEARCH

Disengagement versus Activity Theory

Historical Background
Some of the earliest work on adaptation among elderly people grew out of the Kansas City Studies of 2,000 healthy aging persons living in midwestern, metropolitan communities. These studies gave rise to two opposing views of optimal aging—that of "disengagement" linking adaptation to personality discontinuity, as opposed to "continued activity" relating adaptation to continuity in one's perceived sense of self.

In the case of disengagement theory, Cumming and Henry (1961) theorized that people adapt to being old by voluntarily withdrawing from society so as to cope with biological decline and the imminence of death. The individual's "personal disengagement" was held to precede or accompany society's withdrawal from the aged through its retirement policies. Such policies, by lessening a person's social participation, also lessen the person's social independence—and, hence, the sense of personal control. Proponents of the contrary view, that of activity theory, supported the notion of personality continuity in old age when, they argued, the elderly retain their middle-aged wish for social involvement and therefore disengage only when society disengages from them (Maddox, 1965).

In research designed to evaluate these competing theories, studies by Havighurst, Neugarten, and Tobin (1968) and by Neugarten, Havighurst, and Tobin (1968) repeatedly assessed among aging persons the extent of their personal engagement (i.e., their assertive coping and emotional involvement in everyday life) and their social engagement (i.e., their daily activity and ego involvement in 11 of their current roles, such as those of spouse, parent, and neighbor). Engagement or disengagement, in turn, was linked to adaptation, as inferred from measures of the subjects' psychological well-being (their affect relative to past life roles and to current ones) and also from measures of their life satisfaction (their self-image, mood, satisfaction with current roles, and overall satisfaction with life).

From these studies emerged two trends. One was the finding that in some aging women (and men), adaptation was linked not to disengagement or activity per se, but to personality features. A second trend was the retention in old-agers of the personality dispositions and preferred levels of activity of their earlier adult years. These two findings led the authors to conclude that a relevant theory of aging is marked not by personality change, but by "personality-continuity" (Neugarten et al., 1968, p. 176).

In the research that follows, the notion of personality broadly conforms to the definitions of Walter Mischel and Gordon Allport, for whom personality represents "distinctive patterns of behavior (including thoughts and emotions) that characterize each individual's adaptation to the situations of his or her life" (Mischel, 1976, p. 2), and "the dynamic organization within the individual of those psychophysical systems that determine his [or her] characteristic behavior and thought" (Allport, 1964, p. 28), with behavior and thought directed toward survival, adjustment, and growth (Allport, 1964, p. 29).

The Case for "Continuity Theory"

Personality Continuity

A spate of studies followed the research by Neugarten et al. (1968) and Havighurst et al. (1968). These studies varied as to personality inventory (*Guilford-Zimmerman-Temperament-Survey* [GZTS] versus *California Test of Personality* [CTP]), the assessment approach (self-report versus knowledgeable observer), and the scope of personality features (individual traits versus personality dimensions or domains). Nevertheless, they all indicated considerable constancy of personality across the adult years, including old age.

Longitudinal studies that used self-report measures found personality stability with diverse personality measures. For example, in a study which included comparable numbers of women and men in three age groups—young adults, middle-agers, and old-agers—Costa, McCrae, and Arenberg (1980) found an average retest correlation of .70 over a 12-year period in response to the entire 10 scales of the GZTS. Then, in their 25 year follow-up study, Woodruff and Birren (1971, cited in Conley, 1984) discovered correlations of .65 for women as well as men on the self-adjustment portion of the *California Test of Personality.* And, in their 40 year follow-up of a group of 50 mothers from the *Berkeley Human*

Development Studies, Mussen and colleagues (1980) found consistency correlations of .34 for neuroticism (worry, dissatisfaction) and .24 for extraversion-introversion (talkativeness, energy, self-assurance).

Continuity of broad personality domains up to and through old age is also suggested by studies by Conley (1984, 1985). He applied a "multitrait-multimethod-multioccasion" analysis to a 45 year longitudinal study, whose original pool of subjects included 300 females and 300 males, all of whom were advantaged European Americans with a mean IQ of 113 and one or more years of college.

Data were gathered at three testing periods (1935–36, 1954–55, and 1979–81) and involved three assessment methods (self-reports, acquaintance, and spouse ratings), as based on first- and third-person versions of the *Kelly Rating Scale* (1940) and the *Cornell Medical Index* (Brodman, Erdmann, Lorge, Wolff, & Broadbent, 1949). Not all persons and not all methods and measures were used at each testing time.

Factor analyses of subjective and spouse ratings revealed that when personality domains of neuroticism or social extraversion appeared in early adulthood, they tended to persist through adulthood and old age in both women and men (Conley, 1985).

Both before and after Conley's studies, Costa and McCrae (1988) also investigated the longitudinal stability of discrete and non-overlapping personality domains across adulthood. Based on cluster analyses of Cattell's *16 Personality Factors* (16PF) and factor analyses of the GZTS scales, Costa and McCrea devised their *Neuroticism-Extraversion-Openness* (NEO) inventory, with each personality domain assessed according to six facets.[2] Then, after adding an agreeableness scale (A) and a conscientiousness scale (C), they held that their *Neuroticism-Extraversion-Openness Personality Inventory* (NEO-PI) encompassed all facets of personality.

In their longitudinal studies, Costa and McCrea included 270 females (aged 21–96) and 365 males (aged 25–91), all of them healthy, well-educated, and predominantly European Americans who worked in or were retirees from positions in science, the professions, or business. In 1980, NEO inventory assessments involved self-reports and spouse ratings of 308 of the subjects (151 of the women, and 157 of the men). Then, in 1986, over 60% of the original participants again gave self-reports while a subsample of 78 wives and 89 husbands were re-rated by their spouses. Also, so as to qualify as sequential studies, additional samples of 311 women (aged 19–93, M = 56.4) and 241 men (aged 21–92, M = 62.4) were drawn (Costa & McCrae, 1988).

Results of these studies revealed that despite some variability as a function of the type of analysis (cross-sectional, longitudinal, cross-sequential, or time-sequential), the self-reports of both women and men proved longitudinally stable with respect to all five personality domains. Buttressing the findings from these self-reports were indications of appreciable self/spouse agreement, especially among the older subjects (aged 57–84).

---

[2] In Costa and McCrae's *Neuroticism-Extraversion-Openness* (NEO) personality inventory, each of the three personality domains comprised six personality facets. Thus, their neuroticism (N) scales measured the six personality traits of anxiety, depression, hostility, self-consciousness, impulsivity, and vulnerability. Their extraversion (E) scales measured the six personality facets of warmth, assertiveness, positive emotions, activity, gregariousness, and excitement-seeking; and their openness (O) scales measured fantasy, aesthetics, feelings, actions, ideas, and values.

In sum, these findings of Costa and McCrae (1988; Costa, McCrae & Arenberg, 1980), when combined with those of Conley (1984, 1985) and other researchers (see Schaie & Parham, 1976; Siegler, George & Okun, 1979) all suggest support for the notion that certain personality patterns are stable across adult life and old age, among both women and men.

Well-Being and Its Relationship to Personality

Costa and McCrae (1984) found evidence of stability not only in personality domains, but also in psychological well-being. The latter was assessed according to five measures:

1. *Satisfaction Index,* composed of ranking scales for each of 14 features of life (self-respect, faith, health, appearance, sex, marriage, family, friends, finances, work, leisure, housing, city, and government)
2. Andrews and Withey's (1976) single-item *Delighted-Terrible Scale* for evaluating the quality of life as a whole; and the three scales making up Bradburn's (1969) *Affect Balance Scales—*
3. *Positive Affect Scale* (PAS)
4. *Negative Affect Scale* (NAS)
5. *Affect Balance* (the difference between PAS and NAS)

A stable sense of subjective well-being was inferred from retest correlations among the five measures, ranging from .47 to .63 (N = 473, p < .001).

Well-being, after having been shown to be relatively stable, was examined in terms of its relationship to personality. In a study which included an examination of the responses of 256 women (aged 24–96) and 350 men (aged 25–91) to the NEO inventory and to the five measures of well-being, Costa and McCrae (1984) discovered stable relationships between well-being and the personality domains of extraversion and neuroticism. Extraversion was strongly associated with positive well-being, with the extraversion components of warmth, assertiveness, and positive emotions most closely tied to high life satisfaction and positive affect. Neuroticism, by contrast, was tied to a low degree of life satisfaction and negative affect, with depression proving to be the strongest correlate of low feelings of well-being.

Costa and McCrae (1984) also found that, whether measured either by the 16PF or the GZTS, *extraversion and neuroticism "predicted" later subjective well-being.* Extraversion scores were positively associated 10 and 12 years later with high subjective well-being (high scores on Bradburn's Affect Balance Scale and his Positive Affect Scale). Neuroticism scores were linked 10 and 12 years later with negative affect and with a sense of hopelessness and low feelings of personal security.

Gender Differences

Costa and McCrae (1984) reported that while trends were similar for both sexes, depression in women was more predictive of women's negative affect than was the case for men. Moreover, women had higher neuroticism scores and a higher incidence of depression than did men.

Implications

Considered as a whole, the research by Neugarten et al. (1968), Conley (1984, 1985), and Costa and McCrae (1984, 1988) suggests considerable continuity of personality. Certainly, the patterns of personality and well-being in healthy and advantaged aging women as well as aging men appear to be continuous with and predictable from patterns laid down during earlier adult years. However, this body of research also suggests a need to explore a more general theory of continuity as an explanation of aging. It is to such a theory that we now turn.

CONTINUITY THEORY AS AN EXPLANATION OF AGING

The idea of "continuity" grew out of activity theory research which, as noted earlier, showed that in old age people continue the patterns of personality and psychological well-being of their middle years. Implicit in this research, and in the theory guiding it, was the notion of a homeostatic model; for a person's response to change (say, that brought about by retirement or physical or social losses) was held to prompt efforts to restore a pre-existing state of equilibrium. In other words, active middle-agers sought substitutes to replace the activities and social relationships terminated by retirement, the death of loved ones, or physical impediments (Havighurst et al., 1968; Neugarten et al., 1968; Palmore & Maddox, 1977).

Unlike the activity hypothesis from which it emerged, *continuity theory* speaks of adaptation as a process of "dynamic equilibrium" because of the belief that, within a stable framework, people strive to avoid breakdown and to maintain effective functioning in the face of new demands or conditions (Atchley, 1989; Lieberman & Tobin, 1983; Tobin, 1991).

To be more explicit, continuity theory holds that when we confront change, we achieve a dynamic equilibrium because we perceive inner and outer changes as being assimilable within our own individual personal history (Cohler, 1982). Thus, external continuity comes from our perceiving new outer-world events as being connected with remembered past environments, activities, and role relationships. Then, through repeated exposure to these new conditions, we experience them as increasingly familiar and gradually incorporate them into our evolving concept of the outer world. Similarly, internal continuity is possible because we perceive inner changes as being linked to and supportive of a remembered inner structure of our "self" and our "identity" (Atchley, 1989).

Self and Identity

Our self consists of the thoughts and feelings we have when we contemplate not only our appearance and experiences, but also all the salient features of our personality—our temperament and dominant emotions, ideas and values, cardinal dispositions and skills. Other features are also related to our self. For example, there is our self-concept, the thoughts we have about our self; and there is our self-esteem, the sum of our feelings of self-liking and self-disliking.

Somewhat differentiated from our self is our identity. For the latter encompasses all those global (and ofttimes contradictory) aspects of our self and our personality that we perceive to be constant across differing social situations (Whitbourne, 1986).

In sum, because we interpret our experiences of outer and inner changes in terms of remembered features about ourselves and our world, we are able to retain a sense of inner continuity (of self and identity) and outer continuity (of roles, activities, and external environments) (Atchley, 1989; Lieberman & Tobin, 1983).

There is one important caveat: continuity theory is offered as a general theory of normal aging—that is, of aging in which people are assumed to have retained the autonomy and self-reliance upon which their perceived sense of continuity in self and identity depends. Yet, can similar assumptions apply to those elderly persons whose severe physical, psychological, or social losses have effectively stripped them of much of their self-reliance? Are such persons able to retain a perceived continuity of self and identity?

In seeking an answer to this question, let us turn to the major studies of stress undertaken by Lieberman and Tobin (1983).

ADAPTING TO STRESS IN OLD AGE: CONTINUITY OR CHANGE?

Continuity and activity theories had guided and been affirmed by research involving *advantaged elderly,* in other words, old-agers who enjoy excellent physical and mental health, economic security, social supports, and physical mobility. However, a different theory might be required if, in studies of the elderly, attention is shifted away from everyday behavior and onto responses to the crises that customarily confront the aged during the last 10 or 20 years of their lives. Among these crises are

1. some type of loss involving the subjective experience of a severed attachment to valued persons, activities, places, ideas, and things
2. the need for relocation owing to ill-health, impoverishment, loneliness, or lack of self-reliance
3. the increasing awareness that one's own life is finite and that personal death may be on the horizon

Focusing on the stress of relocation among four groups of aged persons—two relocated from community homes to nursing homes, and two others shifted from one institution to either nursing homes or boarding houses—Lieberman and Tobin (1983) defined adaptation as the capacity, when facing stress, to continue to maintain homeostasis or stability (or to avoid malfunctioning, psychological distress, deterioration, or breakdown).

Regardless of age or life stage, the subjective experience of stress relates to the nature of the stressor and its meaning to the individual. The consequences of stress vary according to the perceiver's social resources (informal and formal supports), and inner capacities, including the cognitive appraisal of the stress and the internal resources for dealing with it. The resources encompass the person's

1. pre-stress functioning ego strength or mental health
2. capacities needed for coping—for example, health, cognitive abilities, and social supports
3. management strategies (Lieberman & Tobin, 1983)

In terms of the association between the stress of relocation and the type of adaptation made to it, management strategies appear to be crucial. This was especially true in the Lieberman and Tobin study of the relocation of the "unwilling old ladies"—42 widows and 3 singles (mean age = 78.1, range = 61–91 years). These elderly ladies were compelled to move from a small, flexible, and centralized facility to a large, highly structured, decentralized facility that necessitated the break-up of friendship groups.

Extensive research shows that an undesired move, especially to an institution, is usually highly stressful. However, dissimilar response patterns among Lieberman and Tobin's "unwilling old ladies" traced mainly to individual differences in their use of three sets of management strategies—namely, coping effort; the integration or cognitive structuring needed for satisfactory coping; and, most importantly, the felt degree of mastery or perceived control over the relocation. The latter was important to preserving feelings of self-respect and effective self-reliance.

These aging women all experienced their move as stressful, and over half had failed to adapt nine months following relocation. However, maladaptation over a two-year interval was substantially less great for those elderly ladies who absorbed considerable information prior to the move. Maladaptation was also ameliorated by a perception of control, especially for those women who perceived a mythical congruence between their preferred environment and their actual one. Indeed, their misperceived mastery culminated in fewer adaptive failures and more adaptive successes because their perceived control served to lower the anticipated threat and loss prior to the move. It also lessened the extent of a short-term or long-term depression following the move (Lieberman & Tobin, 1983).

Paradoxically, these women's psychological traits that facilitated their successful adjustment to the stress of relocation were unlike those that normally predict an adaptive success to stress in younger adults or that conduce to adjustment to non-stressful events in adults of all ages. Specifically, the possession of high ego strength and high personal and social resources did not contribute to optimal functioning following relocation. Instead, the most successful adaptations were achieved by elderly ladies who were aggressive.

Another paradox was the fact that aggression yielded maladaptive as well as adaptive outcomes. For even though aggressive actions contributed to homeostasis and continued functioning following relocation, it also undermined a coherent, consistent sense of identity.

The fact that the adjustment of the "unwilling old ladies" entailed traits that diverge from those that predict adaptation at earlier life stages led Lieberman and Tobin to conclude that there is a seeming disparity between the traits that promote adaptation in old age and those that foster optimal functioning during earlier adult periods.

In view of the divergent research findings of Lieberman and Tobin (1983), Conley (1984, 1985), Costa and McCrae (1988), Havighurst et al. (1968), Neugarten et al. (1968), Mussen, Eichorn, Honzik, Bieber, and Meredith (1980), Palmore and Luikart (1972), and Palmore and Maddox (1987), we wonder whether an understanding of aging requires a theory involving both continuity and discontinuity. Is continuity theory appropriate as an explanation of only advantaged people? Some other theory, one that includes discontinuity, seems needed to explain the aging of persons suffering from severe stress. Thus, we propose a theory of integration, one involving the integration of stressful new experiences with familiar old ones such that elderly women and men who experience severe stress may have to revise their sense of self and identity.

Before exploring a theory of integration, we shall first consider the view of adaptive aging advanced by Erikson, Erikson, and Kivnick (1986). For this work on old age bears on the mastery and retention of a sense of autonomy and identity in the face of threats to the essential features of the self in late adulthood. Thus, we turn now to Eriksonian theory and research focusing on the experiences and adaptation of people in old age.

REVISITING ERIKSON'S LIFE SPAN THEORY

For Erikson, the importance to psychological well-being and adaptation of preserving the sense of self and of identity relates to a continuing sense not only of basic trust, but also of autonomy (personal control) across the life span. After noting the role of epigenesis, we shall review basic trust and autonomy in the context of all eight of the life-span crises or tasks that must be mastered in order to be adapted in old age. Then we shall explore empirical evidence of the reworking of ego tasks in old age and of the implications of this evidence for a theory combining continuity and discontinuity. Admittedly, Erikson's theory was applied to both males and females. However, our focus will be on the implications for women of his theory.

Epigenesis, the view that later development builds on earlier growth, is part of Erikson's belief that, at each succeeding life phase, adaptation depends on the ego strengths gained from resolving the crises of earlier phases, starting with those of basic trust in infancy and of autonomy in toddlerhood.

Basic Trust and Autonomy: Effects and Later Crises

Basic Trust
The physical and psychological well-being that comes from having received consistent and loving care from a mature caregiver, called *basic trust,* permits the hope and confidence needed to motivate efforts to cope with the tasks of all remaining stages. Moreover, if the other childhood tasks are mastered, basic trust in a female will flower into self-trust and loving feelings for a mate and offspring (Erikson et al., 1986).

Autonomy
Basic trust, along with realistic mistrust of dangerous things, endows toddlers with the necessary hope and realism to strive for *autonomy*—for enough control over their body to offset feelings of self-doubt or shame over experiences of nonpersonal control over toileting, walking, and self-feeding, or over the cognitive skills needed to communicate and understand others (Erikson, 1950). It would appear, then, that just as the basic trust of infancy enables self-trust and loving feeling during later phases, so too might the autonomy of childhood foster personal control and self-esteem in adulthood and old age.

Initiative
At differing phases, personal control is wielded in differing ways (Erikson, 1950). For example, as motor and psychosocial skills improve, young girls as well as boys seek control through asserting *initiative*. They initiate relationships with siblings and other children. They initiate intellectual discoveries with their perpetual questions. And they initiate oedipal drives, that later become repressed and give way to the superego.

Industry

During latency, girls as well as boys seek further control when, in their school work and other pursuits, they strive to combat feelings of inferiority and to gain a sense of *industry* (task mastery or competency) by competing effectively with peers, and by measuring up to the standards imposed by significant others and by their ego-ideal (Erikson, 1950).

Identity

Adolescents seek personal control when they struggle to gain their identity and independence from the family of origin and to achieve the economic and psychosocial self-reliance that they need to experience self-trust (Erikson, 1968). The latter is the adult version of infancy's basic trust, just as an *autonomous identity* is the adult version of the toddler's autonomy.

Intimacy

By early adulthood, psychosocial well-being comes from replacing a sense of isolation with feelings of both emotional and sexual *intimacy* with a mate. This, however, depends on the prior attainment of *ego identity* (a sure sense of one's values and preferred adult roles) and also of *sexual identity* (an identification with members of one's own sex and a fusion of tender and erotic feeling directed to members of the opposite sex). When such conditions are met, young adults add to their sense of separate identity a *shared identity* with their mate (Erikson, 1968).

Generativity

In middle age, both women and men achieve psychosocial well-being when, instead of being self-absorbed, they feel *generative* in the sense of being productive and creative in their work, their ideas, and their care of younger persons.

Integrity

Finally, elderly women as well as men experience psychosocial well-being when they gain a sense of *integrity* (inner unity and completeness) and resolve feelings of despair that may be occasioned by awareness of eroding physical and mental abilities and the approaching end of life.

Crises Reworked in Old Age: Empirical Evidence

The trust and autonomy of childhood assume different forms for females when earlier crises are reworked in ways appropriate to later stages (Erikson et al., 1986). Thus, the focus of autonomy for toddlers is control over body functions and accommodation to parental control. Then, as skills and spheres of interest expand across girlhood and womanhood, so do ways of exercising control. But the potential for autonomy among elderly women, especially those over age 80, may be undermined by impaired health and/or sensorimotor and cognitive functioning, or a self-perception of helplessness owing either to having internalized negative stereotypes of old age or to feelings of defeat over cumulative losses—the loss of significant others, one's job or other valued activities, and, perhaps, one's adult home and neighborhood.

In turning to the qualitative study noted below, it will become apparent that individual differences are found not only in the sources of lost autonomy, but also in their effects.

The Guidance Study

In their guidance study, Erikson et al. (1986) studied surviving parents of Berkeley, California children—those who had been part of the Berkeley longitudinal study—through detailed records of their visits (twice-annually from 1928 to 1945, and intermittently from 1945 to the 1980s), and also through taped records of two hour, open-ended interviews when the parents were 40 to 57 years old (in 1945–1946); 63 to 75 years old (in 1968); and then 76 to 90 years old (in 1981), at which time there remained only 29 persons, of whom 19 were women, including 10 widows. All of these aging women and men resided in or around Berkeley, living in their adulthood homes or in luxury retirement communities, small apartments, congregate housing, or the homes of daughters (Erikson et al., 1986). Interview materials yielded the following information about how the elderly women dealt with the life span's ego tasks.

The Eighth Stage Crisis: Integrity versus Despair.   Most of the elderly people evidenced *integrity* (a sense of inner unity and acceptance of the life cycle) by virtue of being more compassionate and tolerant of others and themselves. But they also felt some *despair* (depression and powerlessness) over one or more of the following unwanted changes: impaired health, past failures and an uncertain future, and the imminence of death. However, despair was minimal for those elderly women who underplayed past failures and frustrations and emphasized past joys and successes.

One wonders whether those of the elderly women who selectively focused on past pleasures and achievements would have shown up in Costa and McCrae studies not as neurotics, but as extraverts, and whether these women had enjoyed positive attitudes during middle age as well as in old age. If this were true, it would afford support for the position of continuity theory.

Reworking the Seventh Stage Crisis: Generativity and Care versus Stagnation.   When they resisted or resented their shrinking physical and mental powers and their lost social roles, the old-agers failed to retain their sense of generativity. By contrast, this maladaptive response was avoided by those aging persons who, because of their helpfulness to others, especially young people, maintained a sense of being valued and needed (Erikson et al., 1986). In so doing, they appear to have found a useful means of keeping alive their sense of self, and of their *valued* self.

Reworking the Sixth Stage Crisis: Intimacy and Love versus Isolation.   For some of the elderly women who had been widowed, the struggle to retain feelings of intimacy was undermined by the loss of companionship and sexuality that had been shared with the departed spouse. Some widows used reminiscence to help offset the felt loss of the spouse—a response which affords support for continuity theory. However, in those instances where the marriage had been intimate and of long duration, the widows continued to mourn and feel isolated for many years following widowhood, with the passage of time merely serving to diminish the depth of grief (Erikson et al., 1986, pp. 118–121).

This response conforms with empirical findings from other studies in which widows appeared to persist in their grieving (Bowlby, 1980; Parkes, 1985). Mourning and feelings of isolation were found to be especially strong when the psychological hardships of widowhood were exacerbated by economic and social losses (Babchuk & Anderson, 1989; Keller, Leventhal, & Larson, 1989; Lopota, 1973; Parkes, 1985). In contrast to the widows whose pleasurable memories of their marriage afforded a sense of continuity with their past, the perpetually grieving widows felt cut off from their past lives and thus experienced an unbridgeable sense of discontinuity from their earlier years.

Reworking the Fifth Stage Crisis: Identity versus Identity Confusion. Losses in health, social relationships, and adult roles often limited or prohibited pursuits that previously affirmed the elderly women's sense of identity. Yet some women kept alive through reminiscence the memory of past pursuits and roles involved in their sense of identity, while others identified with the activities and roles of younger persons whose values resembled their own (Erikson et al., 1986). These women, by substituting memories for their losses, appear to have preserved their sense of self—and, hence, to have acted as continuity theory would have predicted.

Reworking the Fourth Stage Crisis: Industry and Competence versus Inferiority. Biological and cognitive declines sometimes undermined feelings of competency which had originated in latency. Nevertheless, some aging women and men retained their sense of task mastery by recalling earlier accomplishments and by actively coping with their personal impairments and approaching death (Erikson et al., 1986). Here, again, is an indication that reminiscence helped to keep alive in these old-agers an important feature of their identity and self.

Reworking the Third Stage Crisis: Initiative versus Guilt. The sense of initiative gained during early childhood was often impeded by declining physical and mental powers, and also by society's frowning on playfulness in old age. Yet some of the elderly women continued to show initiative and purposefulness in their daily lives, thus preserving their sense of initiative, an important feature of identity in Western society.

Reworking the Second Stage Crisis: Autonomy versus Shame. Of central concern to the elderly women and men in this study was their need to exercise some autonomy (personal control) over their body, mind, behavior, and life circumstances. Indeed, so as to defend against shame and doubt over limited or lost control, some of these elderly people sought a balance between their opposing toddlerhood tendencies of "holding on to control" (Freud's anal-retentive tendencies), and their "letting go of control" (Freud's anal-expulsive tendencies).

For some of these old-agers, physical deterioration led to increasing dependence on others, as when their visual and reflex impairments prevented them from driving. Yet, subjective factors also affected their perceptions of autonomy. One wheelchair-bound elderly woman described herself as being healthier than average despite her "sick leg" (Erikson et al., 1986, p. 197). Other elderly women denied their physical problems, sometimes because of vanity, but more often so as to maintain an illusion of independence.

Unfortunately, some of these aging people failed to recognize that mechanical aids often conferred greater autonomy. For example, one elderly woman who was crippled by arthritis refused to use a wheelchair because, for her, it symbolized helplessness; yet her refusal doomed her to actual helplessness. Similarly, a hard-of-hearing woman, by denying the benefits of a hearing aid, limited her autonomy more than was necessary. In these examples of self-defeating behavior, we again see evidence of continuity—but, sadly, of maladaptive continuity.

Reworking the First Stage Crisis: Basic Trust versus Mistrust.   The basic trust of infancy derives from love and fosters throughout life a sense of hope, confidence, and faith in self and the world. In old age, however, continuing self-trust requires a continued perception of autonomy despite biological declines and external environmental obstacles, such as a crime-ridden neighborhood.

In the face of deteriorating health and physical powers, the elderly women and men in the study who seemed to retain considerable feelings of well-being and life satisfaction were those who accepted their actual condition, remained in a familiar environment, provided for their own health care, and maintained the valued relationships and activities of their earlier years.

In other words, these elderly persons were more apt to achieve some form of equilibrium through recognizing a realistic degree of discontinuity in their sense of self (as when there was a loss of complete physical self-reliance). Doing so allowed for a realistic appraisal of their situation, one that could lead to steps that would help them retain a limited amount of independence and some feelings of continuity with their past sense of self and their past identity.

Theoretical Implications of the Guidance Study

With respect to the issue of continuity, there seem to be two opposing ways in which the guidance study's aging women sought to maintain continuity as they reworked in old age the ego tasks of earlier life phases. Some elderly women sought to preserve a sense of inner and outer continuity through *reminiscence.* They reminisced about lost loved ones (e.g., dead husbands) so as to keep alive the feelings of intimacy and companionship they had enjoyed with their spouses. Similarly, they reminisced about skills or activities that were denied them because of external prohibitions or internal impairment. Then, too, some of the aging women sought to preserve their sense of self by identifying with younger people and, sometimes, by working with them, especially with those who, by virtue of having similar values, seemed to be similar to themselves.

Certain of the aging women's efforts to maintain continuity had a maladaptive element. Consider the elderly women who refused essential help—say, that of a wheelchair, cane, glasses, or hearing aid—and did so in order to maintain the illusion of autonomy, self-reliance, or a youthful appearance. From the viewpoint of these women, the refusal to accept help may have reinforced their subjective feelings of continued self-reliance and self-trust. However, from the viewpoint of Erikson and his associates (1986), the actions of these women were self-defeating; for, by seeking to perpetuate the appearance of continuity, they limited their actual possibilities for continued personal control and independence.

From our vantage point, there is yet another interpretation. Maintaining the illusion of continued autonomy may have value for some people, at least for some of the time. However, because self-deception often breaks down, adaptation over the long term may require that elderly women as well as elderly men acknowledge their actual losses and the feelings of discontinuity they engender. Thus, integration rather than illusory continuity might be the solution. When we face the reality of undesired but irrevocable changes, we increase our chances of dealing effectively with them, especially if we integrate them into a somewhat revised sense of self.

There are some constructive ways of coping with reductions in autonomy and basic self-trust. When aging women (and men) require help from younger kin or neighbors with transportation or other activities, they can retain their self-trust through cognitive restructuring in one or both of the following two ways. First, they can reconceptualize aid from others as being but one of the many interdependencies that occur not just in old age, but all through life. Second, they can increase their sense of perceived self-trust if they focus less on their decreased autonomy and more on their retained autonomy owing to the help afforded by other people or mechanical aids.

Cognitive restructuring is only one way to bolster an aging woman's (or man's) sense of personal control. Another way involves practical steps. Physically impaired old-agers can increase their independence by paying others (e.g., home healthcare workers) to perform for them what they cannot do for themselves. Of course, such an option is more readily open to those aging women and men who have the necessary economic resources to engage healthcare workers. But having others provide help is also feasible for impoverished elderly persons who reside in states or countries which provide government-supported home health care. Thus, in cases where reliance on government-paid or personally-paid workers is possible, infirm elderly women can avoid dependency on family members and can also increase the likelihood of staying on in their own residence and outside of a nursing home.

Research by Erikson, and also by Lieberman and Tobin, clearly suggests that the declines and losses afflicting some elderly women may require new bases for a continued perception of autonomy (and of self-trust). So, for a more complete study of this issue, we now turn to the construct of *personal control,* the experimental counterpart to the notion of autonomy advanced by Erikson (1950, 1968) and colleagues (Erikson et al., 1986), and also the idea of perceived mastery put forward by Lieberman and Tobin (1983). It is the personal-control literature that has examined most extensively the conditions under which aging women retain or lose their perceptions of control.

PERSONAL CONTROL AND AGING

Differing Views of Personal Control

Internal versus External Control

While Erikson's concept of autonomy grew out of clinical observations, the counterpart construct of personal control emerged from social learning research and originated in Rotter's (1954, 1966, 1982) notion of *locus of control,* which concerns generalized beliefs about the source of control over pleasurable or painful situational outcomes. When *internally controlled* because of a past history of successful control over situational outcomes, people have the generalized expectation that their behavior determines their receipt of rewards or punishments in most situations. In contrast, when *externally controlled* because of past experiences in which luck or powerful figures have seemed to control outcomes, people have the generalized expectation that their rewards or punishments are unrelated to their behavior in most situations (Lefcourt, 1976, 1991).

Unlike externally controlled persons, those who are internally controlled perceive a link between their own behavior and situational outcomes and, as a consequence, they evaluate themselves in terms of their successes and failures (Lefcourt, 1976, 1991). This suggests that being stripped of personal control in old age might be, at least for internally controlled persons, a source of discontinuity of experience and of change in self-concept and self-esteem.

Learned Helplessness

In a variation of Rotter's view of an externally controlled orientation, Seligman (1975) proposed that, if repeatedly exposed to painful and non-controllable events, people acquire a generalized expectancy of *learned helplessness*—of being helpless to control what happens to them. Under such circumstances, only those persons with an internally controlled orientation are expected to feel responsible for aversive, uncontrollable events—and, hence, to become prone to depression and lowered self-esteem.

Perceived Self-Efficacy

Refining Rotter's internality notion and Seligman's learned helplessness construct, Bandura (1977, 1982) distinguished between *perceived self-efficacy,* or expectations of being able to cope effectively with specific situations, and *outcome expectancy,* or expectations about the environment's responsiveness to personal actions. This distinction suggests that learned helplessness may derive from perceptions either of personal inefficacy or of an environment which is unresponsive or negatively responsive (Kuhl, 1986).

Two-Process Model of Perceived Control

Reformulating internal control as *primary control,* the perceived ability to change the world so as to fit it to one's own needs, Rothbaum, Weisz, and Snyder (1982) proposed that when a perception of internal control is lacking, people may seek a substitute form of control, *secondary control,* which is the perceived ability to change oneself so as to conform to one's environment. (Hereafter, we shall designate persons having perceptions of primary control as "primary controllers," and those having perceptions of secondary control as "secondary controllers.")

Both primary and secondary controllers actually seek four types of control: predictive, illusory, vicarious, and interpretive. *Predictive control,* that of predicting outcomes, is used by primary controllers to master situations through effort and ability but, by secondary controllers, to protect themselves against dashed hopes. *Illusory control,* the illusion of having control in chance-determined events, is ascribed by primary controllers to their own ability and effort but, by secondary controllers, to having "luck" in chancy situations. *Vicarious control,* the belief that control is gained through powerful others, is sought by primary controllers through manipulating or imitating powerful others but, by secondary controllers, through identifying with powerful others so as to participate in their wielding of control. Finally, *interpretive control,* the control which comes from "understanding," is used by primary controllers to solve problems but, by secondary controllers, to derive "meaning" and "passive acceptance" (Rothbaum et al., 1982).

In terms of the preceding theories about perceptions of control, it would appear that losses of autonomy among the aged would adversely affect the self-concept and self-esteem of persons with an internal orientation, but not those with an external one. However, the work of Rothbaum and colleagues (1982) also suggests that internally controlled persons could ultimately adapt to their decreased autonomy if they replaced lost feelings of primary control with the indirect form of autonomy implicit in secondary control.

Having noted differing theoretical views about autonomy, let us now draw on some of these views to consider research indications of whether, and to what extent, women may retain in old age their middle-aged perceptions of personal control.

Research on Personal Control and Adaptation in Old Age

At first glance, the research literature paints a confusing picture of the role of personal control in old age. This stems partly from methodological problems. In cross-sectional studies, internality has been shown to increase, decrease, or remain the same as one grows older; but longitudinal studies indicate that internality declines or remains stable with increasing age (Lachman, 1986; Rodin, 1987).

Further confusion comes from comparing studies that use personal-control measures of differing sensitivity. For example, the inconsistent findings noted above came from research relying on Rotter's (1966) unidimensional internal-external (I-E) scale; but more consistent findings seem to emerge in studies utilizing a multidimensional measure, such as H. Levenson's (1981) three-factor measure comprising three scales—Internality, Powerful Others, and Chance (IPC) scales. A single measure of internality reflects personal mastery, whereas when two measures of externality are provided, one deals with "chance," a random influence, the other with "powerful others," a nonrandom influence. As used in Lachman's (1983) two-year longitudinal study of noninstitutionalized old-agers, Levenson's scale revealed stability in the external components of chance and powerful others, but decline in the internal component of personal mastery.

Confusing results may also arise because some research relies on generalized measures rather than on domain-specific measures that separately assess "chance" situations (lotteries) and differing types of "skill" (work or social pursuits), and perception-specific measures that separately assess factors relative to the person. These include perceived personal efficacy or the personal relevance of the situation, and factors which inhere in the environment, such as environmental responsiveness. By way of example, a recent study by Krause (1994) found that the effects of role stressors on a person's perceptions of control varied according to the role and its salience for the individual. Specifically, a loss of personal control was experienced when stressors were associated with salient roles, but not with nonsalient ones.

Beyond these methodological considerations is another complicating factor. With increasing age, people differ more markedly from each other in the timing and severity of their physical, cognitive, social, and economic losses, as well as in their reaction to them. These differences, in turn, may account for greater variations in the stability or change in aging people's perceptions of personal control (Rodin, 1986, 1987).

Despite these methodological and individual differences, three lines of evidence appear to support the view that, for some aging women, well-being or adaptation may depend on retaining at least a minimal sense of personal control. First, among non-institutionalized old-agers, internally controlled persons enjoy greater well-being (i.e., higher life satisfaction, positive affect, morale, and self-esteem) than do externally controlled individuals (Brown & Granick, 1983; Hunter, Linn, & Harris, 1981–1982; Mancini, 1980–1981; Morganti, Nehrke, Hulicka, & Cataldo, 1988; Pohl & Fuller, 1980; Wolk & Telleen, 1975).

Second, perceptions of lost personal control over aversive events (e.g., involuntary retirement, widowhood, institutionalization, or losses in physical or cognitive skills) have been followed by a deterioration in both physical and psychosocial health. Specific adverse outcomes include

1. hormonal changes that contribute to coronary disease and the undermining of the immune and neuroendocrine systems (Rodin, 1986; and Rodin, Timko, & Harris, 1985)
2. feelings of helplessness, anxiety, and stress (Abramson, Garber, & Seligman, 1980; Abramson, Seligman, & Teasdale, 1978; Miller, Rosellini, & Seligman, 1977; Rodin, 1986; Seligman, 1975)
3. sharp declines in psychological well-being, life satisfaction, and self-esteem (Bild & Havighurst, 1976; Edwards & Kleemack, 1973; Kivett, Watson, & Busch, 1977; E. Levinson, 1975; Palmore & Luikart, 1976; Wolk & Telleen, 1976)

Such findings prompted Rodin (1987) and colleagues (Rodin & Langer, 1980; Rodin et al., 1985) to suggest that perceived declines in personal control may trace not to aging per se, but to the many intrapersonal and social losses that so often accompany aging.

A third line of evidence comes from research showing that when deprived of personal control, the sharp health declines suffered by institutionalized aging women can be somewhat lessened by interventions granting them at least a minimal degree of control, as occurs when allowed a voice in decisions about furniture arrangements, the choice of foods, care of plants, and the time when visitors may see them (Langer & Rodin, 1976; Liem, 1975; Rodin, 1983; Rodin & Langer, 1977; Schulz, 1976).

Non-Personal Control and Stress

Declines in perceived personal control ultimately result in reduced efforts to wield control. Over time, the non-exercise of personal control atrophies a person's actual ability to cope with environmental challenges, with the consequent imbalance between personal competency and environmental demands causing undue stress (Lawton, 1977) and precipitating yet further declines in actual and perceived control.

Ironically, even when aging women personally choose to reduce their work or social activity, the effect is to shrink their range of independent behavior and, hence, their resources for coping with any increased environmental stress. For example, when fears of victimization by neighborhood muggers leads to a lessening of activities outside the home, elderly women limit their mobility and their exposure to everyday stimuli. Thereafter, on the rare occasions when they do go out, stimuli that are usually experienced as innocuous, such as honking horns or flashing traffic lights, may be enough to unnerve them (Parr, 1980). Similarly, when elderly women in congregate housing use more services than their physical health warrants, they reduce their self-reliance and they also experience as much more stressful even the slightest increases in environmental demands (Lawton, 1985).

Elderly women are most seriously underchallenged by their environment, and thus are most susceptible to perceived and then real declines in competency when placed in nursing homes. For it is in such institutions that passive, dependent behavior is positively reinforced and independent behavior is either ignored or punished (M. M. Baltes, 1982; Lawton, 1989; Namehow & Lawton, 1976).

In general, stress which is either too great or too little has the effect of undermining both perceived and actual personal control; and, when immoderate stress levels are linked to institutionalization or illness, the result is often a precipitous drop in survival rates (Lawton, 1977).

ADAPTATION IN OLD AGE

"Holding On" versus "Letting Go"

Earlier, we spoke both of the need of internally controlled persons to "hold on" to personal control, and the stress they experience when forced to "let go" of control. However, we also noted that, in the guidance study, aging women who adapted best to losses in self-reliance were those who accepted some help from others and, in so doing, were able to retain a degree of independence that would otherwise have been impossible.

When faced with inner or outer impediments to self-reliance and the resultant need to relinquish some of their personal control, aging women (and men) may at first experience feelings of discontinuity with their past sense of self. Yet, over time, they may seek a new basis for experiencing a continued sense of identity and self-esteem. This new basis for adjustment is not limited to the yielding of some degree of control so as to assure safety and survival. Instead, it may involve an integration between complementary conditions. This may entail the combining of a lesser degree of primary control with some measure of secondary control, and also the relinquishing of some degree of independence in exchange for an increase in conditions of safety and dependence.

Personal Control versus Personal Security

The notion of old-agers arriving at a new basis for feelings of identity and self-esteem in the face of perceived losses of personal control wins support from research on the effect of physical environmental features on the well-being of the elderly. In this connection, Parmelee and Lawton (1990) observed that housing designs must take into consideration two opposing needs of the elderly: their need, on the one hand, for continued feelings of self-reliance, but, on the other hand, their equally great need for environments that are safe and secure and that also afford easy access to personal services and social supports.

In sum, for aging women to cope effectively with their physical and social losses, they must exchange some personal control for some personal security while, at the same time, continuing to exercise whatever capacities for independence they still retain.

Primary Control and Secondary Control versus Non-Control

The idea that benefits derive from relinquishing some personal control also inheres in the two-process control model (Rothbaum, Weisz, & Snyder, 1982), which holds that perceptions of secondary control are useful when primary control is no longer feasible, as occurs for women in old-age homes (Felton & Kahana, 1974).

Of course, optimal adaptation requires a balance between perceptions of primary and secondary control, although this balance varies according to the individual's prepotent values or goals. For example, when personal achievement is a dominant value, people give more weight to primary control; but when the main aim is for health, safety, and inner peace, people attach more weight to secondary control (Rothbaum et al., 1982).

The adaptiveness of primary control versus secondary control is also a function of the situation. For example, in combat conditions, where life and death are at stake, a perception of primary control is initially useful; but once autonomy becomes impossible, a perception of secondary control is more constructive. By contrast, when first subjected to painful and irreversible events, such as paralysis or the loss of vision, an initial perception of secondary control is preferable because failed expectations of primary control may degenerate into perceptions of complete noncontrol. Yet, even in such situations, people benefit from continued strivings to master those skills which are still attainable (Rothbaum et al., 1982).

Finally, as noted in our earlier discussion of the guidance study by Erikson and colleagues (1986), impaired elderly women seem to function best when they accept the help of people or mechanical aids; for, in so doing, they manage to retain at least a modicum of autonomy.

Conclusion

In this chapter we have suggested that continuity theory (Atchley, 1989; Neugarten et al., 1968; and Tobin, 1991), while applicable to advantaged aging persons, may be an inappropriate explanation of the disadvantaged elderly who have an internal orientation. Certainly, the studies of Lieberman and Tobin (1983), Erikson et al. (1986) and Rothbaum et al. (1982) all suggest that persons who suffer the stress of severe infirmities, social losses, or relocation to institutions may be stripped of their earlier perceptions of personal control and, hence, of their earlier sense of identity and self-esteem. Among such disadvantaged persons, therefore, the experiences and needs of old age may be discontinuous with those of earlier adulthood and may thus require a new basis for feelings of self-trust and self-worth.

This new basis for the adjustment of disadvantaged aging women (and of similarly disadvantaged aging men) requires a new theory of adaptive aging, that of integration. For such persons may need to integrate into their sense of identity and self-worth a perception of greater interdependence and lesser personal control—or, alternatively, a perception of secondary control when a perception of primary control is no longer possible.

Our consideration of some bases for changed perceptions of personal control in aging women leaves some unanswered questions—and, hence, some issues that invite future research. First, with respect to many of the studies cited earlier (e.g., see Langer & Rodin, 1976; Liem, 1975; Rodin, 1983; Rodin & Langer, 1977; and Schulz, 1976), how does one explain experimental indications of institutionalized aging persons whose feelings of lost personal control were followed by sharp declines in health, psychological well-being, and survival rates? Were such outcomes limited to internally controlled persons who could not substitute perceptions of secondary control for lost perceptions of primary control and who, as a consequence, perceived their life situation as being fraught with *non-controllability?*

Second, our current inferences about the effects of institutionalization on perceived control derive mainly from cross-sectional studies. Such studies compare aging women who were institutionalized (those with functional impairments) with those living in the community (those who were presumably non-impaired). However, longitudinal research might yield different findings. By way of example, suppose that longitudinal studies of control perceptions were to be undertaken, with assessments made both before and several times after institutionalization. Might such studies reveal that some institutionalized aging women are more accepting than others of a loss of perceived primary control? And, if this should be the case, who might prove to be the better adjusted old-agers? Might they be persons who, through much of their adult lives, have had perceptions of secondary control? Or alternatively, might they be flexible, ego-controlled persons whose perceptions of primary or secondary control have customarily varied according to whether the situation allowed for perceptions of primary versus secondary control?

Certainly, it seems worthwhile to investigate these issues so as to move toward the discovery of techniques whereby infirm, lonely, or unhappy aged women (and men) might learn how to minimize the aversiveness of perceived losses of primary personal control by replacing them with forms of secondary control.

There is one more area which requires exploration. Most of the studies of perceptions of control among aging persons have focused primarily or exclusively on European-American middle-class or working-class persons. Moreover, when studies of aging women have included ethnic minorities, little or no information has been given as to the number, demography, and economic status of such minorities, and no separate assessment has been made of the extent to which aging minority women and men experience stability or change in their perceptions of control (or non-control) and in feelings of continuity or discontinuity in their sense of self and identity. Thus, future longitudinal studies need to address these issues within aging minority persons.

REFERENCES

Abramson, L. Y., Garber, J., & Seligman, M. E. P. (1980). Learned helplessness in humans: An attributional analysis. In J. Garber & M. E. P. Seligman (Eds.), *Human helplessness: Theory and applications* (pp. 3–34). New York: Academic Press.

Abramson, L. Y., Seligman, M. E. P., & Teasdale, J. D. (1978). Learned helplessness in humans: Critique and reformulation. *Journal of Abnormal Psychology, 87,* 49–74.

Allport, G. (1964). *Pattern and growth in personality.* New York: Holt, Rinehart & Winston.

Andrews, F. M., & Withey, S. B. (1976). *Social indicators of well-being: Americans' perception of life quality.* New York: Plenum.

Atchley, R. C. (1989). A continuity theory of normal aging. *The Gerontologist, 20*(2), 183–190.

Babchuk, N., & Anderson, T. (1989). Older widows and married women: Their intimates and confidants. *International Journal of Aging and Human Development, 28*(1), 21–33.

Baltes, M. M. (1982). Environmental factors in dependency among nursing home residents: A social ecology analysis. In T. A. Wills (Ed.), *Basic processes in helping relationships* (pp. 405–425). New York: Academic Press.

Bandura, A. (1977). Self-efficacy: Toward a unifying theory of behavioral change. *Psychological Review, 84*, 191–215.

Bandura, A. (1982). Self-efficacy in human agency. *American Psychologist, 37*, 122–147.

Bild, B., & Havighurst, R. (1976) Senior citizens in great cities: The case for Chicago. *The Gerontologist, 16*, 1–88.

Bogue, D. J. (1985). *The population of the United States: Historical trends and future projections.* New York: Free Press.

Bowlby, J. (1980). *Attachment and loss* (Vol. III). New York: Basic Books.

Bradburn, N. M. (1969). *The structure of psychological well-being.* Chicago: Aldine.

Brandtstadter, J., & Rothermund, K. (1994). Self-percepts of control in middle and later adulthood: Buffering losses by re-scaling goals. *Psychology and Aging, 9*(2), 265–273.

Brodman, K., Erdmann, A. J., Lorge, I., Wolff, H. G., & Broadbent, T. H. (1949). The Cornell Medical Index: An adjunct to medical interview. *Journal of the American Medical Association, 140*, 530–539.

Bronte, L. (1993). *The longevity factor.* New York: Harper Collins.

Brown, B. R., & Granick, S. (1983). Cognitive and psychosocial differences between I and E locus of control aged persons. *Experimental Aging Research, 9*, 107–110.

Cohler, B. J. (1982). Personal narrative and life course. In P. B. Baltes & O. G. Brim (Eds.), *Life-span development and behavior* (Vol. 4, pp. 205–241). New York: Academic Press.

Conley, J. J. (1984). Longitudinal consistency of adult personality: Self-reported psychological characteristics across 45 years. *Journal of Personality and Social Psychology, 47*, 1325–1333.

Conley, J. J. (1985). Longitudinal stability of personality traits: A multitrait-multimethod-multioccasion analysis. *Journal of Personality and Social Psychology, 49*, 1266–1282.

Costa, P. T., Jr., & McCrae, R. R. (1984). Personality as a lifelong determinant of well-being. In C. Z. Malatesta & C. E. Izard (Eds.), *Emotion in adult development* (pp. 222–265). Beverly Hills, CA: Sage.

Costa, P. T., Jr., & McCrae, R. R. (1988). Personality in adulthood: A six-year longitudinal study of self-reports and spouse rating on the NEO personality inventory. *Journal of Personality and Social Psychology, 54*, 853–863.

Costa, P. T., Jr., McCrae, R. R., & Arenberg, D. (1980). Enduring dispositions in adult males. *Journal of Personality and Social Psychology, 38*, 793–800.

Costa, P. T., Jr., McCrae, R. R., & Arenberg, D. (1983). Recent longitudinal research on personality and aging. In K. W. Schaie (Ed.), *Longitudinal studies of adult psychological development* (pp. 222–265). New York: Guilford Press.

Cumming, E., & Henry, W. H. (1961). *The process of disengagement.* New York: Basic Books.

Edwards, J., & Kleemack, D. (1973). Correlates of life satisfaction: A reexamination. *Journal of Gerontology, 28*, 497–502.

Erikson, E. (1950). *Childhood and society.* New York: Norton.

Erikson, E. (1968). *Identity: Youth and crisis.* New York: Norton.

Erikson, E., Erikson, J., & Kivnick, H. Q. (1986). *Vital involvement in old age.* New York: Norton.

Felton, B., & Kahana, E. (1974). Adjustment and situationally-bound locus of control among institutionalized aged. *Journal of Gerontology, 29*, 295–301.

Havighurst, R. J., Neugarten, B. L., & Tobin, S. S. (1968). Disengagement and patterns of aging. In B. L. Neugarten (Ed.), *Middle age and aging* (pp. 161–172). Chicago: University of Chicago Press.

Hubley, A. M., & Hultsch, D. F. (1994). The relationship of personality trait variables to subjective age identity in older adults. *Research on Aging, 16*(4), 415–439.

Hunter, I. K., Linn, M. W., & Harris, R. (1981–82). Characteristics of high and low self-esteem in the elderly. *International Journal of Aging and Human Development, 14*, 117–126.

Keller, M. L., Leventhal, E. A., & Larson, B. (1989). Aging: the lived experience. *International Journal of Aging and Human Development, 29,* 67–81.

Kelly, E. L. (1940). A 36-trait personality rating scale. *American Psychologist, 9,* 97–102.

Kivett, V., Watson, J., & Busch, J. (1977). The relative importance of physical, psychological, and social variables to locus of control orientation in middle age. *Journal of Gerontology, 32,* 203–210.

Krause, N. (1994). Stressors in salient roles and well-being in later life. *Journal of Gerontology: Psychological Sciences, 49*(3), P137–P148.

Kuhl, J. (1986). Aging and models of control: The hidden costs of wisdom. In M. M. Baltes & P. B. Baltes (Eds.), *The Psychology of control and aging* (pp. 1–33). Hillsdale, NJ: Erlbaum.

Lachman, M. E. (1983). Perceptions of intellectual aging: Antecedent or consequence of intellectual functioning? *Developmental Psychology, 19,* 483–498.

Lachman, M. E. (1986). Locus of control in aging research: A case for multi-dimensional and domain-specific assessment. *Psychology and Aging, 1,* 34–40.

Langer, E. J., & Rodin, J. (1976). The effects of choice and enhanced personal responsibility for the aged: A field experiment in an institutional setting. *Journal of Personality and Social Psychology, 34,* 191–198.

Larson, R. (1978). Thirty years of research on the subjective well-being of older Americans. *Journal of Gerontology, 33,* 109–125.

Lawton, M. P. (1977). The impact of environment on aging and behavior. In J. E. Birren & K. W. Schaie (Eds.), *Handbook of the Psychology of Aging* (pp. 276–301). New York: Van Nostrand Reinhold.

Lawton, M. P. (1985). The elderly in context: Perspectives from environmental psychology and gerontology. *Environment and Behavior, 17,* 501–519.

Lawton, M. P. (1989). Behavior-relevant ecological factors. In K. W. Schaie & C. Schooler (Eds.), *Social structure and aging: Psychological processes* (pp. 57–58). Hillsdale, NJ: Erlbaum.

Lefcourt, H. M. (1976). *Locus of control: Current trends in theory and research.* Hillsdale, NJ: Erlbaum.

Lefcourt, H. M. (1991). Locus of control. In J. P. Robinson, P. R. Shaver, & L. S. Wrightsman (Eds.), *Measures of personality and social psychological attitudes* (Vol.1, pp. 413–499). New York: Academic Press.

Levenson, H. (1974). Activism and powerful others: Distinctions within the concept of internal-external control. *Journal of Personality Assessment, 38,* 377–383.

Levenson, H. (1981). Differentiating among internality, powerful others, and chance. In H. M. Lefcourt (Ed.), *Research with the locus of control construct* (Vol. 1, pp. 15–63). New York: Academic Press.

Levinson, E. (October, 1975). Correlates of internal-external locus of control scale in an aging population. Paper presented at annual meeting of Gerontology Society, Louisville, KY.

Lieberman, M. A., & Tobin, S. S. (1983). *The experience of old age: Stress, coping and survival.* New York: Basic Books.

Liem, G. R. (1975). Performance and satisfaction as affected by personal control over salient decision. *Journal of Personality and Social Psychology, 31,* 232–240.

Lopata, H. Z. (1973). *Widowhood in an American city.* Cambridge, MA: Echenkman.

Maddox, G. L. (1965). Fact and artifact: Evidence bearing on disengagement theory from the Duke Geriatric Project. *Human Development, 8,* 171.

Mancini, J. (1980). Effects of health and income on control orientation and life satisfaction among aged public housing residents. *International Journal of Aging and Human Development, 12,* 215–220.

Mischel, W. (1976). Introduction to Personality (2nd ed.). New York: Holt, Rinehart and Winston.

Miller, W. R., Rosellini, R. A., & Seligman, M. E. P. (1977). Learned helplessness and depression. In J. D. Maser & M. E. P. Seligman (Eds.), *Psychopathology: Experimental models* (pp. 104–130). San Francisco: W. H. Freeman.

Moody, H. R. (1994). *Aging: Concepts and controversy.* Thousand Oaks, CA: Pine Forge Press.

Morganti, J. B., Nehrke, M. F., Hulicka, I. M., & Cataldo, J. F. (1988). Life-span differences in life satisfaction, self-concept, and locus of control. *International Journal of Aging and Human Development, 26,* 45–56.

Mussen, F., Eichorn, D. H., Honzik, M. P., Bieber, S. L., & Meredith, W. (1980). Continuity and change in women's characteristics over four decades. *International Journal of Behavioral Development, 3,* 333–347.

Namehow, L., & Lawton, M. P. (1976). Toward an ecological theory of adaptation and aging. In H. M. Proshansky, W. H. Ittelson, & L. G. Rivlin (Eds.), *Environmental psychology: People and their physical setting* (2nd ed., pp. 315–321). New York: Holt, Rinehart and Winston.

Nehrke, M. F., Bellucci, G., & Gabriel, S. J. (1977). Death anxiety, locus of control, and life satisfaction in the elderly: Toward a definition of ego-integrity. *Omega—Journal of Death and Dying, 8,* 359–368.

Neugarten, B. L., Havighurst, R. J., & Tobin, S. S. (1968). Personality and patterns of aging. In B. L. Neugarten (Ed.), *Middle age and aging* (pp. 173–180). Chicago: University of Chicago Press.

Palmore, E., & Luikart, C. (1972). Health and social factors related to life satisfaction. *Journal of Health and Social Behavior, 13,* 68–80.

Palmore, E., & Maddox, G. L. (1977). Sociological aspects of aging. In E. H. Busse & E. Pfeiffer (Eds.), *Behavior and adaptation in late life* (pp. 464–489). Boston: Little, Brown.

Parkes, C. M. (1985). Bereavement in the elderly. *Geriatric Medicine Today, 4*(5), 55–64.

Parmelee, P. A., & Lawton, M. P. (1990). The design of special environments for the aged. In J. E. Birren & K. W. Schaie (Eds.), *Handbook of the psychology of aging* (3rd. ed., pp. 464–489). New York: Academic Press.

Parr, J. (1980). The interaction of persons and living environment. In L. W. Poon (Ed.), *Aging in the 1980s: Psychological issues* (pp. 393–406). Washington, DC: American Psychological Association.

Pohl, J. M., & Fuller, S. S. (1980). Perceived choice, social interaction, and dimensions of morale of residents in a home for the aged. *Research in Nursing and Health, 3,* 147–157.

Rodin, J. (1983). Behavioral medicine: Beneficial effects of self-control training in aging. *Review Internationale, 32,* 153–181.

Rodin, J. (1986). Aging and health: Effects of the sense of control. *Science, 233,* 1271–1276.

Rodin, J. (1987). Personal control through the life course. In R. Abeles (Ed.), *Life-span perspectives in social psychology* (pp. 103–116). Hillsdale, NJ: Erlbaum.

Rodin, J., & Langer, E. (1977). Long-term effects of a control-relevant intervention. *Journal of Personality and Social Psychology, 35,* 897–902.

Rodin, J., & Langer, E. (1980). Aging labels: The decline of control and the fall of self-esteem. *Journal of Social Issues, 36,* 12–29.

Rodin, J., Timko, C., & Harris, S. (1985). The construct of control: Biological and psychological correlates. *Annual Review of Gerontology and Geriatrics, 5,* 3–55.

Rothbaum, F., Weisz, J., & Synder, S. (1982). Changing the world and changing the self: A two-process model of perceived control. *Journal of Personality and Social Psychology, 42,* 5–37.

Rotter, J. B. (1954). *Social learning and clinical psychology.* Englewood Cliffs, NJ: Prentice-Hall.

Rotter, J. B. (1966). Generalized expectancies for internal versus external control of reinforcement. *Psychological Monographs, 8*(1), (whole No. 609).

Rotter, J. B. (1982). Social learning theory. In N. T. Feather (Ed.), *Expectations and actions: Expectancy-value theories in psychology* (pp. 242–255). Hillsdale, NJ: Erlbaum.

Schaie, K. W., & Parham, I. A. (1976). Stability of adult personality: Fact or fable. *Journal of Personality and Social Psychology, 34,* 146–158.

Schulz, R. (1976). Effects of control and predictability on the institutionalized aged. *Journal of Personality and Social Psychology, 33,* 563–573.

Seligman, M. E. P. (1975). *Helplessness: On depression, development, and death.* San Francisco: W. H. Freeman.

Siegler, I. C., George, L. K., & Okun, M. A. (1979). Cross-sequential analysis of adult personality. *Developmental Psychology, 15,* 350–351.

Tobin, S. S. (1991). *Personhood in advanced old age: Implications for practice.* New York: Springer Publishing Co.

Turner, B. F. (1987). Mental health and the older woman. In G. Lesnoff-Caravaglia (Ed.), *Handbook of applied gerontology* (pp. 201–230). New York: Human Sciences Press.

U.S. Bureau of the Census (1988). "Projections of the population of the United States by age, sex, and race: 1988 to 2080." *Current Population Reports,* Series P-25, No. 1018, Washington, DC: U.S. Government Printing Office.

Whitbourne, S. K. (1986). *The me I Know: A study of adult identity.* New York: Springer-Verlag.

Wolk, S. (1976). Situational constraint as a moderator of the locus of control-adjustment relationship. *Journal of Consulting and Clinical Psychology, 44,* 420–427.

Wolk, S., & Telleen, S. (1976). Psychological and social correlates of life satisfaction as a function of residential constraint. *Journal of Gerontology, 31,* 89–98.

Woodruff, D. S., & Birren, J. E. (1971). *Age and personality: A twenty-five year follow-up.* Unpublished paper, University of Southern California.

8

FURTHER REFLECTIONS
ON AUTONOMY

JOHN D. HOGAN[1]
St. John's University

The foregoing discussions of autonomy make few claims for universal meaning or description. They are, in many ways, an artifact of a particular time and a particular branch of social science. The time is the end of the 20th century and the branch of social science is psychology. Without either of these elements, the discussions could go in very different directions. But temporal meanings can be of enormous significance. What follows are some of the considerations which have helped to shape the discussions and some of the interpretations which can be made of them.

THE FOCUS ON AUTONOMY ACROSS THE LIFE SPAN

The study of development, at least from the perspective of psychology, has gone through many significant changes in the last two decades. Although the bulk of questions being asked are familiar, the manner in which the issues are conceptualized has been transformed. Many theorists and researchers have moved away from static, unidirectional, and unidimensional approaches to behavior. The current approaches tend to be dynamic, bi-directional, and multidimensional, with an appreciation of many variables which were ignored only a generation or two ago. (For one example of the complexity of these newer approaches, see Bronfenbrenner, 1996.)

At the same time, there has been a competing trend in developmental psychology—its increasing fragmentation. In fact, that splintering has been happening throughout psychology, occurring in several ways. The "grand theories" are dead or dying and the era of the

---

[1] I am grateful to Naa Oyo Kwate for her help and advice on this section of the chapter.

"mini-theory" has emerged. Developmental psychology has become increasingly separated from other areas of psychological study, such as clinical and school psychology, with which it holds strong alliances. And often, rather than making an attempt to consider human behavior within some larger framework with all of its complex and interactive biological and social systems, behavior is studied from a very limited perspective.

The reason for such a narrow focus is easy to understand. The complexity of human behavior can be too overwhelming for coherent study. In fact, it has been so typical of science to limit the number of variables under study at any one time that the approach might be considered part of the scientific method. Still, the question remains: Does it make sense to select out a single variable such as autonomy and attempt to consider it in isolation? Is there anything to be learned from such an approach? Isn't it more realistic to research behavior as viewed from a more systematic position?

The reality is that no matter how many variables are employed, they still represent a shorthand for our actual experience. It would be impossible to consider all of the potential influences on any piece of behavior, as the causes of behavior are too complex. But in the early stages of exploration, a more narrowly focused investigation can be very useful. Not only can it help to point out the areas of most importance, it can also aid in forming the very questions to be asked. That is undoubtedly one of the roles of the present volume.

There is a danger in this approach, but gratefully, it does not find expression here. The danger would be that, after having considered autonomy in women separately from other variables, it is left in isolation, unintegrated with the other aspects of development that give it meaning. In each case here, the authors have tried to address the meaning of autonomy, but they have tried to place it alongside a larger view. Perhaps it is impossible for psychologists of this era not to do so.

SOME "POSTMODERN" CONCERNS

Social science, in general, and developmental psychology, in particular, are now said to have entered the "postmodern" era, complicating their study more than ever (Bronfenbrenner, Kessel, Kessen, & White, 1986). Where science was once regarded as objective, now the questions it asks are more likely to be viewed as a reflection of current social and political forces. Hence, it is not only the child who is seen as a "cultural invention" (Kessen, 1979), but developmental psychology itself. With this perspective, it is fair to question the meaning of developmental psychology. In parallel fashion, one may ask of this volume: What is its social meaning? What is the political role of its authors?

Certainly the volume is meant to convey an expression of the value of women. In one of the more common criticisms of developmental psychology, it is argued that male behavior is too often taken as the standard, and women are given meaning only in relation to male norms. In a related corollary, women's behavior is sometimes seen as deficient when compared to men, according to these male-centered standards. Gilligan (1982) has been especially vocal in exposing this bias.

Selecting women and women's developmental standards as the principal focus of a volume such as this is an effective way to avoid the bias of male norms. The reader would have to search hard throughout this book to find an instance where women are not seen as valued in themselves. Within this largely all-female context, there is little room for deficient behaviors, only alternative behaviors. Women can be more explicitly viewed in terms of their own norms.

Recent developments in one branch of the new men's movement have taken some of these "normative" ideas and used them as their own (e.g., Levant & Pollack, 1995). Several writers in the men's movement argue that they, too, have been victimized by norms and social expectations. Men, they argue, must be allowed greater expression of other aspects of themselves, particularly those aspects having to do with intimacy, relatedness and emotional expression. In short, just as there are women who do not wish to be judged by male norms, so too are there men who don't wish to be judged by them either.

This volume might also be seen as an attempt to further validate "women's studies." While many such courses and programs have been well-integrated into the college curriculum, they are still vulnerable to attack. In some cases, they suffer from their own success. (See Kessler-Harris and Swerdlow, 1996, for a recent discussion of some of these issues.) The book may serve as a reminder that this young field has become a powerful political force, challenging and redefining many important social issues of the day.

DEFINITIONS, TIMING, AND CULTURE

There are many obstacles to be faced when choosing a project such as this. For example, autonomy is subject to various meanings throughout the life span. The meaning is clearly different for an infant attempting to determine what is "self" and what is not, for a recently married young woman trying to find her role in this new relationship, or for an elderly person struggling to maintain an independent existence. All three cases could be said to involve autonomy, but our language betrays us. While the behaviors may have some elements in common, they mostly involve qualitatively different components. Care must be taken not to create artificial links and, thereby, obscure the reality.

Yet, there are overarching themes which connect many of these behaviors, as Nadien and Denmark point out in the first chapter. Julian Rotter was the first of the social learning theorists to clarify this issue when he proposed the notion of an internal versus an external locus of control (1966). Albert Bandura (1989) developed the idea further in his discussion of self-efficacy. Now Martin Seligman (1991) has become one of the most prominent contemporary psychologists through his research and writing in "learned helplessness" and "learned optimism." At their center, all of these proposals are concerned with aspects of autonomy.

Kaufman, in her chapter on adolescence, points to another developmental issue of autonomy. Since adolescents possess several characteristics that encourage risk-taking behavior, perhaps too much autonomy is a bad thing at this point in the life cycle. It may be that the full expression of autonomy is best saved for a time when the organism can handle it more effectively, perhaps in young adulthood. Likewise, there are other periods in the life span that may be peculiarly sensitive to the degree of expressed autonomy. Too much autonomy in the elderly, for instance, as shown by ignoring failing capacities, could be dangerous—even life-threatening. Each period of life generates different expectations and behaviors related to autonomy, and any discussion of autonomy should reflect these developmental realities.

The value to be placed on autonomy is another issue of fundamental concern. Autonomy is not necessarily seen as a good thing, even within Western culture. (See Guisinger & Blatt, 1994, for example.) Similarly, Harvey, in her chapter on autonomy in young women, emphasized the necessity of achieving balance between autonomy and relatedness, including the observation that different degrees of balance may be achieved in different arenas of life. A woman who finds a suitable degree of autonomy on the job may not be equally comfortable with the level of autonomy in her marriage, or in dealings with her parents.

It has even been argued that "individualistic" approaches or emphases to life, of which a consideration of autonomy is part, are primarily Western positions and, therefore, represent a minority view. The people of the world, at least in terms of numbers, are better represented by a "collectivist" approach, such that considerations of autonomy are the exception (Triandis, 1996). In an attempt to develop a universal psychology, it is argued, the exceptional nature of autonomy needs to be recognized. Moreover, the value-based nature of autonomy must be underlined.

CURRENT CONCEPTUAL ISSUES IN DEVELOPMENT

The remarkable changes in contemporary developmental psychology are probably best seen in the underlying conceptual issues that govern the practice of the discipline. These issues not only dictate the manner in which research is conducted, but determine the very questions to be asked and the manner in which research results are to be interpreted.

Context

Modern developmental theory has seen a reawakening of interest in temperamental styles and other biologically based correlates of behavior. Echoing some of the earliest pronouncements of developmental psychology, there has even emerged an area of study known as evolutionary psychology (e.g., Buss, 1990) that examines traits and strategies as they relate to the development and adaptation of the species through the history of humankind. Some of these discussions focus specifically on evolutionary aspects of female development (e.g., Gangestad & Simpson, 1990). But despite these biological and evolutionary perspectives, more than anything, modern theory has been characterized by a spotlight on context.

An emphasis on behavior as context-dependent is not new. Several early developmentalists including James Mark Baldwin and, particularly, Lev Vygotsky, also made this point. But their ideas have not always been front and center. In the current way of thinking, an individual does not carry around a behavior, waiting to express it. Rather, there is no behavior until the predisposition and the context meet.

Such considerations underline several of the points made by the chapter authors. Autonomy, like many other psychological variables, can be viewed largely as a social construction. It has no existence independent of an agreed upon definition, and that definition reflects not only the culture but the historical period in which it is found. Moreover, what has been constructed can be reconstructed.

Social constructionism is a particularly appropriate model to use in interpreting research on women since many of the basic points of the approach are similar to those made by feminist critics (Bohan, 1990). In addition, it has been charged that the discipline of psychology itself has been a major force in constructing woman, and some feminists have taken it as their role to help psychology "deconstruct" the female (Herman, 1995).

Cultural and Historical Considerations

Some cultures may choose not to ask questions about autonomy in women because they view it as unimportant. Some historical periods also have ignored the question for lack of perceived significance. The fact that this volume was proposed and completed says a great deal about a general cultural view of women in the United States at the end of the 20th century. It also says a great deal about what women of this time and place are thinking about themselves.

While questions about autonomy in women appear to be strongly correlated with the emergence of modern technological societies, such interest should not be seen merely as a by-product of these societies. Perceptions of women and their roles are more deeply imbedded in culture. Modern Japan, for instance, has achieved a technological modernity that is rivaled by few other countries, yet it has retained a view of women and their autonomy that is usually referred to as "traditional." Autonomous behavior, in general, and in women, in particular, is simply not highly valued in Japanese culture.

On the other hand, the government of China, a nation significantly less well developed in any technological sense, has promoted a view of women that is, in some ways, closer to current Western thought. Certainly the governmental egalitarian view of women, now valued in communist China, is very far removed from that of many traditional Asian nations.

Such disparities are not to be seen within Asian nations alone. As mentioned earlier, even within Western culture, the over-emphasis on autonomy, at the expense of relatedness, has been questioned (e.g., Guisinger & Blatt, 1994). These authors argue that women and men are missing valuable experiences by limiting themselves to culturally assigned emphases in behavior. In their view, genuine maturity involves a more equal mix of autonomy and relatedness. Of course, not all men and women agree. Harvey, in her chapter, cites several studies indicating that samples of both genders are sometimes quite comfortable with their historically assigned roles.

In any case, the point should be clear. Both the specific and general context (i.e., culture) are major forces in defining the roles that women (and men) play. Any discussion of autonomy—including whether it is to have any value at all—is probably best discussed only in terms of the worth assigned to it by the culture and the historical period from which it arises.

Bi-Directional Development

Several researchers, particularly Bell (1979), have made us sensitive to the bi-directional nature of development. While previously it was common to think of the infant or young child as being raised by the parent, it is now common to speak of the role of the child in its own development, or even in raising the parent. It is recognized that neither parent nor child are lumps of clay. They modify their responses based on input and experience from one another.

A parent does not typically impose one style of child-rearing on their progeny. In a larger sense, there is no style of child rearing, at least not one that a parent dictates relentlessly, without regard to particular circumstances. Rather, there is an interaction between parent and child, a constant series of negotiation and renegotiation involving temperament and personal style, what Chess and Thomas call a "goodness of fit" (1984).

It is recognized that such bi-directional influences on development are not relevant only to children. Neither are they confined to parent–child interactions, although the data for other developmental periods are meager. Just as an infant is able to adjust its behavior to the style and temperament of the caregiver—and simultaneously have an effect on the behavior of the caregiver—so too can a young woman establish an interactional loop with the important points of her environment, whether occupation, spouse, or parents. Other periods in life present their own idiosyncratic opportunity for establishing behavioral feedback.

In this way of thinking, autonomy may be less a trait than a potential. At varying times during the life span, a woman (or man) may learn that certain behaviors are not useful, and change behaviors accordingly. This is consistent with a view of development usually referred to as a life-span approach. In this case, "life span" refers to more than just a term of years. It refers to a position that argues that each period of life is an opportunity for genuine development. Humans are not infinitely plastic, but neither are they bound to live out some pattern imposed by early experience. Instead, they are involved in a continuing dialogue with the environment, changing and developing as the circumstances warrant.

Some of this potential for development and change may not be so obvious. Individuals may be content with their marriages and jobs—with themselves in general. The feedback, rather than being a spark for change, is a recommendation for the status quo. Hence, the general picture is one of continuity, as Nadien and Denmark suggest. But the potential remains.

Similarly, the capacity for feedback and change may be one of the reasons that studying autonomy in women in isolation has some inherent limitations. Without specification of the context, the reasons for a change in behavior are likely to be masked. In some cases, the more important unit of study would be women in specified but varied contexts, an idea consistent with the proposals of Bronfenbrenner (1996).

Nature/Nurture Revisited

Psychological research on women's issues has come a long way since the first studies on periodicity and the "variability hypothesis" were conducted at the turn of the century. (See Russo and Denmark, 1987, for an overview of some of the important issues through the years.) But in some ways, the basic questions still remain. Does women's development differ from men's development in substantial ways? And, if so, what is the source of that difference?

In a larger sense, these questions reflect the oldest of questions in psychology—the nurture/nature issue, and their answers usually take a limited number of forms. In one version, the development of women and men are held to be different due to biological differences. They are programmed to play out different patterns largely determined by underlying biology. Even their brains are dissimilar, bathed in different levels of hormones, virtually from the beginning of life.

In the opposing version, developmental differences are really the result of variations in social roles imposed by society. Biological differences are minimal, with enormous overlap in behavior between the sexes. If society were structured differently, it would be obvious that female behaviors and male behaviors are little different from one another.

The third position is the interactionist position and these days almost everyone gives it lip service in one form or another. Whether they truly believe in it or not is a different matter. An interactionist position itself can take many forms, several of which have emerged only recently. Some of its forms redefine the argument itself.

Anastasi (1958) and Lerner (1986), for example, have both argued that in most nature/nurture arguments the wrong question is asked. The question should never be about the relative contributions of heredity and environment—the most frequently queried issue. The answer to that question, contend Anastasi and Lerner, is unknowable.

In a more recent variation of the problem, Plomin (1994) and others have taken the interactionist position a step further. They argue that one of the roles of the genotype is to help select the environment. The choice of environment is not inevitable; for some, the range of environments available may be limited or non-existent. Still, research has found significant relationships between genotypes and traditional environmental measures, suggesting another form of nature/nurture interaction. Further, Plomin (1994) has provided evidence that genes respond to the environment even at the molecular level.

What are some of the implications of the new nature/nurture proposals? For one, they suggest it is time to get rid of our outdated ways of looking at the issue. Simplified notions of independent contributions of experience and genes to behavior do not reflect reality. Even behavioral geneticists, who are committed to understanding the genetic basis from which species behavior and individual differences emerge, frequently write about the extent to which these ideationally separate notions are inextricably enmeshed. Efforts are better spent in looking at the range of behaviors between the sexes across the life span, including differences in autonomy. For instance, a more relevant question might be: What environments do women wish they could choose, but to which they are denied access?

Still, this kind of research may open up avenues that some wish to leave closed. By arguing that genes may affect our choice of environment, aren't we simply talking about another kind of "biology as destiny" argument? Plomin (1994), one of the world's leading behavioral geneticists, says no. He has argued that the more we learn about genes, the more they demonstrate the importance of the environment.

AUTONOMY ACROSS THE LIFE SPAN

Autonomy has different roles and meanings across the life span. At least one researcher has contended that, for the young child, the search for autonomy is the very essence of human existence. Further, he argues, it is to be found in the infant's cry and in locating the nipple (Bettelheim, 1967). Without an appreciation that the infant has some power over the environment, the child's growth will be limited, in the extreme case resulting in such devastating disabilities as infantile autism.

Erikson (1963) places the advent of autonomy a little later than Bettelheim, but still sees it as a crucial step for the developing child. But in a larger sense, the battle for autonomy may be fought many times throughout the life span, although the circumstances may vary enormously. Dramatic physical changes, whether they are the emerging functions of adolescence or the decline of old age, usher in significant changes in the person and require adjustments.

Maccoby (1995) has argued that the relevance of gender waxes and wanes through different periods of development. But even within periods of the life span that are deemed to be relatively homogeneous, say in adulthood, there are constantly shifting patterns in autonomy among women. The goals of a woman in her reproductive years tend to be different from those of a woman in her post-reproductive years, and her views of herself reflect the new issues and problems.

Moreover, the nature of the changing environment must always be a consideration. And it is not only the environment at large that may limit the opportunities to express autonomy, but the more personal environment as well. Roberts and Newton (1987), for example, discuss the degree to which husbands may limit autonomy in their spouses by disrupting their efforts toward occupational goals.

In addition, Levinson (1996) has made the point that women (and men) are in a constant state of renegotiation throughout the life span. While many individuals may exhibit a superficial consistency, lives are marked by periodic and inevitable patterns of stability and change. Some of these same points were made in the chapter by Babladelis, in her discussion of Hornstein's research.

WHEN AUTONOMY IS NOT ACHIEVED

There is a wide range of maladaptive behaviors associated with difficulties in achieving autonomy. In some cases, these behaviors are closely associated with gender. Certain eating disorders, for example, although not unknown among men, are much more likely among women. Anorexia nervosa is one example. While social emphasis on thinness in Western culture clearly plays a central role, a young woman's ability to develop a sense of effectiveness in the world has also been implicated as a key variable.

Gordon (1990) has suggested that a family that places an intense emphasis on achievement but that simultaneously denies the adolescent female the necessary opportunities for self-initiated behavior places the child at risk for developing the disorder. This lack of autonomy fosters a dangerous dependency on the family. A crisis may develop when the young girl is faced with situations that demand a healthy sense of self-efficacy, such as going to college or entering an intimate relationship. As a result, going on a diet, and ultimately starving herself, become expressions of power for a person aware of her own sense of powerlessness. Initial social approval obviously adds to the picture.

In her chapter on adolescence, Kaufman points out that there is frequently an enmeshed relationship with the mother who, ironically, also demonstrates a lack of autonomous functioning in her need for her daughter to achieve a sense of completeness. Also,

Harvey cites research indicating that young women with anorexia, as well as bulimia, have more external locus of control, as well as less self-assertion. In the case of bulimia, Harvey discusses findings in which young women with bulimia were found to have a higher rate of dependency conflicts.

Infantile anorexia has also been described as a failure of the organism to achieve age-appropriate autonomous functioning. Chatoor (1989) has described the etiology of this disorder from an object-relations perspective. The disorder begins between 6 months and 3 years of age, and is characterized by food refusal or extreme food selectivity. Again, a dysfunctional style of interaction between mother and child is hypothesized, in this case at the stage of individuation. If the mother is over-solicitous, in the form of cajoling or forcing food into the child's mouth in order to ensure food intake at this stage, it is believed that there will be an interference with the development of somatopsychological differentiation.

The result of difficulties in establishing autonomous functioning is not limited to eating disorders. The relationship between a lack of autonomy and depression has also received a good deal of attention. Of particular interest has been the presence of severe dependency patterns. For example, Beck's cognitive theory of depression dichotomizes interpersonal patterns into sociotrophy, which places a high value on relatedness and being accepted by others, and autonomy. An excess of sociotrophy, which correlates with "traditional" ideals of femininity, is thought to predict a higher occurrence of depression, a prediction supported by the literature.

As noted by Kaufman, the higher frequency of depression among women begins during middle adolescence, during which girls experience depression at three times the rate of boys. As an explanation, she points to the paradoxical abdication of control in an apparent effort to be in control. Kaufman also relates autonomy to suicidal behavior in adolescence, an outcome that she describes as a result of the "autonomy of inner impulses."

Vulnerability to depression for women in middle age was discussed by Babladelis. Her discussion relates more to a woman's sense of self generally, and indirectly to the focus of this volume. Middle age presents significant challenges, such as the "empty nest" and its effects on the sense of womanhood. However, it appears those women who demonstrate self-control over their lives, particularly those in the workforce, may be better prepared for such inevitabilities. Therefore, autonomous functioning may serve as a buffer against middle-aged depression or other psychological problems.

It is important to realize, as Babladelis points out, that when a woman enters her middle years she is not necessarily more vulnerable to psychological problems. A study by Mitchell and Helson (1990) supports this point. In a longitudinal sample of college alumnae, women in their early 50s most frequently described their current lives as "first rate." These authors hypothesized that this period represented a time of autonomy and relational security.

It should be noted that while this discussion has focused on difficulties that may emerge in the development of autonomy, psychological maladjustment may also occur if it is developed to the exclusion of relatedness. Helgeson (1994), for example, has pointed out that the real question to ask when addressing psychological well-being is the degree to which one possesses the traits of agency, or the focus on the self and forming separations, and communion, or the focus on others and forming connections. Her definitions of these two constructs were based on conventional measures of masculinity and femininity, respectively. The lesson, therefore, appears to be that for psychological well-being to exist, the individual, male or female, must have a good measure of both "traditional" masculine and feminine traits.

WOMEN OF COLOR

There are many paths to autonomy and many consequences of its achievement or lack of achievement. One of the threads running through several of the chapters is the different routes to autonomy taken by women of color. Some of the richest differences in achieving and expressing autonomy may be found in comparing different ethnic and racial groups.

Some have argued that a discussion of women of color must have a foundation in a context different from that used for European American women. Azibo (1994), for example, maintains that a discussion of African American women must be anchored in African-centered black studies as a distinct discipline of its own, rather than as an arm of women's studies in general.

It is interesting to note that while autonomy is generally valued in this society, in some instances it has been used to pathologize those who are not of the dominant culture. For example, Dietrich (1975) describes the myth of black "matriarchy," or female dominance, and argues that social scientists such as Moynihan have attempted to ascribe black poverty to a pathological family structure—one in which the woman is head of a single parent household.

Autonomy in African American women can be conceived of in different ways, given the complex interaction of cultural characteristics (both African and American) and oppression (both racist and sexist). Some argue that for African American women, there exists a more flexible orientation to gender roles (Boyd-Franklin, 1989; Greene, 1994). This flexibility contrasts with African women from the Caribbean who are socialized in fairly stereotyped and rigid sex roles where women are expected to be bright, refined, and cultured, but not to outstrip men (Brice-Baker, 1994; Gopaul-McNichol, 1993). Many researchers have described the ways in which black women develop a healthy sense of an autonomous self, while simultaneously maintaining significant relationships as well as independence (Gibbs & Fuery, 1994).

Nobles (1974) argues that in spite of African American women's flexibility, they are socialized to be caretakers, a result of the African worldview that highly values children as representing the continuity of life. Many African American women internalize the stereotype of the strong matriarch and, as a result, attempt to bear all burdens, acknowledge no personal pain, and take care of everyone (Greene, 1994).

Native American women may also experience greater flexibility and power than do European American women in terms of gender roles. According to LaFromboise, Berman, and Sohi (1994), this occurs as a direct result of the roots of traditional Native American women's identity which is firmly rooted in spirituality, extended family, and tribe.

For Asian and Asian American women, autonomy occurs within a particular constellation of traditional culture and assimilation into the dominant culture. Women who come from cultures built on the social philosophies of Confucius experience a more oppressive socialization in which they are indoctrinated to embody deference, suffering, and personal sacrifice (Bradshaw, 1994). This is not the case for other Asian groups, such as Filipinos, who live in the context of a more egalitarian distribution of power. Acculturation to American values exerts an added pressure to subscribe to an Eurocentric notion of independence and autonomy.

Often, the literature on women of color occurs in a United States context. That is, a particular group may be described as adhering to certain ideologies and exhibiting particular behaviors described at face value. This focus is limiting because it fails to consider more distant historical forces. Even in cross-cultural studies, ethnographic accounts of women of color do not address how the culture has been influenced by European domination, colonization, and slavery. For example, Obbo (1986) argues that the goals of most African women on their native continent include the establishment of their own economic and social credibility historically eroded by colonialism. Further, Kettel (1986) asserts that among the Tugen of East Africa, male dominance can be attributed to the effects of colonialization. Finally, Strobel (1984) illustrates how female subordination and polarized spheres among men and women are a function of the gender ideology maintained by Western education and promulgated by Christian missionaries.

Conclusion

It is clear from these essays that the authors of this volume did not choose an easy task. Nonetheless, they brought excitement to their journey, along with the promise of many possibilities, and their ambitious project would have to be judged successful. One of the most important of the thoughts presented here is that women as well as men may take different things from the same environment, and that they create and select environments by which they are then affected (Maccoby, 1995). In short, the authors argue—consistent with much contemporary theorizing—that we are all active in our own development.

Kaufman, in her chapter on adolescence, poses a challenge that could be applied to the entire life span. Her challenge is to create a "wellness model" upon which successful adaptation strategies could be based. At the very least, such a model would provide a base from which further research and writing could develop. During a period of changing community standards and expanding ethnic diversity in the United States, such thoughtful guidelines would be welcome.

A word of caution is in order. One of the lessons of modern developmental psychology is that there are many paths to health and happiness. The preceding chapters return to that theme several times. Whatever our prescriptions for "model" ways in which we may live out our lives, at base there must always be a respect for individual differences and the potential for successful idiosyncratic choices. The role of a "wellness" model would be as a reference point and guide, not as a requirement.

One thing to be learned from the social constructionist position is that science is not neutral. It is value laden. As a result, even the priority given to research topics is in most ways a matter of choice. It is no longer satisfactory for the social scientist to be content simply doing science. If there is to be any kind of guarantee that the general public will pay attention to the topics that the scientist values, the scientist must engage in a bit of public political activism.

REFERENCES

Anastasi, A. (1958). Heredity, environment, and the question "how?". *Psychological Review, 65,* 197–208.

Azibo, D. A. (1994). Selected issues in black women's studies from the perspective of the African worldview: Towards African women's advancement. *The Afrocentric Scholar, 3,* 28–51.

Bandura, A. (1989). Social cognitive theory. In R. Vasta (Ed.), *Annals of Child Development* (Vol. 6, pp. 1–60).

Bell, R. Q. (1979). Parent, child and reciprocal influences. *American Psychologist, 34,* 821–826.

Bemporad, J. R., & Herzog, D. B. (1989). *Psychoanalysis and eating disorders.* New York: Guilford.

Bettelheim, B. (1967). *The empty fortress: Infantile autism and the birth of the self.* New York: Free Press.

Bohan, J. (1990). Social constructionism and contextual history: An expanded approach to the history of psychology. *Teaching of Psychology, 17,* 82–89.

Boyd-Franklin, N. (1989). *Black families in therapy: A multisystems approach.* New York: Guilford.

Bradshaw, C. K. (1994). Asian and Asian American women: Historical and political considerations in psychotherapy. In L. Comas-Diaz & B. Greene (Eds.), *Women of color: Integrating ethnic and gender identities in psychotherapy* (pp. 72–113). New York: Guilford.

Brice-Baker, J. R. (1994). West Indian women: The Jamaican woman. In L. Comas-Diaz & B. Greene (Eds.), *Women of color: Integrating ethnic and gender identities in psychotherapy* (pp. 139–160). New York: Guilford.

Bronfenbrenner, U. (1996). Developmental ecology through space and time: A future perspective. In P. Moen, G. H. Elder, & K. Luscher (Eds.), *Examining lives in context: Perspectives on the ecology of human development* (pp. 619–647). Washington, DC: American Psychological Association.

Bronfenbrenner, U., Kessel, F., Kessen, W., & White, S. (1986). Toward a critical social history of developmental psychology. *American Psychologist, 41,* 1218–1230.

Buss, D. M. (1990). Toward a biologically informed psychology of personality. *Journal of Personality, 58,* 1–16.

Chatoor, I. (1989). Infantile Anorexia Nervosa: A developmental disorder of separation and individuation. *Journal of the American Academy of Psychoanalysis, 17*(1), 43–64.

Chess, S., & Thomas, A. (1984). *Origins and evolution of behavior disorders.* New York: Brunner/Mazel, Inc.

Dietrich, K. T. (1975). A reexamination of the myth of Black matriarchy. *Journal of Marriage and the Family, 37,* 367–374.

Erikson, E. (1963). *Childhood and society* (2nd ed.). New York: W. W. Norton.

Gangstad, S. W., & Simpson, J. A. (1990). Toward an evolutionary history of female sociosexual variation. *Journal of Personality, 58,* 69–96.

Gibbs, J. T., & Fuery, D. (1994). Mental health and well-being of Black women: Toward strategies of empowerment. *American Journal of Community Psychology, 22,* 559–582.

Gilligan, C. (1982). *In a different voice.* Cambridge, MA: Harvard University Press.

Gopaul-McNichol, S. A. (1993). *Working with West Indian families.* New York: Guilford.

Gordon, R. A. (1990). *Anorexia and bulimia: Anatomy of a social epidemic.* Cambridge, MA: Basil Blackwell, Inc.

Greene, B. (1994). African American women. In L. Comas-Diaz & B. Greene (Eds.), *Women of color: Integrating ethnic and gender identities in psychotherapy* (pp. 10–29). New York: Guilford.

Guisinger, S., & Blatt, S. (1994). Individuality and relatedness: Evolution of a fundamental dialectic. *American Psychologist, 49,* 104–111.

Helgeson, V. S. (1994). Relation of agency and communion to well-being: Evidence and potential explanations. *Psychological Bulletin, 116,* 412–428.

Herman, E. (1995). *The romance of American psychology: Political culture in the age of experts.* Berkeley: University of California Press.

Kessen, W. (1979). The American child and other cultural inventions. *American Psychologist, 34,* 815–820.

Kessler-Harris, A., & Swerdlow, A. (1996, April 26). Point of view. Pride and paradox: Despite success, women's studies faces an uncertain future. *Chronicle of Higher Education, 42*(33), A64.

Kettel, B. (1986). The commoditization of women in Tugen (Kenya) social organization. In C. Robertson and I. Berger (Eds.), *Women and class in*

Africa (pp. 47–61). New York: Africana Publishing Company.

LaFromboise, T. D., Berman, J. S., & Sohi, B. K. (1994). American Indian women. In L. Comas-Diaz & B. Greene (Eds.), *Women of color: Integrating ethnic and gender identities in psychotherapy* (pp. 30–71). New York: Guilford.

Lerner, R. M. (1986). *Concepts and theories of human development* (2nd ed.). New York: Random House.

Levant, R. F., & Pollack, W. S. (1995). *A new psychology of men.* New York: Basic Books.

Levinson, D. J. (1996). *The seasons of a woman's life.* New York: Knopf.

Maccoby, E. E. (1995). The two sexes and their social systems. In P. Moen, G. H. Elder, & K. Luscher (Eds.), *Examining lives in context: Perspectives on the ecology of human development* (pp. 347–364). Washington, DC: American Psychological Association.

Mednick, M. (1989). On the politics of psychological constructs: Stop the bandwagon, I want to get off. *American Psychologist, 44,* 1118–1123.

Mitchell, V., & Helson, R. (1990). Women's prime of life: Is it the 50s? *Psychology of Women Quarterly, 14,* 451–470.

Nobles, W. W. (1974). African root and American fruit: The Black family. *Journal of Social and Behavioral Sciences, 20,* 1–18.

Obbo, C. (1986). Stratification and the lives of women in Uganda. In C. Robertson & I. Berger (Eds.), *Women and class in Africa* (pp. 178–196). New York: Africana Publishing Company.

Plomin, R. (1994). *Genetics and experience: The interplay between nature and nurture.* Thousand Oaks, CA: Sage Publications.

Roberts, R., & Newton, P. M. (1987). Levinsonian studies of women's adult development. *Psychology and Aging, 2,* 154–163.

Rotter, J. B. (1966). Generalized expectancies for internal versus external control of reinforcement. *Psychological Monographs, 8,* (1, whole No. 609).

Russo, N. F., & Denmark, F. L. (1987). Contributions of women to psychology. *Annual Review of Psychology, 38,* 279–298.

Seligman, M. E. P. (1991). *Learned optimisim.* New York: Knopf.

Strobel, M. (1984). Women in religion and in secular ideology. In M. Hay and S. Stichter (Eds.), *African women south of the Sahara* (pp. 87–101). New York: Longman.

Triandis, H. (1996). The psychological measurement of cultural syndromes. *American Psychologist, 51,* 407–415.

INDEX